The Pursuit of Sustainable Leadership

Becoming a Successful Strategic Leader through Principles, Perspectives, and Profesional Development

The Pursuit of Sustainable Leadership

Becoming a Successful Strategic Leader through Principles, Perspectives, and Profesional Development

David L. Rainey

Rensselaer Polytechnic Institute

Dan

I sincerely thank you for all of your insights and contributions to the concepts in this book. You are my inspiration and guiding light. With love and appreciation. David

David L. Rainey

April 6, 2013

IAP

INFORMATION AGE PUBLISHING, INC.

Charlotte, NC • www.infoagepub.com

Quotes

I have tried where necessary to give full details of the sources for all data and information and am grateful to the authors. If I overlooked providing the appropriate citation, I apologize and thank the source.

Library of Congress Cataloging-in-Publication Data

Rainey, David L., 1946-
The pursuit of sustainable leadership : becoming a successful strategic leader through principles, perspectives, and professional development / David L. Rainey.
p. cm.
ISBN 978-1-62396-126-8 (pbk.) – ISBN 978-1-62396-127-5 (hardcover) – ISBN 978-1-62396-128-2 (ebook) 1. Leadership. 2. Strategic planning. 3. Organizational effectiveness. 4. Success in business. I. Title.
HD57.7.R35 2013
658.4'092–dc23
2012042637

Printed in the United States of America

I would like to dedicate this book to my loving wife, Elizabeth, who supports me in all my endeavors and encouraged me in articulating the principles and philosophies expressed herein.

Contents

List of Figures

List of Tables

List of Abbreviations

CEO	Chief executive officer
CERES	Coalition of Environmentally Responsible Economies
CSR	Corporate social responsibility
DAD	Decide, announce and defend
dad	Discuss, analyze and decide
Dow	Dow Chemical Corporation
EPCRA	Emergency Planning Community Right-to-Know Act
EU	European Union
FLA	Fair Labor Association
FMC	Ford Motor Company
FSL	Full-spectrum strategic leadership
GM	General Motors
GMAC	General Motors Acceptance Corporation
GRI	Global Reporting Initiative
ICT	Information and communications technologies
IP	Intellectual property(ies)
J&J	Johnson & Johnson
KISS	Keep it simple stupid
LCA	Life cycle assessment
MBA	Master of Business Administration
NBC	National Broadcasting Company
PERI	Public Environmental Reporting Initiative
PC	Personal computer
PP	Precautionary principle
PSL	The pursuit of strategic leadership

RCA	Radio Corporation of America
R&D	Research and development
SBU	Strategic business unit
SEC	Securities and Exchange Commission
SMEs	Small and medium sized enterprises
SOA	Sarbanes Oxley Act
SSL	Sustainable strategic leadership
TV	Television
UN	United Nations

Introduction

Overview

Leadership is an essential element of an organization's pursuit of its strategic direction, desired outcomes, sustainable success and survival. It is easy to comprehend, but very difficult to truly realize. Leadership has been studied and written about for centuries, yet it is still one of the most elusive topics because many of the concepts, methods and techniques developed by scholars and business practitioners are simply too narrow or they quickly become outdated, especially in today's fast-paced and turbulent world. Most of the business scholars and authors who teach leadership to existing and aspiring leaders generally focus on how to manage problems, people, processes and practices. The perspectives are usually on contemporary situations and the near term. Most of the theories and methods pertain to organizational behavior and determining the best ways to achieve objectives and obtain targeted results. While there are numerous concepts and propositions about how to be a leader, the prevailing methodologies are usually on how to exploit one's natural talents, to employ certain "proven principles and practices" that "always work," and to learn the "leadership process." There are many other common themes as well. For instance, one of the most popular themes in books pertaining to leadership is the notion of focusing on one's core competencies and strengths. While such a theory may help in the short term, the results often leave the individuals unprepared for the future when their strengths are rendered meaningless due to changes in the business world. For example, strategic leaders in the automobile industry were totally unprepared to manage the dramatic drop in demand during the Great Recession. Their strengths in operations, marketing and finance did little to provide them with the requisite skills and knowledge in managing the complexities of excess capacity, surplus inventories, the lack of consumer credit, and consumer reluctance to buy. Conventional methods simply did not work and the strategic leaders had very little time to learn the requisite requirements for leading in a more turbulent business environment.

The Pursuit of Sustainable Leadership, pages xvii–xxii

In a conventional sense, leadership is having a position of being the leader of some organization or part thereof or having the ability to lead people and organizations. Such individuals typically focus on their roles and responsibilities for managing their organizations and on their abilities to obtain the required outcomes. However, many of the supposed leaders who have been selected to occupy strategic and operational positions are not true leaders at all; they are managers and/or administrators. They deal with and manage functions, activities, resources and things. While such perspectives and approaches are not necessarily bad, they are limited and often focus on the here and now, i.e., what reality is, instead of what it could be or has to be. In simple terms, many of the prevailing theories are really about management, not leadership.

Leadership is a complex and dynamic construct that involves leading people, organizations, and business enterprises, realizing the aspirations and goals, orchestrating positive change, obtaining the desired outcomes and achieving sustainable success. Leadership is multifaceted requiring the incumbent to be competent and knowledgeable in many different subjects and disciplines, especially in the relationships with employees, peers, superiors, partners, enterprise contributors, customers, stakeholders and, in certain cases, shareholders. It involves staying ahead of the demands, expectations and changes of the business world. It is the never-ending pursuit to become a sustainable leader who has the capabilities, confidence and courage to lead organizations and people in their quests for positive outcomes, satisfaction, growth and development, happiness and success.

Leadership has many facets from the underlying principles and philosophies to the perspectives and qualities that a leader has to have for inspiring people and energizing them into taking positive actions and realizing outstanding results and excellent performance. It is also about insights, imagination and innovativeness. Leadership involves broad array of perspectives and constructs that include leading, governing, managing, making decisions, taking care of people, developing innovative ways of achieving outcomes and making people successful. In simple terms, leadership is a continuum that is all encompassing.

The Pursuit of Sustainable Leadership

The Pursuit of Sustainable Leadership (PSL) involves the ongoing learning and development of business leaders and students to become true strategic leaders who have the proper principles, philosophies, values, capabilities and perspectives for achieving sustainable success. True leaders are dedicated to their endeavors and never stop making transitions and transformations to higher levels of sophistication. Most leadership theories pertain to how an incumbent or an aspiring leader progresses through stepwise processes from managing activities and operations and leading teams and groups of people to strategic management and leadership of business units and companies. The recommended process entails going from being a supervisor and department manager to a strategic business unit (SBU) leader and possibly a C-level leader (chief executive, chief financial officer, etc.).

The PSL is based on learning the foundation of leadership, having the right principles, developing personal philosophies, using broad perspectives, adapting openness and honesty, engaging in continuous learning, embracing life-long personal and professional development, and being a sustainable leader. The key to success involves acquiring new knowledge, seeking profound experiences, expanding one's understanding of realities and possibilities, and developing positive mindset through demanding roles and responsibilities, interactive engagements and profound learning. While much has been written about the "Peter Principle," many promising leaders often create their own limitations and/or demise, because they stop learning and developing the means, mechanisms and thought processes to become sophisticated and capable strategic leaders. Many strategic leaders reach a certain point in their development in which they believe that they have obtained the requisite skills and know-how to be an effective leader and simply rest on their laurels. While such leaders may believe that they are competent and can effectively and efficiently manage their organizations and enterprises, the business world continues to change and such individuals eventually fall out of synch with reality. By the time they recognize that they need additional learning and development and more experience and that they have to be more capable and sophisticated, it is too late or they do not have the time or inclination to improve. There are many other barriers that are often self-induced such as being arrogant or assuming that they know everything.

Sustainable leadership involves a rich mosaic of principles, philosophies, perspectives, styles, mindsets, experiences, methods and constructs. The recognition that one needs ongoing learning and development in itself is a powerful insight that helps the person to achieve ongoing success. For most of the twentieth century, leaders developed their skills and knowledge during the early stage of their careers and then exploited their capabilities as they assumed more responsible positions, especially within large corporations. Even though the business world did change and their backgrounds became less relevant per the new conditions and trends, such individuals were still able to succeed for the most part because the underlying conditions and trends did not radically change. In a slow-paced business world, the half life of one's knowledge and capabilities may be pertinent for a decade or two, sufficiently long to cover the tenure of most leaders, especially those in senior level positions. However, in a fast-paced world of the 21st century, leaders of all persuasions have to be extremely careful to ensure that they continue to be relevant and have the requisite skills, knowledge, capabilities and perspectives to lead in a more dynamic and less predictable world.

The question of whether leaders are born or they are developed has perplexed scholars and authors for generations. It follows the "nature or nurture" debate. The "nature" theory suggests that leadership is in one's genes, either one has or not; the "nurture" theory argues that one can develop the requisite qualities to be a competent, capable and successful leader. However, the answer is not an "either-or" situation; one having only two possibilities that are generally mutually exclusive. Leadership is multifaceted. In most cases, certain leaders have inborn qualities like charisma and personal attractiveness that propel them toward becoming effective and successful leaders, especially in dealing with people, while others have to acquire qualities like having wisdom and empathy that connects them with people. In most situations, leadership is about taking advantage of one's natural talents and concurrently developing new capabilities, competencies, experiences and other learned qualities. Indeed, PSL would not make sense if leadership was purely inherent to the individual and could not be developed through learning and experiences. The good news is that even individuals who are not well endowed with natural attributes can become exceptional leaders and achieve great outcomes, if they engage in PSL and build a broad-base repertoire of leadership qualities.

The PSL is not simple or easy. It takes concerted efforts and dedication to become a sophisticated leader in today's complex global economy and the ever changing global landscape. While there are many elements that are part of the basics of leadership that are easy to obtain and follow, the PSL becomes more challenging as one proceeds from the basics of leadership, also called the foundation of leadership, to the more sophisticated and demanding requirements of being a strategic leader. The former includes the underlying principles and values of leadership that are appropriate regardless of the situation or circumstance and the time frame in which one is involved. The basics include imperatives like honesty, openness and transparency that are timeless and fit every situation and endeavor. All leaders can adapt solid principles, philosophies and values that are respected in society and provide a firm basis for leading, managing and making decisions. For instance, respecting people and protecting human rights are critical factors for achieving success. Every leader can quickly embrace fundamental truths and employ them in one's endeavors. On the other hand, being a strategic leader is very challenging because it requires more and more sophistication as one grows and matures in leadership positions and over the course of one's career. Strategic leaders are normally in senior positions that require precise actions and flawless execution.

Young and aspiring leaders have much to learn and develop, but time is on their side and often great latitude is provided to them because they do not have a lot of experience and knowledge. As they develop, they acquire more capabilities and know-how and more is expected of them. Astute young leaders take every opportunity to learn, to acquire the requisite skills and capabilities and to make ongoing progress. They take prudent risks and learn from both the positive experiences and the mistakes they make along the way. Early on mistakes are often overlooked and understood in most situations to be part of the learning experience. As young leaders mature more is expected of them and their seniors and mentors, if they have them, become less forgiving. Eventually, aspiring young leaders have to stand on their own and be competent and capable of developing strategies and solutions, making good decisions, and taking actions. They have to transition from being a specialist or competent leader with narrow perspectives to multi-specialists and generalists with global perspectives that are beyond their existing roles and responsibilities. As one assumes strategic leadership positions, the quest continues toward even higher levels of sophistication. Such leaders have to continue over their careers to develop all aspects of leadership qualities and capabilities. In today's complex world, corporate leaders, SBU leaders, public sector leaders and other senior leaders cannot assume that they are just generalists who have a sense of the "big picture" but they do not have to worry about the details. They have to be competent and wide-ranging: visionaries who set direction; generalists who have a sense of the broad aspects of their domains; and multi-specialists who have the knowledge and capabilities to deal with the critical elements of their roles and responsibilities. Sustainable strategic leaders have to be very well qualified and have a comprehensive repertoire that allows them to understand and engage in whatever is necessary. Such perspectives are demanding, yet they are exciting and full of opportunities for confident and dedicated leaders.

Purpose of the Book and Philosophical Perspectives

This book examines how leaders and managers, especially aspiring young business leaders and management students, can make dramatic improvements in their endeavors, enrich their knowledge, and learn the essential perspectives of leadership. In today's world, business leaders regardless of the venue have to be aggressive in their aims, holistic in their perspectives, and lead change ahead of the prevailing driving forces. The PSL is about being out front and ahead of change, seeking new opportunities, dealing with the challenges and developing new solutions and achieving the desire outcomes even before their contemporaries are aware of the changes in the business environment.

The business world of today is not an "either-or" situation, but a global landscape of realities, possibilities and exciting opportunities with numerous challenges, difficulties, problems, risks and vulnerabilities. True leaders understand and deal with the realities, take proactive actions, make courageous decisions and exceed expectations in performance and outcomes. The basic premise is that astute leaders can create extraordinary value and achieve sustainable success through sustainable leadership and multifaceted perspectives and by leading change and inspiring people. This premise holds that true leadership requires an all encompassing perspective that is open to scrutiny and efficient, effective and flexible in design and execution. Leaders have to build their own "brand" and portfolio and exercise the skills and competencies every opportunity they have.

The book describes theories, principles, philosophies models, constructs, insights, guidelines, and practices of sustainable leadership. Given the level of sophistication in theories and practices, the discussions represent the beginning of the dialogue on the PSL. The book consists of six chapters. The first two chapters focus on the foundations of leadership and the related principles, philosophies and values that are pivotal in achieving sustainable success in today's complex world. Chapter 3 explores the concepts of openness, transparency and accountability and how they lead to trust and integrity. Chapter 4 discusses the requisite qualities of leadership. It explores how leaders are developed, what leaders do and how they provide the means for achieving success. Chapter 5 examines the key elements of strategic leadership. Chapter 6 discusses selected leadership constructs and includes concluding comments. The following provides a general flow of the essential topics:

Chapter 1: Foundations of Leadership: Underpinnings and Context

☐ Precepts ☐ Underpinnings and concepts ☐ Context ☐ Perspectives

Chapter 2: The Principles, Philosophies, Values and Cultural Aspects of Leadership

☐ Principles ☐ Philosophies ☐ Responsibilities ☐ Personal values ☐ Cultural considerations

Chapter 3: Openness, Transparency and Accountability: The New Imperative

☐ Openness ☐ Transparency ☐ Honesty ☐ Trust ☐ Stakeholders ☐ Accountability

Chapter 4: Qualities of Leadership and Leadership Development

☐ Qualities ☐ Innate and learned aptitudes ☐ Leadership development ☐ Learning

Chapter 5: Sustainable Strategic Leadership

☐ Fundamentals ☐ Styles ☐ External and internal perspectives ☐ Full-spectrum strategic leadership

Chapter 6: Concluding Comments

☐ Leadership constructs ☐ Dynamic of leadership ☐ Concluding comments

1

Foundations of Leadership

Underpinnings and Context

Introduction

Leadership involves the abilities, skills, talents, knowledge and mindset to lead people and organizations and positively affect change. It is an exciting challenge when met using the proper perspectives and reflections on reality and innovations to create a sustainable future. It involves subordinating one's own personal standing and advantages to elevate and support the positions and circumstances of all of the people involved. Leadership involves making other people successful and ensuring that they have the means and mechanisms for achieving success.

The foundations of leadership include two broad areas: underpinnings and context. Underpinnings are the tangible and intangible aspects of leadership. They involve the micro-world of leadership and the organization: what the leaders are, the people they engage, and the fundamental elements of leadership: principles, philosophies and values. Context involves the macro-world of leadership: how leaders are developed and how they respond to the internal and external dimensions: the opportunities and challenges. It involves understanding what is necessary and required, and what the strategies, tactics and actions are necessary for achieving success.

The tangible aspects pertain to the physical realities of the organization and the enterprise. The tangible aspects include guiding, developing, supporting and leading the people of the organization and building relationships across the organizations and the whole enterprise. They are easily identified and characterized and are often thrust upon leaders by their positions and the underlying missions and agendas of

The Pursuit of Sustainable Leadership, pages 1–23

their organizations. Business leaders generally acquire many of the tangible aspects of leadership through learning and experience. They can be taught the roles and responsibilities of their positions and learn the theories and practices for managing people, organizations and enterprises. While acquiring such skills, talents and capabilities is neither easy nor learned quickly in a classroom, most experienced leaders enjoy many of the requisite elements of the tangible aspects and are usually able to perform reasonably well. Moreover, most leaders tend to become more competent in these areas as they gain additional knowledge and experience.

The intangible aspects relate to the intellectual and psychological foundation of the leaders themselves. They include their personal values and beliefs, the overarching principles, their leadership philosophies and underlying mindset, and their willingness to succeed. Personal values and beliefs provide the foundation for leading and directing people of an organization. Without well-established values and beliefs leaders are forced to examine the underlying aspects each time they engage people and make decisions. It is akin to living in a society without rules in which government officials have to ascertain what the precepts and criteria should be in adjudicating every conflict, problem and/or misdeed. Clearly in such situations leaders would be slow to act and would be perplexed, if not overwhelmed, when trying to determine right and wrong and how people should behave and act in such a society. Principles are the standards that are used in decision making and in carrying out actions, especially ones that are important and relevant. They are similar to values and beliefs except that they are usually more universal and apply to the whole and the individual. Philosophies include such viewpoints as using the logic of value creation to guide decision making, being people-oriented when leading the organization, and managing in the best interests of people including shareholders, stakeholders, customers and employees. Principles and philosophies are discussed in more detail in Chapter 2. Having a positive mindset is one of the most powerful qualities of a great leader. It includes focusing on supporting people rather than acquiring personal power and wealth is a fundamental intangible aspect. Having the proper perspectives implies that the leader is willing to take on all the responsibilities of leadership; the good and the bad; the simple and the complex; the glory and tribulations; the rewards and blame; etc. Leadership implies that leaders are holistic in their views and take on the full spectrum of their roles and responsibilities, expressed or implied. Unfortunately, many leaders take the opposite approach; they exploit the people of the organization or external contributors for their own personal and/or professional advantages and gains. Moreover, they want their positions to be one sided; they obtain the positives and force others to handle the negatives. These comments are not intended to suggest that all leaders are one sided, but, there are still many leaders who are self-interested and arrogant. Such leaders have narrow perspectives about their duties and obligations. They often focus on their own success rather than the success of their companies and others. They usurp the glory, rewards and shun undesirable duties to their subordinates, and blame others when they fail to achieve the desired outcomes.

Intangibles also include personal perspectives, one's emotional makeup, the ability to inspire people, and many other more complicated mechanisms such as a sense of connection with people. Intangibles are more difficult to define, but are just as critical as the tangible aspects. Understanding and utilizing these more esoteric elements are often the most powerful qualities exhibited by effective leaders. For instance, most leaders have difficulties orchestrating change because they try to be in synch with the mainstream "school of thought" like trying to maximize profits; they often lack an entrepreneurial spirit to think in unconventional ways and lead change. Intangibles involve the leader's individual characteristics, predispositions and personal values when engaging people, making decisions and dealing with complex challenges. Intangibles involve a rich mosaic of intellectual capital and aptitudes that are defined by a leader's unique constitution, his or her background, life experiences and thought processes. Many people want to be leaders, but are unwilling to subordinate their own aspirations for others, to make personal sacrifices or to take good care of the people in their charge. Having solid values and fundamental beliefs are crucial for succeeding as a leader. Leaders must have well-established core values and beliefs that guide them and their organizations in making decisions and managing performance and outcomes.

The perspectives and foundations of leadership depend on context as well. Context involves the external situations and circumstances that relate to the leader, his or her organization, the management aspects, and the means and mechanisms for leading and managing. Context is framed by defining the scope of the business environment and market spaces and the key variables therein. It also includes the internal management systems and organizational structures for managing the strategic and operational aspects. Context defines and identifies what the leaders have to consider and respond to in their analysis of the business environment and in their decisions and actions. True leaders take proactive efforts to understand the underlying conditions and trends in the context of the prevailing situations. For instance, being responsible for a nuclear power plant requires different perspectives than what is necessary for running the marketing department in a fast-paced industry like consumer electronics. Leaders engaged in the former have to be good at ensuring stability and control, realizing the expected performance, taking due precautions, and maintaining the health and safety of the employees and the communities surrounding the plant among a plethora of stringent technical and legal requirements. Leaders engaged in the latter have to be creative in developing new means and mechanisms and proactive in leading change as new technologies and products are introduced. They must be able to adapt to changing circumstances as well.

Leadership requires broad perspectives that consider the direct and the indirect linkages with the business environment, market spaces and extended enterprise. It involves high-level strategic direction and decision making. Business leaders who take a broad view of the business landscape face the complex realities head on. This makes decision making more complicated; however, such leaders usually increase their prospects for finding exciting new opportunities, mitigating negatives, creating advantages and achieving sustainable success.

In a global business environment with powerful competitors in the developed countries and emerging ones in developing countries in far-flung regions of the world, business leaders need a holistic perspective of the realities and possibilities and use more inclusive and integrative approaches. They have to consider and manage the social, economic, ethical, technological and environmental conditions and trends on a global basis, if they want to truly understand the driving forces of change and what they need to do to lead change. The external context of the business world is expanding dramatically as the world's population expands, as people everywhere seek to improve their well being, and as leaders in many different fields from government agencies to social organizations contribute to the needs of people and the requirements to protect the natural world.

Leadership is about serving people and making them successful. Great leaders have the ability to glean insights from the external business environment, to take advantage of the myriad of the opportunities available, and to deal effectively with the numerous challenges. They also have the instinctive ability to connect personally and professionally with people in the organization and to inspire them to accomplish great things. They examine every perspective and ensure that they fully understand all of the implications and ramifications. True leadership involves being open and honest with everyone and being accountable for one's decisions and actions. It also involves being creative and innovative in strategy formulation and implementation. Leadership includes many qualities and characteristics; some may be classified as innate and others as learned. The qualities and characteristics of leadership are discussed in Chapter 4.

The intent of this book is to provide insights and guidance for developing and implementing innovative ways of leading organizations. Given the growing diversity of global corporations and small and medium size enterprises (SMEs) and the increasing complexities of the business environment, today's business leaders need the ability and knowledge to tailor their thinking and approaches to the realities of their business situations and the future needs and expectations. They must have global perspectives, holistic frameworks and enhanced qualities of leadership. They must understand the underpinnings of sustainable leadership. They have to be adaptive. They must explore and examine perspectives from horizon to horizon and they must focus on achieving success. Leadership is not about winning battles and engagements, but succeeding across the business landscape and over the course of time. True leadership is about sustaining success in the short term and the long term.

This chapter pertains to the concepts, constructs, perspectives and theories that apply to all leaders from supervisors to executives. The chapter includes the following main topics:

- Defining the precepts of leadership and underpinnings of strategic leadership
- Identifying the underlying aspects of external context.
- Introducing the pursuit of strategic leadership.

The Precepts of Leadership and Underpinnings of Strategic Leadership

Precepts of leadership

Leadership is about building trust and having integrity. Trust binds people together across the organization and business enterprise in the knowledge that the proper governance, direction, strategies and actions are being taken and that all due considerations and precautions have been included in the decision-making process. Customers buy products and services because they trust the producers and providers. People within the organization generally follow the leaders they trust because they believe that such leaders are acting in their best interests. Trust links people across the broad spectrum of the business environment and strengthens relationships among people who may or may not even know each other. Integrity entails the soundness and completeness of one's being, decisions, strategies, solutions and actions. It is the sum of the trust relationships, positive actions and fruitful outcomes. It is based on the presumptive belief that the leaders and their organizations have ethical and moral standings. Integrity is essential for preserving the corporate image and reputation. It takes huge efforts to acquire and build integrity, but it can be easily lost due to one or a few misdeeds by the leaders or employees.

Outstanding leaders share success with others and ensure that everyone gets his or her fair share of the rewards. They do not take rewards when the organization is having difficulties nor do they take disproportional rewards when it enjoys financial success. Effective leaders obtain a diverse set of views and voices so that decisions, strategies, objectives and action plans are inclusive of multiple considerations and responsive to alternate perspectives. They create stability and continuity as they lead change. Stability involves balancing the needs of present customers, stakeholders, and key contributors, meeting the needs and aspirations of the future, and ensuring outstanding performance over time. The logic is simply; investors provide capital assets and other resources because there is evidence and a belief that the anticipated rewards justify the investments. If the corporation has a high degree of volatility relating to negative aspects, investors and supporters are less likely to make ongoing commitments and/or stay the course. Stability in this context does not connote resistance to change. Stability means that ongoing success is the norm and that the organization will not become static in its plans and actions. It implies dependability and reliability in the near term and continuous success over the long term. Continuity implies that the leaders are connected to the organization and the enterprise and that the connections are enduring.

Good leaders are multifaceted. They have a solid core of precepts and beliefs that provide steadfast guidance and direction in everything they do. These precepts are essential elements of the foundation of leadership upon which everything lies. Successful leaders have the forbearance to rely on their precepts; ones that guide them over time at the same time they provide the guidance to adapt to changing or new conditions when necessary without compromising their values and beliefs. The main precepts are:

- ***Truthfulness, candor, integrity and trust***—Truthfulness and honesty imply telling the whole truth in every situation. Candor involves making full disclosures of appropriate facts and details under the proper circumstances. Integrity means protecting the whole business enterprise and ensuring that no one is caused to suffer losses due to inappropriate actions. Integrity is the result of having high standards, ethical practices and methods, and proper actions. Trust binds people together in the knowledge that the proper decisions and actions are being taken.
- ***Openness and transparency***—Openness is essential in building trust, integrity and awareness across the enterprise. Information and data are shared with all appropriate constituencies to ensure that plans, actions, and outcomes have peer review and are generally acceptable internally and externally. Transparency implies that companies provide pertinent facts and information to customers, stakeholders, employees and shareholders. It means providing disclosures about relevant details to the public pertaining to products, services, operations and activities.
- ***Accountability***—Leaders are ultimately accountable for their decisions and actions. They are answerable to the shareholders, directors, corporate officers and their organizations for their achievements and failures. This includes their lack of action when such actions are required.
- ***Ethics and responsible behaviors***—Ethical practices are directly related to building trust. Companies and their contributors are expected to police themselves and ensure that best practices and approaches are employed and that individuals, groups, departments, business units, organizations and enterprises act and behave in a responsible, prudent, and safe manner. Responsible behaviors include complying with laws and regulations, mitigating problems and negative impacts and informing people about the full implications (positives and negatives) of products, services, processes and operations.
- ***Value creation and innovativeness***—Leaders ensure that they are making improvements, enhancements and ongoing developments to make the world a better place. Value creation includes incremental improvements to existing technologies, products and processes, radical innovations and new discoveries for creating new solutions through cutting-edge technologies and products that meet the needs and wants of customers, stakeholders and constituents. Innovativeness includes developing new business models, systems, processes methods, and techniques for creating sustainable solutions and producing successful outcomes.
- ***Inclusiveness and connectedness***—Inclusiveness implies that leaders integrate the internal strategic and operating systems with the external entities, partners, allies, supply networks, customers, stakeholders, related industries, infrastructure and other support relationships. It is based on a holistic thinking, in-depth analysis and proper execution of all of the systems and processes involved from the raw materials to the disposal of the residuals and waste

streams. Connectedness involves building linkages and solid relationships with people.

- ***Dual-sided perspectives and sustainable success***—Leaders create sustainable success using a balanced perspective of the driving forces and mandates impinging on the organizations and the enterprise. The overarching objective is to create outstanding value for everyone by improving the positive outcomes, reducing the negative impacts and ensuring that all contributors and recipients are successful.

Collectively these precepts enhance the well being and reputations of the leaders and their organizations. The percepts are discussed in more detail in the chapters related to the specific topics.

Great leadership involves envisioning and creating a more positive future and orchestrating its reality well before anyone else has any inkling about what can and must be accomplished. It is also about inspiring people to develop their skills, talents and intellectual capital to realize their potential, to contribute to the organization, and to accomplish their own ambitions. Great leadership also involves proactively changing the underpinnings of the organization to enhance its capabilities and positions to be even more powerful and successful in the long term. It is about leading change without disrupting stability and continuity. This is possibly the most complicated aspect of leadership, because it inherently involves the tension between stability and change. It is this tension that makes leadership complex, dynamic and exciting. It also invokes the notion of the dual-sided/multifaceted perspective. True leadership takes on every factor from multiple perspectives and ensures that all facets are considered and successful dealt with.

Underpinnings of strategic leadership

The underpinnings of strategic leadership are derived from the legal, ethical and moral obligations of the social, political, technological and economic dimensions. Strategic leadership pertains to the whole domain of the company, business units, the extended enterprise and all of the strategic leader's direct and indirect duties, roles and responsibilities. It involves exploring the whole business environment, integrating the entire extended enterprise, discovering and exploiting new opportunities, managing and mitigating challenges and risks, developing innovative solutions, maximizing value creation and investing in the future. The notion of an ***extended enterprise*** is relatively new construct. It includes all of the important contributors to the success of the company and its business units and all of the recipients of its solutions and outcomes into a holistic framework. The contributors include supply networks, partners, allies and other value networks. Contributors are also supported by the external infrastructure of roads, electricity, water systems, etc. The recipients include customers, stakeholders and related industries. It also includes the actions of competitors to the extent they add to the success of the enterprise.

Being a strategic leader of an organization does not automatically mean that such a person engages in strategic leadership. Strategic leadership is a much more profound and compelling concept and reality. It involves connecting with and inspiring people, learning and knowing how to lead, developing people, being innovative and adaptive, crafting strategies and solutions, establishing systems, building relationships, orchestrating change and achieving success. It implies giving others the opportunity to excel and to be successful within their definition of success.[1] There are many strategic leaders who exhibit strategic leadership at its best. Jim Collins in his bestseller, *Good to Great,* describes exactly what it takes to be a strategic leader and to exhibit true strategic leadership. Collins suggests that the most critical element in developing a great company is to develop great leadership.[2] Collins identifies "Level 5 Leadership" as the highest level of leadership development and thinking. He describes "Level 5 Leadership" as the starting point in the process to becoming great.[3]

> "*Level 5 leaders*" channel their ego needs away from themselves and into the larger goal of building a great company. It's not that Level 5 leaders have no ego or self-interest. Indeed they are incredibly ambitious–but their ambition is first and foremost for the institution, not themselves.
>
> "*Level 5 leaders*" are fanatically driven, infected with an incurable need to produce sustained results. They are resolved to do whatever it takes to make a company great, no matter how big or hard the decisions.

The concepts of strategic leadership and being a strategic leader converge at Collins' Level 5. Such leaders are driven by achieving extraordinary results for their organizations, being successful over the long term and making other people successful. They are individuals who believe in the underpinnings of leadership and embrace and execute the full spectrum of their duties, roles and responsibilities.

On the other side, many strategic leaders in business and other settings do not measure up to Collins' standards of a Level 5 leader. Often such leaders are individuals who are designated as the leader of the organization, but they do not exhibit leadership qualities or have the proper precepts and perspectives. Many are conceited and self-serving. Many are mainly interested in their own success and personal objectives like becoming wealthy, famous and powerful. While the business objectives and the success of the organization occasionally coincide with those of such leaders in the short term, narrow-minded, personally-focused strategic leaders often cause significant harm to their organizations in the long term. For instance, there are strategic leaders who engage in corruption and bribery saying that they are just trying to do what is necessary to achieve the company's objectives, but in reality they are just thinking about their own personal gains like big bonuses and not the overarching goals of the company. They try to obtain outstanding performance so that their compensation is improved. The questions arise: Whose profits are they trying to maximize? Do they think about the harm to the organization due to their misdeeds? Prudent leaders of any organization know that the risks associated with wrongdoings and unethical practices are high and that the probabilities of discovery increase over time. They implicitly know that such behaviors are not in the best interest of the company regardless of the possible outcomes or profits involved. So why do some business leaders get involved in such activities? The answer may lie in the perceived benefits to themselves and not to the company. These views are explored in more detail in Chapter 3.

Strategic leaders who have true strategic leadership qualities and abilities inspire others to achieve and to go beyond their perceived boundaries of capabilities and realities. Inspiration is one of the most compelling qualities of true strategic leaders who can convey their passion for achieving success to other people in the organization and extended enterprise. True strategic leaders work to:

- Influence and inspire people across the broad spectrum of transactions, interactions and relationships to realize positive outcomes and to contribute to each other's success. They get contributors and recipients to become excited about the possibilities and the potential outcomes.
- Promote harmony and stability within the organization and extended enterprise at the same time they obtain proactive actions and extraordinary achievements. They do not hide difficulties, but bring them to the forefront so they can be resolved and eliminated.
- Encourage people to be open and to address both positive and negative aspects of the organization and the leadership thereof. They channel the energy of the organization toward mutual gains, ensuring that everyone is succeeding to the extent possible.

Strategic leadership is based on the recognition that high-level leaders in an organization are not just superiors in the hierarchy who have command and control authority over the lower levels of the organization, but are fiduciaries that have the overall duties and responsibilities to sustain the organization and direct, facilitate and support the people, strategies, actions and outcomes. Outstanding strategic leaders are not at the top of the pyramid, but are really the foundation of leadership upon which the organization is developed, built, led and sustained. Strategic leaders are the architects and developers of the organization and business enterprise. They are responsible to a broad array of people from external customers and stakeholders to internal employees and shareholders. They design, build and enhance the management systems and organizational structure for the people therein.

Strategic leaders are facilitators in establishing strategic direction and obtaining results as well as having the vested authority in strategizing, leading change, taking actions and ensuring proper execution and financial performance. In today's fast-paced business world, the old top-down attitudes based on superior and subordinate relationships are being or have to be replaced with more engaging and interactive approaches that have more participation and empowerment in discussions, decisions and actions. Top-down methods are usually single-sided approaches that have some positive aspects and many negative ones as well. Traditional top-down leaders often rely on what is called the big "DAD" approach.[4] DAD stands for "Decide, Announce, and Defend." If strategic leaders make decisions without very much input from their organizations, it is relatively easy to obtain agreement. However, resistance to the changes may result because the leaders did not allow others to have a voice in the process. Strategic leaders announce their decisions and then spend a lot of time defending the logic of the decisions. While strategic leaders may ultimately convince people within the organization that the decisions are sound or they simply force people to take the requisite actions, the process is less efficient and effective because time is loss during implementation and execution. Moreover, if the strategic leaders cannot bring the organization together, implementation and execution suffer and results are often sub-optimal, if not worse. Even if there is no resistance, time may be loss because people do not understand the underlying aspects of the decisions and/or they do not know what to do. In my book on *Enterprise-wide Strategic Management: Achieving Sustainable Success through Leadership, Strategies, and Value Creation,* the small "dad" approach is offered as a profound alternative:[5]

> The alternate method is the small "dad" approach, in which the organization is engaged throughout the strategic management process. Small "dad" stands for "discuss, analyze, and decide." While not everyone may ultimately agree with the final decisions, people generally respond more favorably if they had a chance to voice their views during decision making and have sense of the logic of the decisions. It may take additional time during strategic formulation to engage more people, but the time saved during implementation may more than compensate for the investment. While each strategic situation has its own particular requirements and needs for confidentiality, being open and honest, sharing in decision making encourages people to perform at the highest level.

The philosophical perspectives of strategic leaders bear upon their ability to create and realize a compelling strategic direction for the company and to ensure the fulfillment of the mission(s) and objectives of the organization. Strategic leaders encourage people to follow their lead through interactive and proactive methods in which people are engaged and succeed through mutual gains. Strategic leadership involves getting people to participate because they want to. Great strategic leaders share the benefits of the efforts, contributions and accomplishments with the full array of the participants. People often contribute more in the long term when they are given the means and mechanisms to perform and are encouraged and supported in realizing their own personal and professional development. Moreover, the competencies and capabilities of the contributors should not be viewed from a static perspective of what is, but from ones that are dynamic including the potential developments and expected enhancements. The key question regarding personal development is not what a person is, but what he or she can become. People have enormous facilities to learn and become more important contributors when given the opportunities to do so. It takes exceptional strategic leaders to afford them the opportunities to realize their full potential. Again, it requires dual-sided or multi-sided perspectives in which the strategic leaders facilitate the opportunities and the participants make the efforts to achieve the objectives and outcomes.

Strategic leaders often expect that the people of the organization to respect them given their stature as the appointed leaders of the organization. While it is customary and proper for people to show respect for the designated officials and authorities of an organization, respect is also a dual-sided perspective in which strategic leaders owe respect to people in the organization and the enterprise. Effective strategic leaders recognize achievements within the organization and reward people accordingly. Respect and recognition are critical elements in which leaders and the people within the organization are all viewed to be important contributors to the overall success.

Strategic leadership involves personal interactions with people. In today's world of instantaneous communications and continuous connectedness, many strategic leaders believe that they are effectively communicating with the organization through tens, hundreds, even thousands of emails and electronic messages. While people may be better informed using such mechanisms, they may not feel the personal touch of face-to-face or personalized interactions. Often it is not the quantity or depth of the communications that counts, but the quality and the degree of interactions. Strategic leaders who take the time to visit their employees and open a dialogue with them are often viewed to be more communicative than those who send hundreds of one-way messages that are full of details, but lack personal attachment or commitment. However, care has to be taken by strategic leaders to ensure that their approaches are not viewed as self-serving, single-sided, or superficial. Employees are often reticent to express their opinions in one-way mechanisms when there is a lack of feedback or they are unsure about who is getting the information. In a dialogue people get a better sense of how their thoughts are being received and are often more likely to be candid, especially if they do not feel threatened. While every form of communications has limitations, the more personal the engagement is, the more likely the people will believe that they are important contributors to organizational success and act in ways to support the desired outcomes.

People need constant reaffirmation of their worth to the organization and the quality and value of their contributions. Annual performance reviews may help the employees understand their strengths and weaknesses and the meaning of their efforts and contributions, but people generally appreciate more direct and ongoing feedback on a real time basis. If the feedback is positive, it provides encouragement and motivation. If it is negative, it allows the individual time to make improvements and turn negatives into positives. Most importantly, providing reaffirmation of an individual's importance and discussing the value of his or her contributions are significant ways to exhibit the positive aspects of true strategic leadership.

As a related aside, conducting annual reviews tends to be a management function that is performed by managers and administrators. While annual performance reviews may have positive outcomes if they are used to promote improvements, they are often used to rank people and determine who stays and who leaves or how people are viewed in the pecking order. Many strategic leaders rely heavily on such management constructs and instruments, because they lack the ability or fortitude to deal more directly with employees. If changes have to be invoked, good strategic leaders provide direct feedback with suggested corrective actions based on the notion that they want to keep their employees and make them more successful. If the new initiatives that employees have worked on diligently have to be cancelled or significantly modified, then strategic leaders should engage the people directly to inform them why the changes are necessary. And, then they should take affirmative steps to move onto the future prospects.

Strategic leaders encourage creativity and change. They allow people to make mistakes and even to produce failures along the road to achieving success. They encourage people to think out-of-the-box or in ways that may be contrary to the norm. They provide opportunities for people at the core levels of the organization to originate ideas and concepts for new solutions. For example, 3M has employed its "15 percent" rule for more than a half century. It allows employees to spend fifteen percent of their paid time on programs or projects initiated by the employee(s).[6] This philosophical perspective has created numerous new solutions for 3M over the years including Posit-it and 3M's Pollution Pays Program in which the company saved over one billion dollars from environmental management initiatives by employees between 1975 and 2000.

On the other side, many strategic leaders tend to be dictatorial, barking out orders and expecting to be perceived as being right all of the time. They may think that they are always correct, but it is rare for anyone to be correct all of the time. Dictatorial types have a tendency to accept all of the praises and push blame down the organization causing even more harm. They seemingly win all of the time; however, other people unfortunately end up losing most of the time, especially those at the bottom of the organization or ones that are defenseless. In dysfunctional organizations, credit for the good work of the lower level contributors is often usurped by the strategic leaders, while on the negative side the lower level participants are blamed for the poor decisions and actions of the strategic leaders when things turn out poorly. In the long term, people in such organizations may stop working or only do what is required of them. Creativity and the organization's energy typically decline.

Good strategic leaders are fair-minded and open to positive critiques. Positive critiques involve employees making suggestions or recommendations about the decisions or approaches that they believe are incomplete, defective, or even flawed. Good strategic leaders are part of the organizational team and are willing to take constructive criticism. Exhibiting faith in the people is a great motivator. Giving people an opportunity to lead and to take initiatives encourages learning and participation. W. Edwards Deming believed that people want to do their best and engage in productive and successful work and outcomes.[7] They just have to be given opportunities. While it is not prudent to simply give people work that they are not ready to perform, most employees have the skills and capabilities to be successful; they simply need the chance to prove themselves. Good strategic leaders delegate decision making and actions to the lowest levels reasonable in a given situation. They ensure that the incumbents are not only properly educated and developed, but they are provided with the means and mechanisms to achieve success. This includes the requisite information, decision making criteria, and feedback.

Good strategic leaders achieve results through people and ensure that successful employees are recognized and rewarded. They help those that are underperforming to realize their potential and do as much as possible to make everyone successful. Such leaders have many responsibilities including assuring the survival and sustainable success of the company and the organization. They have powerful roles and awesome responsibilities. They have an absolute duty to protect human health and safety and to ensure that everything they or their organizations do is fundamentally sound and in keeping with ethical, moral, and generally accepted practices. They are the stewards of their enterprises and have the overarching responsibilities to provide the best solutions possible given the state of the art of the technologies, the underlying social and economic conditions and trends, and the capabilities and resources of the organization. Moreover, they have implicit and explicit duties to preserve and protect the natural environment and ensure that future generations inherit a world that is more fruitful and sustainable than the world of today. These are shared responsibilities with many other leaders in government and social settings.

EXAMPLES OF CONTRASTING PERSPECTIVES OF HISTORICAL "STRATEGIC LEADERS"

Strategic leaders have made large impacts on history from the early days of civilization to the modern era. Most stories reflect positively on the leaders involved and provide a sense of what true leadership really involves. It is always difficult to characterize exactly what the traits of great leaders are or should be. In absolute terms, they should put their duties, roles and responsibilities above themselves. They should serve others and ensure that other people realize their own successes. They should be fair and honest and support the best interests of the whole as well as support each individual in his or her endeavors. Leaders create harmony and accord. They avoid selfish behaviors and conduct their affairs in the sunshine. They do not deceive people through misinformation, false statements, or lies. They are above the fray and operate as if everyone in the world is watching them. They are open to the discussions and information and data.

Strategic leaders focus on getting results and investing more time and energy for achieving even more results in the long term. They assure that all aspects of their roles and responsibilities are considered, acted upon and executed properly.

The following are examples of contrasting perspectives of some historical figures:

- George Washington lost most of the battles he engaged in, but protected and preserved the Continental Army and eventually prevailed and won the American Revolutionary War. General Washington understood that keeping the army intact and taking care of his soldiers to the extent that he could given the meager resources available were pivotal aspects in maintaining his position and achieving success. Washington realized that it was the army (people) that was most precious and not geography, even if the sacrifices included the cities of Boston, New York and Philadelphia.
- Napoleon Bonaparte won many battles including defeating the combined Russian and Austrian armies at the famous battle of Austerlitz. He was head of state and enjoyed many pleasures because of his power and position. Yet with all of his resources and capabilities, he was ultimately

driven from his lofty heights, because he failed to take care of his armies and the citizens of the republic. He lost more than two hundred thousand soldiers in his ill-fated conquest of Russia. He failed to take due care of his responsibilities and sacrificed people for his own personal glory. He achieved nothing and caused incredible suffering along the way.

- Winston Churchill sacrificed his political capital to stand up against the tyranny of Nazism and was unwavering in his commitment to protect democracy and freedom. He put his personal well being and political life on the line to save his country and its citizens from Hitler and his war machine.
- Adolf Hitler usurped political power and destroyed the lives and fortunes of millions of people in Germany, Austria and other countries in Europe, Africa and the Middle East. He used the resources and capabilities of Germany to spread evil and killed tens of millions. He used his position and power for personal gain, which ultimately was fleeting. He gained nothing and ultimately led his country to destruction.
- Alexander the Great was said to eat and sleep with his solders so that he could personally judge their stamina and endurance. He paid attention to their well being and they were loyal and supportive of his initiatives. He never lost a battle and has been well respected over the course of history.
- Louis XVI of France lost his crown and his life, because he did not understand or appreciate the plight of his people. He lived in luxury as they starved and lived in squalor. He could only relate to his personal comfort and did not contemplate the well being of his subjects. He was at the top of the pyramid and the people were at the bottom. He believed that he had preordained rights to power and the riches of his country. He focused on his own well being and failed to take care of his responsibilities. Like most poor leaders he ultimately paid a heavy price for his failures.

Context and Perspectives

External context

Context includes the external dimensions of the business environment and market spaces and the internal aspects of the organization. Strategic leaders have to understand reality before they can make decisions about how to deal with it and the future requirements of their businesses and how to use the capabilities and resources of the organizations in beneficial ways. Understanding external context is usually the initial perspective required for determining the relevancy and usefulness of internal context. The most appropriate perspective is to examine the external context (external dimensions) before the internal ones. Such a perspective is logical since the value and meaning of internal positions, capabilities, resources and assets are determined by the external business world.

The broadest view of the external dimensions includes the whole natural environment and all aspects of the social/human world in general, the business environment and market spaces therein. The natural environment includes all of the ecosystems: the land, the atmosphere, the oceans, freshwater, the minerals, natural resources, and all living species. Ecosystems are the interconnected systems of living organisms and the biological, physical and chemical support structures. They link the material and energy flows. Managing ecosystems is an implicit responsibility of everyone. The business world depends on the ecosystems for mineral resources like metal ores and fossil fuels and on living organisms for materials like wood and food products.

Effective leaders use natural resources prudently and efficiently within their processes and operations. They have to ensure that waste streams are properly treated and that the risks from the wastes and pollution are mitigated to the extent possible and eliminated whenever possible. Failure to do otherwise may negatively affect their business environment and potentially impact the long-term success of their organizations and enterprises. Moreover, leaders have to share in the responsibilities for ensuring that the ecosystems they affect are adequate to serve the needs of both the human communities and nature and to protect them for future generations.

The social/human world includes all aspects of the human condition, human characteristics that facilitate people's interactions with nature and our relationships with each other, and social systems and structures. It is a subset of the natural environment encompassing humankind and our social interactions and exchanges. It is the centerpiece of human endeavors and business activities. The social/human world facilitates human well-being, the quality of life, sustainable success and survival. The social/human world provides the underpinnings for most markets and customer behaviors. Businesses serve people and it is their needs, wants and expectations that provide important driving forces for opportunities and change.

The business environment is a subset of both the social/human world and the natural environment. It specifically relates to the driving forces that are critical for the success of business enterprises. It includes the external forces impinging upon the company: the social, economic, political, technological, environmental, ethical, and market forces. It also includes the external dimensions of the extended enterprise including markets, stakeholders, competition, related industries, supply networks, and the infrastructure. Markets involve specific customer groups and individuals that seek identifiable solutions. The focus of external context is on those elements most critical to business leaders as they manage their organizations and enterprises, perform their overall responsibilities to shareholders and participants of the enterprise, meet expectations of the markets, achieve sustainable success, and fulfill their roles in protecting the natural environment.

The social, economic, ethical, technological and environmental forces directly affect and influence strategic decision-making. For instance, in the social dimension, the living conditions and lifestyles of people everywhere have direct effects on how businesses create, sell and deliver products and services. Such considerations are critical for understanding the emerging opportunities throughout the world and how businesses can create solutions to exceed needs and expectations. The deeper that leaders delve into understanding the requirements of the social and economic dimensions, the greater are their prospects for discovering opportunities for success and for providing solutions that provide extraordinary value for everyone involved including shareholders.

In conventional management approaches, leaders and managers play direct roles in responding to the needs of customers, markets and related parties and they generally concentrate on providing specific products and services for them. But, using conventional thinking leaders and managers are viewed to have only tangential roles in the broader context of the social/human world. Anything outside of the traditional business domain is someone else's responsibility. In the broader context, leaders, especially strategic leaders, must be mindful of all social, economic, ethical, technological and environmental aspects, issues, problems and concerns and they must be helpful in responding to and resolving to critical challenges and difficulties. They are expected to play important roles in providing solutions and in supporting the efforts of non-business related entities like governments, social organizations, non-governmental organizations and local communities.

The preferred external context includes the critical elements of the natural environment, social/human world and the business environment. It is more inclusive than the traditional view of industry structure that focuses on customers, markets and competitors. A broad perspective of external context provides business leaders with a more comprehensive understanding of the realities and possibilities they face. Many of the important changes and new opportunities in today's business world are driven by entities and forces that are outside the traditional industry structures. Historically, business leaders focused on the forces of change within their industry and utilized narrow perspectives on market requirements and competitive actions. They tended to view only the primary markets as the opportunities and direct competitors as concerns or threats. They often focused more on the competitive scene than on customer satisfaction and market conditions and trends. Over time, most business leaders did change in an evolutionary way, which was indicative of how they managed their businesses. They were slow, cautious and deliberate. Often the preferred strategy was to "do nothing" or to maintain the "status quo." For example, the traditional strategic leaders of the American automobile manufacturers viewed the other members of the "Big Three" as the main competitors. While General Motors (GM), Ford Motor Company (FMC) and Chrysler were formidable companies in the 1950s and 1960s, they were unprepared for the onslaught of international competitors in 1970s and 1980s. They failed to fully appreciate the threat of global companies until it was late in the situation. By the time they did respond, the global competitors enjoyed about a third of the US automobile market.

With the rise of globalization and the rapidity of change in technologies, many international corporations as well as smaller, more entrepreneurial organizations are now leading change. They think more broadly about the markets and business environment. And, today's allies may be tomorrow's competitors. Emerging companies may quickly expand to become the giants in their sector. The "Walmart phenomenon" instead of being an exception may become more of the norm. It refers to small insignificant company(ies) that the main competitors pay little attention to during the early years but later on rapidly overtakes the industry leaders. Walmart was a start-up in 1962; a blip on the radar screen in 1972; an insignificant competitor in 1982; an equal in 1992; and the undisputed industry giant in 2002. Today, the situation is even more dynamic. Google was really just a concept in 1997, yet it became a global search engine and household word in less than ten years. EBay was just a San Francisco based software provider in 1998 with limited revenues that has become one of the largest non-traditional retailers in the world accounting for over $50 billion in transactions ten years later. Facebook went from being a concept to industry leader in four years.

Internal context

Internal context includes the positions, portfolios, capabilities, resources and assets of the organization, how it is able to meet and exceed the demands and expectations of the business environment and markets, and how it executes the selected strategies for creating sustainable solutions and achieving success. The power of a business and its enterprise is defined to a large extent by the intellectual capital, capabilities and resources of the company and its strategic partners, alliances, and supply networks. The strengths and limitations of the entire enterprise determine what is theoretically possible and what the strategic direction can be in terms of the external context. But, the analysis of capabilities and resources does not just involve examining the organization's strengths and weaknesses because such assessments focus on the existing context and not future ones. Strengths and weaknesses are meaningful in relation to the prevailing and expected conditions and trends, but existing capabilities and resources are important, if they provide the means for addressing opportunities and creating value and meaningful outcomes. However, they have to be reinvigorated and refined to stay ahead of the needs and expectations on an ongoing basis.

Competencies and capabilities of the people are among the most important strategic assets of the organization. They allow the company to translate objectives and strategies into realities and create new innovations for leading change and staying on the cutting edge in the business landscape. They are the means for crafting strategies, effecting solutions, and sustaining them in the future. The analysis of capabilities and resources helps to articulate and determine the strategies to enhance prevailing and future strategic positions. Managing capabilities and understanding their fit are important requirements. Concentrating only on existing core competencies is a static proposition that may result in antiquated capabilities.

Knowledge and the capacity to learn are also essential ingredients for success. Knowledge represents the present; learning is the future. While capabilities include the know-how, knowledge, intellectual capital, intellectual properties (IP), and processes of the organization, the essence of the organization's capabilities lies in its people. It is the innovative abilities of people that translate core capabilities of the present into superior positions in the future.

The importance of perspectives in today's business world

Perspectives are a person's mental views of concepts, facts, entities, etc. and their interrelationships. They involve exploring, examining, and contemplating the critical elements of the external and internal contexts, how their elements are interconnected and interrelated, and what they contribute to the whole. Moreover, perspectives can be framed by an observer or interpreter. For example, Thomas L. Friedman suggests that the interconnected world of the 21st century is becoming flatter as the internet and telecommunications among numerous other technologies level the playing field among the old-line industry giants and the emerging companies in developing countries.[8] Friedman provides insightful perspectives on how the business world is changing and the opportunities and challenges that are developing as a result. He also describes the rising power of the "individual" who has many more means and mechanisms like the internet to interact and communicate.

Perspectives are informal management constructs that are influenced by the leader's background, experience, knowledge and personal values. They are subject to the pressures, cultural aspects, and personal views of the leader. They do not provide absolutes, but relative views about reality and the prospects for the future. Perspectives trigger insights that help form theories and understandings about business realities. These may be viewed as the grey areas of leadership and management constructs that are not necessarily provable, but ones that help to establish the links between what is accepted in the mainstream of business today and what is evolving to create the mainstream of tomorrow. While perspectives and theories are often eschewed by many strategic leaders as being academic and not of the practical business world, they often foretell change and may be the harbingers of things to come. Theories may lead to new management constructs and practices that become the mainstream approaches of tomorrow. Perspective sets the stage for understanding and dealing with reality.

Perspectives involve rethinking mainstream notions about what is happening and how strategic leaders need to respond. Perspectives may simply be innovative or different ways of thinking about what is happening or what is changing. It can be argued that change is a continuum and that business leaders often lag behind in their interpretation of the implications. However, astute strategic leaders work to understand the nature and potential impacts of changes before their peers and competitors, and they gain insights about what may be as well as focusing on the prevailing aspects.

Perspectives are critical because they provide cutting-edge ways of strategic thinking that does not require absolute proof. Strategic leaders can form and assess their own perspectives on the business environment, markets, and their extended enterprises without having to provide hard evidence that their views are precise or provable. But, perspectives have to be plausible and provide potentially useful outcomes. For example, Columbus's perspectives that the world was round and that he could sail west to reach India gave him useful insights even though many aspects of his perspectives were incorrect. His overarching perspectives provided valuable contributions. On the other hand, a perspective that the Earth is going to crush into the Sun offers no benefits because it is not plausible (at least for billions of years) and it does not contribute to positive actions that could improve or mitigate the situation.

Perspectives are important because they shape the way business leaders view the business world and they help in decision making. Perspectives should include elements that are broad based and realistic. They should include the interrelationships of the elements and determine the dependence and independence among them. And, perspectives should examine the whole as well as the parts. The most compelling aspect is exploring the full spectrum of possibilities and realities.

Business leaders have to work hard and make judgments in the real world. They have to use credible information, data and evidence when making decisions. Moreover, they have to analyze the information and data as thoroughly as possible so that they are making the best decisions possible in generally accepted ways. Yet, in today's fast-paced world business leaders have to be careful to ensure that their management constructs are still relevant. New conditions and trends rapidly change the business landscape and some of the generally accepted ways of making decisions and doing business quickly become obsolete. Given such situations, strategic leaders must use best practices for the present and new perspectives and theories for the future. It is not that one is better or more appropriate, or that practices pertain to the real world and that theories pertain to the academic world. Both are relevant and important in managing the present and leading change in the future.

Strategic leaders, in particular, must be comfortable with developing perspectives, theories, and insights about their businesses, since they may provide road maps for the future and help to improve the methodologies of the present. In a slow-paced world, strategic leaders often had the luxury of following the industry leader, reacting to change or simply doing nothing until the implications of change were obvious and the new direction was clear. Today, strategic leaders have to have the skills and broad knowledge to understand the real world and the implications of change. In many situations, the best approach is to lead change and be on the cutting edge in developing the new mainstream constructs and approaches, rather than trying to catch up after lagging behind. For example, FMC was once a leader in the automobile industry and one of the largest and most successful corporations in the world. Its strategic leaders over time allowed the company's performance to slip and they failed to outpace change. Now, FMC's strategic leaders are trying to get it back on track and regain FMC's former levels of success.

To make real gains on its peers and competitors, proactive companies and their strategic leaders have to make radical changes and/or dramatic improvements that are at rates significantly greater than the overall rate of change in the industry or markets. For instance, assume that company A is ahead of company B by hundred percent in certain metrics like quality, reliable, unit costs, etc. If company B is improving at a compounded rate of ten percent per year, it would double its current positions in seven years. This calculation is based on the rule of 70, in which the rate of change is divided into seventy to obtain the number of years it takes to double (i.e., 70÷10=7 years). If company A also improves at ten percent per year, Company B will never catch up. If Company B improves at an impressive twenty percent per year, it would take seven years to reach parity assuming Company A improves at ten percent. For example, Company A is at 2.0 at the start of the exercise and it doubles in seven years to 4.0; Company B is at 1.0 at the start and it doubles in three and half years to 2.0; it must double again to become equivalent in seven years. (If company B's rate of improvement is fifteen percent it will take fourteen years to catch up). While real world situations are not as simple as the math suggests, it is clear that the lagging company has to make significant gains, if it wants to achieve parity and beyond. For example, Walmart is a $405 billion giant in retailing.[9] If Target Stores, one of its main competitors in the US, wants to become equivalent given its 2010 position of $67.4 billion in revenue, how can it achieve such a goal?[10]

The Pursuit of Sustainable Leadership

Leadership is among the most critical elements for achieving sustainable success in any organization, whether it is a nation state, a corporation, or a simple social group. Sustainable leadership provides a sense of purpose, vision, strategic direction, integration, connection, cohesion, innovation, and exhilaration. It conveys the spirit of being engaged, enthused and excited about what can be created, achieved and sustained. It is a dynamic involving dreams and aspirations for the future.

The pursuit of sustainable leadership (PSL) is difficult to define exactly because it is highly dependent on the attitudes, attributes, qualities, knowledge and learning of the leader, his or her personal values, beliefs, and behaviors, and the circumstances and situations involved. There are no precise definitions because the number of variables is extremely large and depend on the settings and changes over time. For instance, a strategic leader who is more of an administrator may be very competent in stable times, but lack the qualities necessary for managing during recessions or in leading change. As long as the business environment remains stable, such an individual may be perceived to be adequate or even outstanding. But, if the situation becomes turbulent, that leader may be unable to handle the situation. Moreover, many variables are intangibles, which are hard to define, understanding and articulate. It is difficult to map out exactly what the proper perspectives are and how the leader should respond in changing times.

The PSL involves determining what can be or has to be. It is not just about strategic leaders, managers and followers; it is about engagements, relationships and positive interactions. The PSL is not a process that one can prescribe. If it was a process, it would be easy to map out the process so that all leaders could follow a generally accepted pathway for achieving success. But it is not that simple. There are overarching precepts and principles that one can learn and there are values, beliefs and attitudes that a person can adopt, but it is not possible to lay out everything systematically so that anyone can follow to obtain success. The PSL involves designing and developing new approaches that are impossible to define in precise terms. Leaders often do not have the luxury of following well-established pathways, especially when changes necessitate creativity and innovation.

Strategic leaders are often the individuals that develop the vision for the future, identify the frameworks and constructs used by the organization for strategic formulation, implementation and execution and obtain exciting outcomes. They are the architects of the highways and byways to future success. They have the courage and conviction to lead change. For instance, imagine going along with Lewis and Clark during their famous exploration of the Louisiana Purchase. They had a wide-ranging mission from President Thomas Jefferson to explore the vast new territory he bought from France in 1803. Jefferson's orders were simple and open-ended, yet Lewis and Clark fulfilled their mission because they were able to lead people through uncharted waters and over new lands. Moreover, they successfully built relationships with native-American people who helped them in their quest. Lewis and Clark were insightful and open to new ways of doing things.

The PSL is pervasive. It is all encompassing with twenty-four seven responsibilities of the organization and extended enterprise. It involves assuming personal and professional responsibility for what happens in a business context. It requires understanding reality and knowing how to deal with the complexities of achieving success in the short term, preparing and innovating for the long term through a far-reaching strategic direction, and leading an organization into more desirable and sustainable positions. Strategic leadership requires truly imaginative, creative, inspirational, and courageous individuals who want to make a difference. Such leaders are focused on the external context and think about what can be done to change from what is to what can be. They study, research and collaborate to discover ways of accomplishing desired results and leading others within and outside of their organizations to participate in the processes and to expand the possibilities.

Reflections

The PSL is about leading people and change. It involves being proactive in creating a better future for the people and the organization. The underpinnings of leadership are broad and are difficult to precisely define and articulate, but nevertheless they are easy to understand if one has the proper perspectives and mindset. Strategic leaders are directly responsible for leading change and making dramatic improvements overall so that the business world is enriched and the organization becomes more sustainable. Strategic leadership involves making people successful and ensuring that value is created across the entire spectrum of social, economic and environmental aspects. It entails developing sustainable solutions that provide win-win outcomes for the organization, its enterprise and the key entities in the business environment.

Strategic leaders are confident, courageous and dedicated to their organizations and their aspirations. They achieve success through people and ensure that contributors are duly recognized and rewarded. They put the well being of the organization first and their self interest last. True strategic leaders are honest, trustful, have integrity and ethics, and engage in responsible behaviors. They do not compromise their personal values and standards for the sake of short-term gains and personal glory. They protect and preserve the well being of their organization. They focus on value creation and innovativeness and build solid relationships with people in the business environment.

Strategic leaders have a great sense of context. They understand the business environment, seek out opportunities and challenges, and create positive outcomes for all. If a strategic leader is the architect of great solutions, it is because he or she embraces the needs and expectations of the markets, customers, stakeholders and society. Moreover, strategic leaders know that great solutions are dual sided, whereby the positive aspects are maximized, as the negatives are minimized.

The PSL involves earning the respect of the organization and external entities and respecting the key contributors to success. The PSL is a multi-sided construct that promotes respect of others in the organization. Being a strategic leader of an organization involves more than occupying positions. Strategic leaders who are appointed by boards of directors, other strategic leaders or committees thereof must also authenticate their positions by exhibiting true leadership and providing support and encouragement within the organization.

Notes

1. Success is a far-reaching concept that often has to be defined in the context of the individual or organization. It cannot be solely based on making a lot of money or becoming the head (like being the CEO) of a powerful corporation. For example, Dr. Martin Luther King, Jr. was very successful in changing the views of many Americans and leading change across the civil rights movement. Mother Teresa became world famous for her charity and dedication in helping the poor worldwide. The leaders of the Apollo Program were successful because they integrated the multiple teams of players at NASA and the supporting entities into a coherent and effective enterprise.
2. Jim Collins, *Good to Great: Why Some Companies Make the Leap . . . and Others Don't* (New York, NY: Harper Business, 2001, p. 142).
3. Id, pp. 21 and 39. While some of the concept discussed in *Good to Great* fit the constructs of FSL, the premise of success using Collin's methods depended on meeting financial objectives rather than achieving multifaceted performance and outcomes.
4. Lawrence Susskind and Jeffrey Cruikshank, *Breaking the Impasse: Consensual Approaches to Resolving Public Dispute* (New York, NY: Basic Books, 1987, p. 260). Their note states that the "decide-announce-defend" approach was first used by Dennis Ducsik. The big DAD approach was described by Lawrence Susskind and Jeffrey Cruikshank as tool in disputes resolution.
5. David L. Rainey, *Enterprise-wide Strategic Management: Achieving Success through Leadership, Strategies, and Value Creation* (Cambridge, UK: Cambridge University Press, 2010, p. 316)
6. Ernest Gundling, *The 3M Way to Innovation: Balancing People and Profit* (Tokyo, Japan: Kodansha International, 2000, p. 58). 3M's innovative capabilities derive from its corporate culture and management philosophy that rely on customer input and employee contributions. 3M promotes creativity and decentralized thinking. William McKnight, the Chairman between 1949 and 1966, encouraged delegating responsibility and taking initiative. He was credited with 3M's famous "15% rule" that permeates the culture today, allowing its technical employees the flexibility to use fifteen percent of their time at work on their own projects.
7. W. Edwards Deming, *Out of the Crisis* (Cambridge, MA: The MIT Press, 2000, pp. 77–86).
8. Thomas L. Friedman, *The World Is Flat: A Brief History of the Twenty-first Century* (New York, NY: Farrar, Straus and Giroux, 2005).

9. http://www.walmartstores.com/AboutUs/
10. http://sites.target.com/images/company/annual_report_2010/documents/Target_Annual-Report_2010.pdf Target 2010 Annual Report.

References

Collins, Jim (2001) *Good to Great: Why Some Companies Make the Leap... and Others Don't.* New York, NY: Harper Business.

Deming, W. Edwards (2000) *Out of the Crisis.* Cambridge, MA: The MIT Press.

Friedman, Thomas L. (2005) *The World Is Flat: A Brief History of the Twenty-first Century.* New York, NY: Farrar, Straus and Giroux.

Gundling, Ernest (2000) *The 3M Way to Innovation: Balancing People and Profit.* Tokyo, Japan: Kodansha International.

Rainey, David L. (2010) *Enterprise-wide Strategic Management: Achieving Success through Leadership, Strategies, and Value Creation.* Cambridge, UK: Cambridge University Press.

Susskind, Lawrence and Jeffrey Cruikshank (1987) *Breaking the Impasse: Consensual Approaches to Resolving Public Dispute.* New York, NY: Basic Books.

2

The Principles, Philosophies, Values and Cultural Underpinnings of Leadership

Introduction

Successful leadership is based on principles, unshakable beliefs and proper constructs that are supported by convictions, commitments, courage, determination, proper behaviors and personal development. Astute leaders have to have a solid foundation of well-established principles, philosophies, personal values, and cultural underpinnings Principles provide stability based on the underlying values and tenets of the individual leaders and their organizations. One's beliefs include the principles, philosophies and personal values that guide the strategic leader's view of reality and provide the underlying strategic logic for leadership and management. Beliefs are solidified and modified through knowledge, experience and learning. Well-conceived and validated beliefs and known truths are crucial for effective leadership. They provide the logic and rationale for decisions, actions and behaviors. True leaders have the capacity to select the best means and mechanisms for leading their organizations and enterprises though building relationships and developing solutions, systems and structures that are in concert with the needs, expectations and dynamics of the world.

Principles are the agreed truths, standards and basic suppositions that form the basis for personal ethics, proper behaviors and good decision making; ones that do not vary much over time and. Principles are easily articulated and are based on generally acceptable standards. They should resonate in society and with people and be in line with acceptable behavior in civil society. For instance, telling the whole truth is one

The Pursuit of Sustainable Leadership, pages 25–52

of the most crucial principles. Most people are honest and fair; therefore, the related principles reinforce their personal views and the ones that they would want their leaders and business organizations to have. While there are differing perspectives about what some of the principles are or how they are framed and interpreted, the most basic principles generally have common ground among the leaders and most people within the organization and the outside communities.

Leadership philosophies are the general approaches used by individual leaders in forming strategies, making decisions, taking actions and leading people. Leadership philosophies involve the underpinnings of thought, the logic for decision making, the system of overarching values, and the conceptual views pertaining to life and proper behaviors. They are broad leadership perspectives that are often difficult to prove because most of them are intangibles, yet they are generally accepted because they are perceived to be correct, valid and appropriate. They provide comfort to leaders and people within the organization. For instance, determination, dedication and steadfastness are often keys to success in which leaders stay the course through difficult and trying times. George Washington prevailed though the harsh winters, limited resources and numerous lost battles because he was resolute in his convictions. While he did not originate the saying, "never give up," he clearly invoked it throughout the difficult days of the Revolutionary War. Winston Churchill was determined to fight the Nazi to the "bloody end" regardless of how bleak the situation appeared.

Values are based on knowledge, experiences and emotional makeup. They affect the choices that people make over the course of their lives and careers and support them in making decisions and developing behaviors. Personal values guide implicit judgments and the determinations that individuals make based on their family, ethical, and personal backgrounds. For instance, people select a religion and follow its beliefs based on the views of their parents or the historical context.

Cultural underpinnings are the norms and values of the group, clan, community, and/or society. They are the shared beliefs and approaches that form over time and are sanctioned by a majority of the people within a community. Cultural underpinnings are broad generalizations that define the essence of the culture and explain why things are done a certain way. They facilitate behaviors within an organization or community, i.e., they provide people with an understanding of the norms and standards. However, care has to be used when considering cultural underpinnings because they do change over time and most importantly they typify a general situation and not specific ones. People may be part of a community or culture and behave according, but they also act as individuals based on their own views and beliefs.

The principles, philosophies, values and cultural underpinnings are critical elements of leadership. The terms "leadership" and "leaders" used in this chapter apply to all levels from the bottom to the top. The term "strategic" is not always used even though it may be implied.

This chapter includes the following main topics:

- Identifying and describing the main principles of leadership.

- Discussing the underlying philosophies of leadership and management.
- Highlighting the importance of personal values and the cultural underpinnings.

Principles of Leadership

Axiomatic principles of leadership

Principles of leadership provide guidance in leading and managing organizations that reduce some of the fuzziness when dealing with complex situations, dealing with critical issues and problems, and making difficult decisions. They help one chart the course toward the proper perspectives, directions and outcomes. Principles include the truths and fundamental beliefs that establish the foundation for decision making and provide the temperance for the organization. They provide consistency in strategic thinking and alignment in actions and outcomes.

The ***axiomatic principles*** are overarching or universal ones that fit most contexts and realities. They include the precepts of leadership discussed in the previous chapter. They help to link the leaders' and organization's perspectives with the prevailing realities of the business environment. Some of the axiomatic principles not covered under the topic of precepts include ensuring:

- Human rights, equality and fairness.
- Responsiveness, due care, precautionary (principle) safeguards and preparedness.
- Good governance, proper disclosures, and full compliance.

Basic ***human rights*** that all people desire and deserve are the most critical principles of leadership. Leaders have an overarching duty to assure that their decisions, actions and behaviors conform to the fundamental human rights and that they promote and protect the human rights of all people. These are absolute obligations that cannot be modified by situations or circumstances. For instance, exploiting workers and condoning harsh working conditions are violations of basic human rights, even if such practices are not against the law in a particular country. In such situations business leaders have the duty to ensure that workers, associates and contractors are treated properly, fairly, and humanely regardless their social, political and legal standings. Principles of human rights have been formulated by a number of organizations from the United Nations (UN) to various special interest groups like the Fair labor Association (FLA). The UN formulated the Global Compact in 1999 to guide business, labor, and society in the quest for social responsibility and equality. While there may not be general acceptance of some of the specifics associated with the Global Compact, many of the principles are similar to those of international social organizations like the FLA The principles of the Global Compact are:[1]

Human Rights

- Principle 1: The support and respect of the protection of international human rights;
- Principle 2: The refusal to participate or condone human rights abuses.

Labour

- Principle 3: The support of freedom of association and the recognition of the right to collective bargaining;
- Principle 4: The abolition of compulsory labour
- Principle 5: The abolition of child labour
- Principle 6: The elimination of discrimination in employment and occupation.

Environment

- Principle 7: The implementation of a precautionary and effective program to address environmental issues;
- Principle 8: Initiatives that demonstrate environmental responsibility;
- Principle 9: The promotion of the diffusion of environmentally friendly technologies.

Anti-Corruption

- Principle 10: The promotion and adoption of initiatives to counter all forms of corruption, including extortion and bribery.

The principles are a mix of codes of conduct, statements of obligations and prescriptions for action. Common themes among most of such constructs include fundamental freedoms, respect for people, abolition of forced and child labor, and the eradication of corruption.

FLA is a non-profit organization dedicated to ending sweatshop conditions in factories worldwide.[2] It is supported by social organizations, universities and about thirty global corporations including Nike, Inc. and Adidas Group. FLA prescribes the following workplace code of conduct:[3]

- Forced Labor: There shall not be any use of forced labor, whether in the form of prison labor, indentured labor, bonded labor or otherwise.
- Child Labor: No person shall be employed at an age younger than 15 (or 14 where the law of the country of manufacture allows) or younger than the age for completing compulsory education in the country of manufacture where such age is higher than 15.
- Harassment or Abuse: Every employee shall be treated with respect and dignity. No employee shall be subject to any physical, sexual, psychological or verbal harassment or abuse.
- Nondiscrimination: No person shall be subject to any discrimination in employment, including hiring, salary, benefits, advancement, discipline, termination or retirement, on the basis of gender, race, religion, age, disability, sexual orientation, nationality, political opinion, or social or ethnic origin.
- Health and Safety: Employers shall provide a safe and healthy working environment to prevent accidents and injury to health arising out of, linked with, or occurring in the course of work or as a result of the operation of employer facilities.
- Freedom of Association and Collective Bargaining: Employers shall recognize and respect the right of employees to freedom of association and collective bargaining.
- Wages and Benefits: Employers recognize that wages are essential to meeting employees' basic needs. Employers shall pay employees, as a floor, at least the minimum wage required by local law or the prevailing industry wage, whichever is higher, and shall provide legally mandated benefits.

- Hours of Work: Except in extraordinary business circumstances, employees shall: (i) not be required to work more than the lesser of (a) 48 hours per week and 12 hours overtime or (b) the limits on regular and overtime hours allowed by the law of the country of manufacture or, where the laws of such country do not limit the hours of work, the regular work week in such country plus 12 hours overtime, and (ii) be entitled to at least one day off in every seven day period.
- Overtime Compensation: In addition to their compensation for regular hours of work, employees shall be compensated for overtime hours at such premium rate as is legally required in the country of manufacture or, in those countries where such laws do not exist, at a rate at least equal to their regular hourly compensation rate.

The Sullivan Principles is another example of overarching principles, which were developed and introduced in 1977 by Reverend Leon Sullivan who promoted fair treatment of disadvantaged workers in South Africa during apartheid.[4] Many international corporations adopted these principles, because they did not want their reputations tarnished by associations with those violating human rights. Many corporations and organizations took even more dramatic approaches and pulled out of South Africa because of the government's violation of basis human rights.

Equality requires that business be conducted using means and mechanisms that are appropriate in all situations; ones that do not disadvantage anyone as a matter of design or execution. It implies equal treatment and justice for all people. It also implies that no one has a superior position from a human perspective and that no one should be treated more favorably or less favorably than anyone else. From a business perspective, ***fairness*** involves ensuring that all people receive proper compensation for their contributions and appropriate recognition for their labor, land, other possessions, or dispositions. It also implies eliminating mechanisms and practices that disadvantage people who are negatively affected by them, especially those with no voice in decisions. For instance, business leaders should not target less affluent communities when building production facilities that have particularly nasty operations, produce toxic substances, and/or have huge negative impacts on the surrounding ecosystems.

Responsiveness and ***due care*** involve upfront and ongoing actions to create the best solutions that provide external entities and individuals with the successful outcomes they seek. Business success depends generally on the ***responsiveness*** of business leaders to the needs and expectations to customers, stakeholders and other constituencies. People expect and demand solutions that provide the full range of benefits and ones that mitigate the defects, burdens, and negative impacts that are associated with the products and services provided. Everyone desires solutions that are safe, effective, affordable and long lasting.

Responsible leaders provide ***precautionary safeguards*** to ensure their solutions are appropriate and safe from every perspective. Precautionary safeguards means that every decision and every action are duly scrutinized and that proper outcomes are assured, considering the current state of the art. Strategic leaders have a duty to use the precautionary principle (PP), if the health, safety and well being of individuals or the social world and natural environment are jeopardized by uncertain and potentially risky outcomes. PP involves taking all appropriate preventive measures, when there are reasons to believe that potential danger, harm, or impacts exist. It simply implies that leaders have an absolute obligation to explore every facet of the situations and ensure proper outcomes before they make decisions and take actions. PP dictates that the most reasonable course is to err on the side of safety, human health, and the protection of the natural environment.

Preparedness involves assessing reasonable possibilities to determine the likelihood of unexpected negative effects and impacts and preparing emergency and contingency plans to deal with the potential consequences and to mitigate likely effects and impacts. While it is impossible to guarantee perfection, strategic leaders are expected to consider negative events and take the associated precautions to provide the best outcomes possible. Moreover, strategic leaders have a duty to be prepared to deal with the unexpected, especially foreseeable possibilities that could affect their businesses and people. This is one of the more difficult areas, since it involves unknowns.

Strategic leaders have an absolute obligation to assure the proper ***governance*** of their organizations and the entire extended enterprise. Good governance is central to leadership, strategic management, operations management, and strategic decision-making. It is a fiduciary responsibility established by the corporate by-laws and by the obligations one assumes as a leader. Strategic leaders are expected to be connected with their business environment, to formulate and implement policies, processes and practices and to make decisions based on providing the best outcomes possible from the every perspective. Ensuring good governance involves broad participation, the effectiveness of the actions and outcomes, and the coherence of the organization. It implies that business leaders assume responsibility and accountability for their decisions and actions. They may delegate the actual implementation to others, but they are still accountable for the oversight and have a duty to ensure that the proper execution is affected regardless of the delegation. Leaders are expected to be honest and open with all constituents, especially the people that they are directly responsible for. Good governance also involves proper reporting. For instance, customers and stakeholders want proper disclosures of all pertinent information to ensure the appropriate and safe use of the products and services. Customers wish to minimize or eliminate the inherent risks associated with buying and using the products. Stakeholders and society expect the principals involved in producing and delivering products and services to prevent adverse difficulties and problems. These principles are especially well articulated in the European Union (EU) and sanctioned by EU directives.[5]

Compliance with laws and regulations is simple to understand, but often complicated and difficult to achieve. It involves complying with all of the laws and regulations that affect the companies, their business units and the leaders and ensuring that the mandates and requirements on the extended enterprise are being fulfilled. The former is a primary obligation, while latter is an indirect obligation that also fits in with the notion of being accountable for the whole. Compliance is not only applies to the company, it is a primary obligation of the strategic leaders. Individual leaders may be held personally responsible for their organization's failure to comply with laws and regulations. Once a leader's personal reputation and standing are damaged it is difficult to recover. On the positive side, a record of full compliance is testimony of a leader's character and integrity.

Business-related principles

Business-related principles involve guiding doctrines for proper conduct and behaviors that facilitate understanding reality, dealing with the driving forces of change and making the most appropriate decisions possible based on the context of external opportunities, challenges, conditions and trends, and internal strategic positions, capabilities, resources and realities. Such principles are intended to provide guidance for making decisions and taking actions, but are not necessarily absolute requirements that must be always be followed. The principles herein differ from the precepts described in Chapter 1 and the axioms discussed in the previous section in that they are more dependent on the prevailing and expected situations. They are not necessarily universal and there may be alternate forms of business-related principles with the many variations in content and the associated implications. The main business-related principles include the following:

- **Embrace the fundamental underpinning that people are always first**—Make people the prime beneficiaries and think about how they can become more satisfied and successful through the decisions and actions of the strategic leaders, the organization and its enterprises.
- **Employ holistic perspectives to explore the full spectrum of space and time**—Focus on opportunities that benefit the whole enterprise and organization using holistic (full spectrum) thinking, i.e., consider every perspective. This implies that the threats and risks should be mitigated as soon as possible so that their effects and impacts are minimized across the whole spectrum of space and time.
- **Develop win–win attitudes**—Encourage people to participate in win-win situations and outcomes that maximize the gains for contributors and beneficiaries; ones that avoid destructive behaviors in which no one wins, especially conflicts with communities and indigenous peoples involving the use of resources, the effects of pollution and the disposal of wastes.
- **Create strong value networks and enduring relationships**—Success depends on the integration of the company and the entire extended enterprise; building long-term relationships with people across the value networks and within the organization; and, creating the means and mechanisms for everyone to become successful.
- **Create sustainable solutions**—Provide solutions that create the most value for customers, stakeholders, constituencies, shareholders and the organization; ones that enhance the positive aspects and eliminate the negative effects, impacts and outcomes on the external business environment and ensure that the recipients of the solutions enjoy success over a considerable time horizon.

These principles are interrelated and critical factors for success that are measured in terms of the realities and practicalities of the business environment and not just the leader's or the organization's perspectives on financial performance and company-centric outcomes.

The business-related principles are based on how the people outside the organization perceive their own needs, requirements and expectations and not just on how strategic leaders think about them. They are more complicated than what many authors writing on leadership suggest and may be contrary to many prevailing views. For instance, keeping things simple as recommended by the archaic "keep it simple stupid" (KISS) principle sounds like a wonderful prescription for success; however, given that the realities of the current business world are extremely complex, the KISS principle may delude business leaders into focusing on narrow perspectives that may lead to success in the short term, but ultimately result in a quagmire in the long term. Most opportunities and challenges are neither simple nor are they just based on a single dimension like making money. Focusing only on the economics or financial aspects misleads many business leaders to think that they can obtain true success by managing only the financial side of their business enterprise rather than managing all of the critical factors including the well being of employees, customer responsiveness, environmental effects and impacts, and numerous others.

Business-related principles are critically important, because they provide strategic leaders with the logic and guidance in managing in the complexities of the business environment. Unlike many of organizational aspects, which are controllable to a large extent, the forces of change in the business environment are often difficult to truly understand and manage. Putting people first is one of the most important perspectives for managing complexities; in other words, making people the prime beneficiaries. This principle involves becoming people-centric instead of company-centric or self-centered. It necessitates strategic thinking from the perspectives of the customers, stakeholders, employees, shareholders, and constituents. While this seems to be straightforward, it is actually a profound change in the strategic thinking about what should be done not just what is being done.

Putting yourself in some other person's shoes as the old adage suggests is an important step for understanding what is needed, required and expected. However, such approaches are extremely hard to actually accomplish given that most views and generalizations are formed with the perspectives of the observers and not the subjects. Nevertheless, it is critical for business leaders to envision the business world and the external dimensions from the other person's perspectives. This becomes more difficult to do as business leaders shift their thinking from individuals to groups and communities. Business leaders can dramatically improve their prospects for developing and implementing the appropriate strategies and solutions and achieving success by understanding external context and the people therein from the broadest possible perspectives. Within a country and the specific communities therein, people have distinct cultural aspects and different ways of thinking about the actual or potential strategies, solutions and approaches. For instance, people in developing countries would like to enjoy the products and services provided by businesses that improve their well being and living conditions. However, most business leaders in the past developed and delivered products and services from the perspectives of their business objectives and not from those of their existing and potential customers. Even today, business leaders often want to produce and sell what is currently in their product portfolio rather than addressing the true needs and expectations of customers; this is a particular concern pertaining to people living in developing countries who often have different situations and circumstances than the people living in the developed countries. Most of the products that are available from global corporations do not fit the context of the indigenous people in many of the poorest countries. The problem is that most of the products were designed and developed based on the conditions that exist in the developed countries. For instance, the current products may require electricity, which is a perfectly fine design consideration for most locations in the US or EU, but not appropriate in many of the poorest countries where electricity is not available or not affordable.

Holistic thinking involves focusing on all of the critical elements for achieving success. Business leaders have to consider opportunities and challenges across space and time. Businesses generally have more opportunities, if they can mitigate the negative aspects of situations. For example, there are enormous opportunities and challenges in the automobile industry associated with climate change and fuel efficiency; think about the strategic advantages General Motors (GM), Ford Motor Company or any of the other global competitors could enjoy, if they had solutions to these difficulties. Weak competitors could become industry leaders by leading change and providing the right solutions to great challenges.

Business success is enhanced when there are many entities and people supporting one's business operations, systems, processes, and activities from producing parts and materials to buying and selling the end products and when they all have the ability to be successful. Today, there are only a very few examples like some of the petroleum companies in which an organization can enjoy success when others may not be. To the contrary, most successful situations involve broad participation of many contributors and recipients who generally obtain positive outcomes and receive various rewards through win-win relationships and outcomes. Success often results from making many others successful. Win-win attitudes involve ensuring that each participant in business transactions, operations and activities obtains his or her fair share of the outcomes. This does not mean that everyone shares equally, but that everyone is respected and recognized for their contributions and compensated accordingly. Developing win-win attitudes requires new perspectives on creating value and enhancing positions. Win-win attitudes are based on the premises that strategic leaders and their organizations become more successful when the other entities in its business enterprise are also successful. This notion is directly related to creating extraordinary value, building solid relationships and focusing on sustainable success. For example, BASF is the world's largest chemical manufacturer that provides the critical materials for other companies in the production of many of the leading products in the world. BASF focuses on making its customers successful and ensuring that the materials used are the best possible for the applications selected. Its success is predicated on the success of its customers. And, the success of Honda over the last several decades is because its supply networks are integrated into its business enterprise and provide the right parts at the right time.

Relationships are the cement that connects people and the elements of value networks to realize exceptional performance and extraordinary outcomes that benefit the contributors and the recipients. Strategic leaders have to be the lynch pins for building relationships and connecting the people who engage in developing, producing, delivering, supporting and using solutions. Building relationships with supply networks, partners, allies and supporting entities on the upstream side of the extended enterprise tends to reinforce and stabilize the value created over time and facilitates the transitions and/or transformations to the higher levels of sophistication that are necessary for continued success. While the systems, solutions, products and services, processes, components and parts thereof may dramatically change or even be replaced over time, building solid relationships among the contributors and recipients is an effective mechanism for developing and maintaining predictable and fruitful situations and outcomes. Relationships are built on trust and trust is enhanced when the people involved realize positive gains from their efforts and experiences.

Creating sustainable solutions is among the most important principles. The concept of a "solution" seems to be straightforward, but in reality it is ever evolving as the requirements of the business world change and new expectations develop. A ***solution*** is multifaceted and involves the product, the service, the underlying technology(s), and all of the tangible and intangible elements of the system(s) and relationships. It involves the contributions of entities in the supply networks and related industries that offer parts and components or complementary products. It also includes providers of end-of-life considerations and supporters who ensure that solutions are sustainable.[6]

The solution is framed in the context of the whole business environment and extended enterprise. Its ultimate form depends on the conditions and trends of the social, economic and environmental factors. Moreover, it is a moving target. Strategic leaders often mistakenly define the desired solutions by what their products are (features, form, and functionality) and not by the needs they address and how they meet or are expected to fulfill the desires and expectations of people or a population.[7] For example, a hydrogen fuel-cell powered vehicle without the availability of a source of hydrogen fuel has little value. The same can be said of a gasoline or diesel powered automobile without the availability of those fuels. A solution requires all of the ingredients and support services provided by its designers and producers and all of the supporting elements that are necessary for success over time, including the complementary products and the related infrastructure. Moreover, it is not sufficient to have a few support products and services, but an interconnected array of such elements and the related facilities that are economically stable, environmental sound, and proven to be safe so that customers and potential customers of the solutions are confident that their choices will prove to be appropriate over time. People realize that when they purchase certain products like automobiles they are buying dependences. It is incumbent on business leaders to ensure that customers' decisions are sustainable over time and that the economic value is maintained.

In business, it is pointless to win a competitive battle or to make a financial "killing" and then lose it all in subsequent periods. The history of business is replete with stories of companies that built great wealth over ten, twenty, thirty or more years, only to give it all back in a relatively short amount of time when their fortunes reversed. For example, during the 1970s Wang Laboratories and Digital Equipment Corporation were stars in the computer industry, but they were unable to sustain their successes during the late 1980s and early 1990s. Although the strategic leaders were successful during the glory years, they failed to ensure that their successes were broad based and enduring over time. Companies that focus on existing products and how they exploit prevailing market opportunities often fail to create sustainable futures.

Underlying Philosophies of Leadership

The importance and implications of leadership philosophies

Leadership philosophies are the personal and professional views and doctrines of the leader. They may be broadly held ones like the old-line perspective that the purpose of business is to maximize profits or they may be more contemporary attitudes toward leadership such as embracing ethical behaviors and endorsing corporate social responsibility (CSR). A particular philosophy does not have to be unique to the leader, but each leader should adapt his or her versions of generally accepted philosophies or create more personalized ones. It is imperative that leaders contemplate what their philosophies are and/or should be. This is particularly crucial when engaged in complex decision making. Leadership philosophies involve fundamental perspectives and prescribe the basic ways of approaching situations, contemplating decisions and entertaining actions. Most leadership philosophies are neither precisely right nor exactly wrong; however, one has to be careful not to think that all choices in realm of leadership philosophies have merit, especially leadership philosophies that are counter to the precepts of leadership and the axiomatic principles. For instance, the philosophies associated with apartheid are contrary to the principles of human rights and basic rights of all people. In reality, such views and perspectives are not philosophies at all, but excuses for malfeasance and illegal behaviors.

Business leaders should determine their primary leadership philosophies as early in their career as possible, since philosophies provide a sense of consistency and a theoretical basis for decision making. Leaders that follow a well-honed set of leadership philosophies can ascertain how well their leadership styles are working in light of the philosophical underpinnings, i.e., beliefs about what is right and proper and what is ethical and moral. Using a philosophical basis eliminates some of the potential difficulties with trial and error approaches. With a sound philosophical foundation, business leaders can test their concepts, constructs and methods and make adjustments whenever outcomes suggest changes are necessary. A simple trial and error approach without a solid foundation either works or does not work. If it does not work, it is difficult to determine how to correct the situation. If a philosophically sound approach proves to be faulty, there is evidence about what needs to be done. Many of the prevailing views of strategic management are real philosophical perspectives that certain leaders believe to be true. For instance, the widely held theory about profits as articulated by Milton Friedman in 1962 is thought to be an axiom of business, but it is really a simple philosophy that still requires validation. Friedman, a Nobel laureate in economics, viewed the role of business and capitalism as follows:[8]

> The view [social responsibility of business and labor] has been gaining widespread acceptance that corporate officials and labor leaders have a "social responsibility" that goes beyond serving the interest of their stockholders or their members. This view shows a fundamental misconception of the character and nature of a free economy. In such a economy, there is one and only one responsibility of business-to use its resources and engage in activities designed to increase its profits so long as it stays within the rules of the game, which is to say engages in free and open competition, without deception or fraud.

Friedman asserted that the primary social responsibility of business is to make sufficient profits to cover all expenses and provide an appropriate return on shareholders' investments. He contended that strategic leaders are rightly guided by the "economic self-interest" and that the purpose and primary objectives of business entities are to maximize profits and shareholder wealth. Such perspectives whether right or not became the primary philosophies for guiding many strategic leaders during the last century in their decision making and actions. However, Friedman's perspectives are not axioms (truths), but are really presumptions with extremely limited perspectives.

Most leadership philosophies are not based on proof or scientific methods, but are validated by actions and outcomes. Some can be shown to be correct or the most appropriate in given situations, but leadership philosophies are really complex views that require extensive data and information and analysis to validate. Validation in the real world provides a sense of proof through compelling evidence based on ongoing success with positive outcomes. Such validations are achieved without going through the rigors of scientific proof. If the latter was done, then the leadership philosophy(s) would possibly become a principle, thus simply redefining it as such. While principles are usually more rigorous than leadership philosophies providing a basis for more generalized use, leadership philosophies are important, since they provide guidance and assistant without having to be precisely proven. Moreover, a leader may adapt new philosophies over the course of time as new evidence becomes available about what is appropriate.

Leadership philosophies pertain to how the leader thinks, decides, behaves and acts. They involve leadership, not strategic management, and the way that the leader views and treats other people; how he or she establishes what is critical and what is less important. Leadership philosophies should be broad and provide more exciting possibilities, not constraints and limitations on choices. For decades there have been numerous debates about certain philosophical differences, some of which are business philosophies as well as leadership philosophies. The tensions often revolve around the "either-or" perspectives. In *The Three Tensions: Winning the Struggle to Perform without*

Compromise, Dominic Dodd and Ken Favaro discuss the philosophical tensions that leaders face.[9]

> More growth damages profitability and more profitability slows growth. Efforts to build for tomorrow distract everyone from producing results today; but when managers shift focus to results for today, they compromise the future strengths of the company. Attempts to create one-company benefits hold back individual business units; then attempts to unleash the individual potential of the business units bar the way to capturing the benefits of being one company. It's like squeezing a balloon in one pace only to find that it expands elsewhere.
>
> These are the three tensions that act on every company; profitability, [versus] revenue growth; results today, [versus] results tomorrow, and the performance of the company as a whole, [versus] the performance of each part of the company.

Dodd and Favaro hit on the classic dichotomies that business leaders struggle with all the time. Historically, strategic leaders made trade-offs when dealing with such tensions; a little of this for a little of that or trying to find the "middle ground." Today, business leaders have to think about how to create and deliver success without compromises or tradeoffs, i.e., success in the present, success in the future, and success for all. Business leaders often fall into the trap of "either-or" thinking. They take philosophical perspectives that are one-sided: short term or long term; the whole or the parts; profits or growth; company success or customer success; and so on. Leadership is not about making compromises or focusing on just one side of an issue or question. From a philosophical perspective such thinking falls under the regime of dictates. Indeed, many of the most famous early to mid- twentieth century business philosophies were really dictates that offered little latitude and were typically highly prescriptive. For instance, the philosophical perspectives of maximizing profits, achieving short-term performance, focusing on core competencies, and the like are actually dictates that constrain strategic thinking rather than facilitating creative thinking and developing balanced solutions.[10] They involve the ***"either-or trap"*** in which leaders are seemingly forced to decide upon achieving a specific outcome at the expense of other valuable outcomes. For instance, leaders focus their attention on short-term profits instead of also building enhancing customer satisfaction and sustainable success. Such leaders often create future liabilities as they try to reduce costs.

Leadership philosophies run the gamut from well-defined, narrow beliefs to the more open-ended and broader perspectives that are customized for the situations and uses of the individual leader. This can be stated in another more direct way; they vary considerable from generic, well-known business philosophies used by the mainstream that are articulated by renowned scholars and practitioners to unique philosophies that are created and developed by the incumbent leaders.

During the twentieth century, the preference was for the generic philosophies, because they were easy to assume and they offered leaders cover. The business leaders could always say that they were simply following the lead of well respected scholars and practitioners and they were in the mainstream of leadership thinking. Such approaches often worked reasonably well in the short term, but created difficulties in the long term. The reasons are simple. If most strategic leaders are following dictates or generic constructs, how do they differentiate their positions? Generic approaches often lead to generic results. For instance, GM was the undisputed leader in the automobile industry during the 1960s with approximately sixty percent market share in the US. However, its strategic leaders let GM's leadership position slip away, because they focused on profits instead of reinforcing the company's strategic positions and engaging in strategic innovations that might have elevated GM to even higher levels of sophistication.

In his book, *The Long Tail: How endless choice is creating unlimited demand*, Chris Anderson highlights product-market opportunities that are beyond the mainstream.[11] He characterizes most product-market situations in terms of the mainstream in which there are several dominant products that enjoy high volume (high frequency of purchase) and many other products that have very low levels of purchases. Using his logic and adapting it to leadership philosophies, strategic leaders can gain insights about using generic philosophies that are in the mainstream versus crafting their own unique ones. An adaptation of Anderson's model suggests that as the selection of leadership philosophies moves from the well-established ones in the zone of mainstream philosophies to the zone of individualized ones at the extreme end, the range of potential outcomes and the quality and satisfaction thereof increases dramatically. Figure 2.1 provides a representation of the implications.[12]

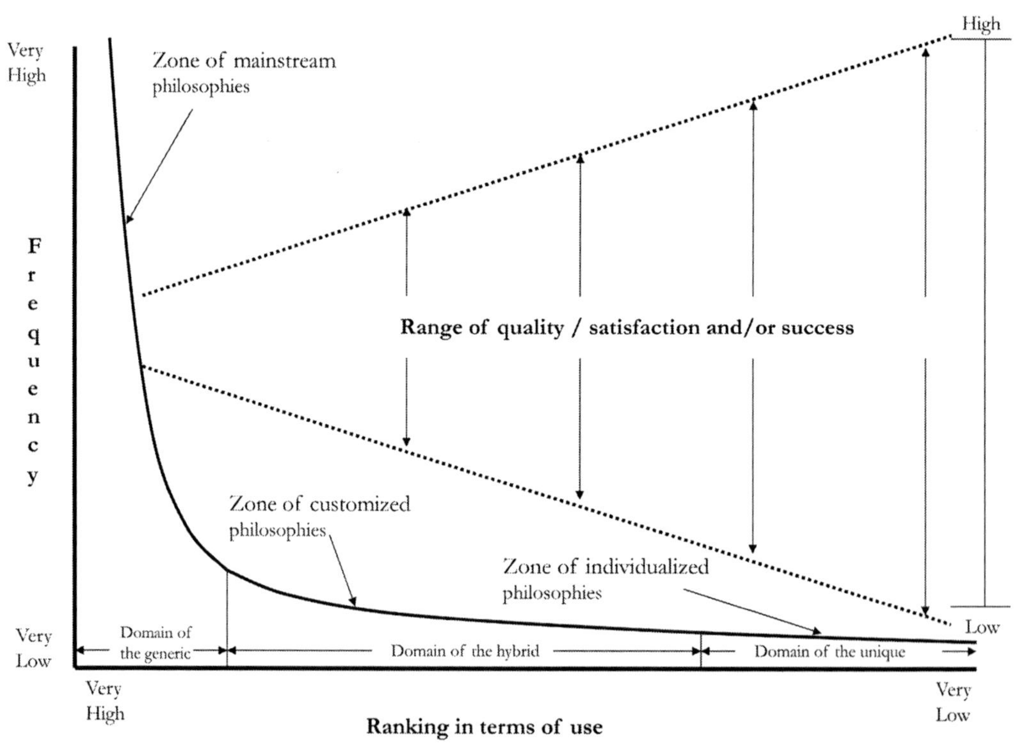

Figure 2.1 A graphical representation of the choices pertaining to leadership philosophies[13]

There are numerous generic leadership philosophies that strategic leaders can adopt. The advantages include being in the mainstream and gaining credibility based on the reputation of the leading scholar and/or expert whose views are widely recognized. The generic leadership philosophies are generally well known and understood and are shared by a relatively large number of other leaders and people. In Anderson's concept of the long tail, he indicates that the generic approaches usually provide a reasonable level of satisfaction that is often acceptable to the mainstream. He also suggests that the range of outcomes is small and that the probability of obtaining greatness is likewise small. The implication is that generic philosophies usually lead to a high probability of achieving reasonable degree of success, but typically do not offer the possibility of realizing an overwhelming degree of success. The disadvantages include being an imitator who just adopts the prevailing views and does not have a distinctive approach. Having generic or mainstream philosophies means that your philosophical approaches are like those of a large number or even a majority in the mainstream. They lack distinctiveness and often are not precise fits to one's situations. Moreover, they often are not in line with the strategic direction so they have to be forced to fit the company's strategic logic. People get what they expect. There are numerous examples of leaders of their industries who followed each other's lead and all suffered the same consequences. The leaders in the banking industry during the last decade are examples how strategic leaders of different companies follow each other. One might ask: how could a large number of strategic leaders in the banking and financial services industries get into the same problems associated with "sub-prime" mortgages?

To offset some of the limitations of being generic, strategic leaders might modify or customize some or even all of their generic philosophies and create "hybrids" that provide some semblance of customization and individualization. Such approaches still have some disadvantages of the generic philosophies because they are derived from generalized approaches; however, as strategic leaders move further to the right in the domain of the hybrid philosophies, they start mitigating some of their problems associated with being an imitator and begin gaining the advantages of being innovators. They are customizing their leadership philosophies to be in concert with their own situations and circumstances. The concept suggests that unique approaches offer many more possibilities and provide a greater range for successes. While creativity and thinking out-of-the-box involve more uncertainties and greater risks, enlightened and competent leaders can outperform peers and competitors through aggressive strategies and actions using innovative constructs.

On the "long tail" or extreme side, the range of outcomes is much larger going from achieving extraordinary success at the high end of the possibilities to the depths of dismal failure at the low end. Strategic leaders who individualize their leadership philosophies can realize exciting outcomes that are unique and distinctive. Of course, they have to be good at finding and taking advantage of opportunities and mitigating challenges and problems. But, that is what makes great leaders. On the far end of the graphic in the domain of unique philosophies, strategic leaders create highly individualized approaches; ones that fit their situation exactly. The advantages and disadvantages tend to be just the opposite of those for the generic philosophies. The main advantage is creating the means and mechanisms to stand out from the enormous number of generic leaders who are basically conformists. The more individualized leadership philosophies allow differentiating oneself from mainstream strategic leaders who are not very dynamic. Leaders with highly individualized philosophies exhibit an aura of distinctiveness and confidence. The main disadvantage is the possibility of a lack of acceptance and the risk of being out on a tangent. There are also the possibilities that the selected philosophies will not contributed to sound decision making in the long term. For instance, Boeing changed its philosophy of designing new aircraft using in-house talent to using global partners for designing and producing many of main components of the Boeing 787 Dream Liner. The new business philosophy was expected to reduce the investment in the design by $4 billion.[14] While the Boeing reduced its design and development investment, delays in production due to global sourcing have more than offset the expected economic gains. It is always difficult to think through all of the potential possibilities upfront; therefore, leaders have to be diligent in ensuring the business philosophies are relevant in terms of reality and that they continue to be relevant over time. In determining and selecting one's leadership philosophies, leaders have the opportunity to become unique and be a person that is dynamic and creative. Leadership philosophies in general have more flexibility and adaptability than principles. The number of possibilities is endless. Each person can select his or her own philosophies in leading and managing. The more choices one has, the higher is the probability of finding success. Remember even great innovators and proactive leaders may fail to reflect on their philosophies and perspectives and become entrenched in outmoded ways of thinking and decision making.

An overview of contemporary leadership philosophies

Fundamentals pertaining to leadership philosophies

Leadership philosophies are self-selected constructs for leading organizations and people. It is important for leaders to adopt leadership philosophies because they are the basis for determining mindset, values and certain decision making criteria. It is crucial that philosophies be far-reaching, i.e., that there are wide range of choices and that the choices are not limited to the "either-or trap." Care should be taken to avoid mapping out choices in terms based just on extremes, e.g., believing one has to be either "top-down" or "bottom-up" in approaches or that one must use only hard evidence or soft interpretations for making decisions. An example of the "either-or trap" is assuming either that success is achieved only through a dictatorial management style in which only profit matters or that success is achieved only by empowering people within the organization to make decisions and to bear full responsibility for their functional areas of the organization. The philosophical perspectives used by business leaders are rarely simple views that can be articulated in a few words or expressed unequivocally. Philosophies are usually more complicated than principles and often lack precise meanings or definitive applications. Nevertheless, leadership philosophies are critical components of the foundation of leadership that provide leaders with a sense of steadfastness and determination without being too rigid. Leaders must know what they believe in and be committed to those beliefs.

Leadership philosophies can provide business leaders with the necessary confidence and courage when making critical decisions, especially under circumstances that have unclear implications and complex consequences. They help strategic leaders make good decisions; ones based on the whole context of the business, the critical elements associated with the decision process, and fundamental beliefs of the leaders. Good decisions do not always turn out to be correct because of possible changes in the business environment and unexpected turn of events. However, if leaders follow the overarching principles and their own well-honed leadership philosophies, they enhance the consistency of their decisions, improving the probability of achieving successful outcomes. Some of the most important leadership philosophies pertaining to business situations involve the overarching purpose and aims of the organization, its views about people, especially customers and employees, and the roles, responsibilities and behaviors of its strategic leaders.

The intent of this section is to highlight some of the philosophies that leaders might embrace. It is impossible to outline all of the possibilities given that most leadership philosophies are based on an individual's perspectives and not just what is popular or well established. Indeed, the notion of generally acceptable is a fit for principles not philosophies as discussed in the previous section. Some of main philosophies include:

- Focusing on value creation and value maximization.
- Leading people and garnering respect.
- Providing success and making people successful.
- Being a good citizen and exhibiting social responsibility.

Value creation and value maximization are overarching aims of an organization and its leaders. They include and are superior to most of the more traditional views like maximizing profits. Strategic leaders who maximize value create benefits across the enterprise and have significant opportunities to enjoy success. People want to be engaged and to perform. Being people-oriented and ensuring that everyone is recognized for his or her contributions are critical elements for energizing the organization and the enterprise to achieve sustainable success. Contributors have to be empowered to do so and be rewarded for their efforts. Making others successful is another philosophical approach for achieving success. If people are successful and satisfied they are more likely to continue their involvements and enjoy the fruits of the relationships. Companies are expected to be good citizen and contribute to the great social good. Each is discussed in the next subsections.

Creating value and value maximization

Value maximization is one of the most important philosophies. The purpose of a business is not just to increase shareholder value; it is to create beneficial outcomes and maximize value the across space and time. In the process of maximizing value, successful companies generate cash flow and profits that sustain their future and create opportunities for growth and further accomplishments. With sufficient cash flow, the company can invest into innovations that provide even more opportunities and rewards in the future. Solid and balanced connections and relationships with customers, stakeholders, and constituents ensure that everyone has the prospects for achieving their goals and aspirations.

The ***value proposition*** is the critical perspective that outlines the meaning and elements of value creation. Business is not a zero sum game where customers and producers win and stakeholders and society loses or any other possible combination of outcomes. For instance, the use of toxic substances like lead and cadmium are examples of low cost material that help suppliers and producers to improve margins and profits; however, such materials increase the costs of disposal and have negative health effects and impacts on employees and users. The value proposition can be expressed in terms of the value equation that examines the benefits of the enterprise in terms of the investments made by all constituents. Figure 2.2 depicts the form of the value equation.

While this equation provides a comprehensive view of the value proposition, it may be impossible to map out all of the implications of what value means. The prevailing view by most companies is the simplified version of performance (ΣBenefits) to price (ΣInvestments). Per this version, value is improved by increasing performance or decreasing price or doing both. The personal computer (PC) era marshaled in the concept of improving benefits (the positive side) and reducing price at the same time (the negative side). Intel lead the way in increasing the positives and decreasing the negatives via Moore's Law which suggested that each new generation would be two times more powerful than the previous. Each new x86 microprocessor provided significant benefits over the older version at the same time the prices in real terms were declining.

Performance is improved by enhancing the benefits, both the tangible and intangible ones. Tangible benefits are the direct outcomes that meet the needs of customers, stakeholders, or other constituents. Intangible benefits are the psychological effects. For instance, the tangible benefit of an automobile is mobility; the intangible benefit may be the pleasure enjoyed by driving the car. For most of the 20th century, the general approach was to increase performance at a rate greater than the increase in the price. The leading effects are the primary benefits sought at inception that are usually apparent and based on the needs and desires of customers and stakeholders. They are usually the main positive considerations when determining whether projects, programs, products, etc. are worthwhile. The value of the benefits is established in

	Leading		**Lagging**		**Limiting**
	ΣBenefits	< *Tangible* / *Intangible*	+ ΣEffects	< *Tangible* / *Intangible*	+ ΣKnowledge
Value ≈					
	ΣInvestments	< Time / Money	+ ΣDefects	< Quality / Liability	+ ΣBurdens

Figure 2.2 Value equation from an enterprise perspective[15]

terms of the investment of time and money to acquire the benefits. Money is viewed as the tangible aspect, since it represents actual resources, or property while time might be seen as intangible, since it cannot be captured or stored. Time may be as critical as money in calculating the investment, given that time can never be recovered.

Lagging effects and defects are a little more difficult to ascertain. Lagging effects are considered to be positive and defects are considered to be negative. Lagging effects are actually benefits that were not contemplated or realized immediately. They are often discovered much later in time, especially after customers have been using the products and services or when the project or program matures. For example, many of Microsoft's products (software) like Windows became really valuable after millions of customers used them and connected with others. It was the interconnectivity that made the products valuable and successful. During the early 1980's, it became apparent to producers and customers alike that defects were a significant cost that had a huge negative impact on value. The total quality management revolution was driven by the need to improve the quality and value of products and processes. The value equation provided the proper perspective of strategic decision making. Producers did not always pay for the defects; often customers pay a high price. Even when producers did rectify the defects through recalls or warrantee claims, if customers were inconvenienced there were costs and negative impacts.

The limiting effects are knowledge and the burdens associated with the outcomes. Human knowledge is a positive that propels us forward. But, there are always unknowns and limits. The notion of "burdens" became a significant consideration when calculating the value of a product, process, transaction or outcome. This recognition is one of the most crucial determinations in the process of creating true value. Burdens are multifaceted and have great negative impacts on the enterprise and its constituents. Burdens reduce benefits to customers, have negative impacts on stakeholders, and/or make society pay for cleaning up the problems. For instance, with the explosion of environmental problems during the last half of the 20th century in the developed countries and the actions of stakeholder groups like the Sierra Club, Greenpeace and others, along with myriad of laws and regulations, burdens took on new meanings and became a significant way to improve value by reducing the associated burdens. Burdens are not always apparent at the inception of a product, process or business venture. While burdens may be difficult to determine during the early stage of an endeavor, it is imperative that a continuous evaluation is used to discover and mitigate such impacts. The negative effects of leaded gasoline and asbestos are just a few examples of very successful products that met their demise because of the burdens that they caused.

The future direction of value maximization involves efforts to improve the sum of the positive aspects and to reduce and/or eliminate negative aspects. The penultimate goal is to move toward ideality; a situation having zero defects, zero burdens and a minimal investment. Ideality is easy to understand from an external perspective. Customers obtain superior solutions at very low costs. Stakeholders do not have to be concerned about negative impacts and their consequences. Society does not suffer with burdens. However, producers might view this approach as a zero sum game. All of the gains benefit the external dimensions at the expense of revenues and profitability. The answer for the producers is to achieve their strategic, market and financial objectives using value creation techniques rather than simple pricing strategies, clever marketing campaigns, or similar constructs. Eliminating defects is the most obvious focus for moving toward ideality, especially ones that provide improved solutions at low costs. Everyone's position is enhanced. Eliminating all burdens is another area where enormous savings are also possible. The question of profitability appears to be the most difficult to address for a win-win scenario. Firstly, if all defects and burdens are eliminated, the costs of the associated corrective actions or cost elements that are added to the cost of goods would not have to be included in calculating the cost and price of the product. The price to the customer would be reduced without any negative implications on profitability. Imagine the potential results! Secondly, as the products and processes are improved using advanced technologies, the cost per unit is typically reduced and volumes increased. Savings are passed on to the customer and the profit margins are actually increased. The profit objective is to achieve the strategic and financial outcomes and not to maximize the profit per transaction or per product.

Strategic leaders should not ask how to make the trade-offs, but how to maximize value creation. Maximum value is the goal. It involves the integration of strategic thinking and operations so that all objectives are achieved in parallel. With parallel processing, the total set of strategic objectives may be achieved. It is the concurrent implementation of the internal and external requirements that leads to successful outcomes. Value maximization is an innovative construct that provides leaders with a powerful perspective on decision-making.

Leading people and garnering respect

For several centuries, business leaders copied many of the leadership philosophies of military leaders. They engaged in command and control approaches in which the superior had the power and authority to dictate to subordinates commands and orders. In business settings the superior was the boss and the subordinate was simply viewed as the person for accomplishing the tasks and doing the work. In traditional business terms, this philosophy was manifested as the leadership pyramid via the hierarchical organizational structure. The bosses resided at the top and the employees at the bottom. Information, decisions, and commands flowed from the top to the bottom. The approach was deemed to be efficient and productive. The focus was on formulating strategies, developing tactics and making decisions by the superiors with the subordinates carrying out actions.

Military-type leadership philosophies were deployed based on the superiority of the authorized strategic leaders. They were in charge and had the power to make decisions, allocate resources and take decisive actions. The underpinnings of such leadership philosophies were based on the strategic leader's superior positions and the inferior positions of their employees, who were treated as subordinates. The latter were simply perceived to be resources (albeit human resources) that could be or should be exploited to maximize the profits of the company. Workers were managed like the plant and equipment and the other resources of the company. While the facets of this discussion are complex and cut across many aspects of leadership and management from many perspectives, such beliefs were commonplace and seemed to be efficient in a time when most companies used similar approaches and when the dynamics of the business world were slow paced.

However, over the last several decades the strengths of these philosophies became weaknesses. They involved one-way approaches that functioned best from the top down, but they did not work very well from a horizontal perspective or from the bottom up. Commands were communicated to employees in a reasonable fashion, but interpretations often required explanations and efforts that were difficult to orchestrate, costly and time consuming. Superiors believed that they were communicating because they sent out numerous messages through various instruments including in more recent times emails and intranet sites. There were numerous filters that colored the messages or their intent, especially as they flowed down the "chain of command." Many messages were lost in translation, not received at all, or were simply deleted. Moreover, employees, supervisors and lower level managers had few feedback mechanisms to articulate their views. Strategy formulation and decision making were possibly enhanced at the expense of implementation and execution. The processes tended to be static. Implementation might be successful, if everything went according to plans. The approaches worked reasonably well, if everything stayed on track. But, if difficulties arose, solutions were time consuming and costly to develop and deploy. The approaches were often optimized in one direction (top-down) and not very flexible or adaptive. As an aside, think about the philosophical perspectives used by strategic leaders of sophisticated corporations when they outsource requirements to companies in developing countries or rapidly industrializing countries where some of the old-line philosophies are being used to cut costs and improve profits. The question arises whether such strategic leaders are more enlightened or whether they have just shifted their perspectives to new ways or locations for maintaining the old paradigms.

The archaic philosophy that strategic leaders are superiors in the sense of having superior rights, privileges and positions often isolates them from the rest of the organization. The perspective becomes one of "us versus them." The strategic leaders assume that they should be respected and followed because they are leaders even when they have done little to garner the respect. Moreover, they often fail to reciprocate with respect and recognition of the employees. They become one-sided in their leadership, which leads to animosity and conflict within the organization. Such difficulties degenerate into internal conflicts that consume energy and time without any benefits.

Today, strategic leaders have to deal with more complexities and a fast-paced business world. They need to be more flexible, adaptable and innovative. They cannot envision all requirements upfront and even if they could, the business environment is moving too quickly to rely solely on top-down management approaches. Strategic leaders need people throughout the organization and across the extended enterprise to fully participate in developing strategies, making decisions, and implementing actions plans and tactics. In a creative organization, success depends on the knowledge, capabilities, creativity and contributions of all of the people; all of the contributors and recipients. People are not static resources that can be used, exploited and then discarded per the dictates of the strategic leaders; they are the essence of an organization and are the intellectual capital upon which the company's success and future relies. Thus, the recognition that people are the most important ingredients in achieving sustainable success and that everyone plays a vital role in sustaining success across the enterprise is perhaps one of the most profound changes in leadership philosophies over the last decade. This includes recognizing that people are unique and that it is their being and contributions that result in extraordinary outcomes and achievements. It is the enlightened recognition that employees are not resources in the conventional sense of labor and workers, but are significant strategic (human) capital that is critical for success. This recognition implies that strategic leaders have a duty to protect, develop and respect this most valuable capital that is unique and difficult to acquire. Business success depends on the talents of the organization.

The contemporary leadership philosophies treat employees and key contributors as important individuals and strategic assets. Such thinking requires respecting everyone, recognizing good contributions, and rewarding the most deserving individuals regardless of position. Strategic leaders who exhibit respect for others are usually respected by others as well. Given that employees are valuable, then it is incumbent upon strategic leaders to facilitate the development and contributions of the employees and to ensure their well being. Strategic leaders should not view themselves as superiors, but as those who have roles, responsibilities, duties and obligations to orchestrate change and lead the organization to its full potential. In today's business world, communications have to have a two-way approach. Employees have to receive the message clearly and understand the meaning and requirements. They need feedback mechanisms to provide input and voice their concerns.

Making people successful begets success

Leadership revolves around positioning for success. It involves making people across the extended enterprise and within the organization more successful. Customers who achieve success through their relationship with strategic leaders and their organization are usually more than satisfied and typically seek additional ways to enjoy even more success. Stakeholders whose perspectives are recognized as important and whose issues and concerns are mitigated through positive actions by strategic leaders are likewise more likely to feel successful in their endeavors and are more inclined to support those leaders who provide successful outcomes. Employees are often inspired by strategic leaders who develop their potential, recognize and respect their value, and encourage them to fulfill their own destinies. And the story goes on with all constituencies. Success begets success.

Leading change requires an interactive leadership style that allows people to participate in strategic and tactical decisions. Astute leaders permit contributors to participate in the discussions and to develop the means and mechanisms for obtaining the best solutions and outcomes. People then become part of the strategic direction and development processes because they understand and appreciate the implications, benefits and rewards. Strategic leaders, in particular, have to go beyond merely motivating employees to improve performance and to work hard; they have to inspire them to contribute to realizing the desired changes, to develop new skills and capabilities, and to achieve personal and company objectives. True strategic leaders seek new opportunities from every vantage point. They drive change toward more favorable outcomes, succeed through cooperation and collaboration, and build the foundation and structures for future success. Strategic leaders must set the tone for the future and encourage the full participation of the whole enterprise.

Leaders can set the stage for success using this philosophy many different ways. One of the most important subsets is always seeking causes and effects when problems, difficulties and challenges arise and avoiding blaming other people or finding the "fall guys." Often effective leadership and goodwill are lost when adverse situations occur because the leaders try to lay the blame on someone else. Rather than mitigating the difficulties and eliminating the causes of the problems, ineffective business leaders often exasperate negative situations by shifting the emphasis toward who is at fault rather than how to fix it and to assure that it would happen again?

Another subset of this philosophy involves treating every co-worker as a unique individual who deserves recognition and respect. From a business perspective it involves treating people as important participants in achieving success. It refutes the conventional thinking that strategic leaders at the top of the organization are more important than people at the bottom of the organization. From a philosophical perspective everyone is important. Each individual has different roles and responsibilities. And, it is clear that there are differences based on the contributions people make and the skills and talents they have, but fundamentally everyone is important and should be treated accordingly. Strategic leaders have a duty to ensure fair and impartial treatment of all employees, customers, stakeholders and constituents. In doing so strategic leaders enhance their own positions and are more likely to earn respect and goodwill from the other people as well.

Philosophical aspects of corporate social responsibility

In today's complex business environment, it is not easy for strategic leaders to determine exactly what their social responsibilities are and how they should behave from an ethical perspective. From a philosophical perspective, the easiest way to handle the complexities of the business world related to CSR is for strategic leaders to have a more inclusive scope of what they are responsible for. Instead of limiting the scope, strategic leaders should be more holistic in considering what they influence and affect. The more inclusive the perspective, the more likely strategic leaders are to create value, develop beneficial solutions, achieve positive outcomes, and meet/exceed the explicit and implicit needs and expectations of all related entities, parties, etc.

CSR is a broad philosophical perspective that all leaders have implicit and explicit duties and obligations to meet the needs and expectations of customers, stakeholders, employees, and other direct and indirect contributors in a socially responsible manner that includes protecting the health and safety of people and the natural environment and preventing negative impacts and their consequences.[16] CSR is a combination of ethics, ethical behaviors, compliance with laws and regulations, implicit protections for people and the natural environment, and requisite actions to create a better world. CSR goes even further and implies that leaders have implicit obligations to be ethical citizens and responsible decision makers and to ensure that their strategies, actions and business solutions are appropriate and viable from social, ethical, economic and environmental perspectives across the entire business environment and the market spaces they address.[17] Astute leaders articulate what CSR means and what it necessitates from their perspectives and realities. It is clear that strategic leaders have responsibilities to perform well, take due care of people and sustain results. They have the challenge to realize substantial gains in the short term and to ensure that the company survives and prospers in the long term.[18] CSR also includes philanthropy, supporting charities and related organizations, contributing to public policy making, and promoting the common good and well being of humankind.

Personal Values and Cultural Considerations

Personal values are strongly-held convictions that shape a leader's perspectives and judgments. They are related to the leader's background, personality, aspirations, integrity and desires for achieving outcomes. They are usually deep seated and entrenched personal beliefs and ideals. While one's personal values may evolve over time, leaders with well developed personal values are unlikely to make radical changes in them unless they are modifying unacceptable values and perspectives.

Personal values are often directly related to the philosophical beliefs of the leader and run the gamut from broadly-held values like honesty and ethical behavior to highly individualized ones such as personal integrity and always doing what is right. While statements on personal values are difficult to characterize because they are the personal beliefs of an individual (they are just what the term connotes-personal), many of one's personal values may overlap with the general principles and leadership philosophies discussed in the previous sections. The more broadly held ones tend to be more closely aligned with principles and philosophies, while the more specific ones are often created and defined by the leader. Table 2.1 provides a listing of selected personal values. The list can be extensive depending on the individual leader and his or her perspectives on reality. The intent herein is not to prescribe every possibility, but to help facilitate an individual's reflections on his or her own personal values. It is a good idea for each individual whether he or she is an existing leader or an aspiring one to reflect on and articulate his or her personal values.

The most important personal values are those the individual has developed and tailored to fit his or her situation and circumstance. However, this does not mean tailoring one's values to justify inappropriate behaviors and practices; some leaders often try to condone poor behaviors by claiming expediency or necessity because of circumstance. For example, in the aftermath of hurricane Katrina the business lead-

TABLE 2.1 Selected categories and insights about personal values

Category	Characteristics	Implications
	Broad	
Being honest	Always telling the full truth; disclosing all positive and negative factors; ensuring that others are truthful; eliminating deceptions.	It takes courage to be totally honest in many situations or in organizations that like operating in the "gray area."
Being good/ moral; using proper behaviors	Proper behavior that follows the generally acceptable practices of a society is difficult to prescribe exactly, but most people recognize and know what the proper behaviors are.	While good moral behaviors depend on societal norm, there are many universal aspects. People in organizations often follow what the leader does; goodness often begets goodness within the enterprise.
Being ethical	Ethics are the standards governing conduct and behavior in a setting or situation. Being ethical implies that the leader adheres to the highest standards of personal and professional behavior.	Being ethical has similar implications as being moral. Moral aspects usually involve the personal behaviors; ethical aspects involve professional behaviors. Morals and ethics go together.
Being fair	Fairness means being impartial and unbiased in decisions and actions. It often pertains to how others are treated and impacted. It implies equal treatment for all.	Being fair is a duty of leadership, especially ensuring that decisions and actions are not skewed toward one's personal position and fortune, those of your friends or against one's adversaries.
	Specific	
Having integrity	Having integrity involves conviction and commitment to one's beliefs and acting in a consistent and sound manner. It involves unwavering adherence to one's values.	Integrity builds trust and others rely on their trust of the leader's personal values and integrity when they decide whether to follow the leader. A lack of integrity may cause others to be wary of leader.
Respecting others	Respect for others involves recognizing the value and contributions of other people and ensuring their views are duly considered and respected.	Leaders who respect others are more likely to be respected by others. It is difficult to obtain the respect of the organization, if one eschews the value and contributions of other people.
Taking care of others	Leadership involves taking care of the people that one is accountable for. Leaders are responsible for the well being of the people involved.	Leaders have a duty to make others safe, secure and successful to the extent possible. This includes ensuring that they are recognized and rewarded for their achievements.
Forgiving others	Leaders focus on positive outcomes and corrective actions. If problems occur they should fix the problems and forgive and forget in a majority of situations.	While it is appropriate to find causes of difficulties, leaders should avoid affixing blame, especially for behaviors and actions that are without negative intent.

ers of some of the petroleum companies dramatically increased the price of gasoline and diesel, rather than trying to mitigate the effects of the disaster. Were these leaders fair in their handling of the situation? Did they act on behalf of the people involved or were they acting only on the basis of their own self interests? Such questions require analyses, discussions and intellectual thought. Key questions pertain to the duties that strategic leaders have in such situations and what kinds of decisions they are obligated to make.

Good leaders have personal values that reinforce their standing in their organizations and communities. They have integrity and are mindful of their obligations to others. Leadership is an awesome endeavor that requires being respectful of people and ensuring that the people of one's responsibilities are duly taken care of. If problems do arise, good leaders take actions to remedy the situation and are careful not to place blame. They resolve the situation and ensure that the people involved are provided with the appropriate learning so that adverse outcomes are alleviated.

Social institutions include the family, community, circles of friends, acquaintances, educational establishments, religious organizations, and social systems that provide stability, cohesion and meaning. There are many other social systems that support people and make life easier, richer, and less risky. In the developed countries there are often additional mechanisms like social safety nets and advocacy groups that complement the primary social institutions and systems. Cultures are usually complex with a rich mosaic of realities, but there are typically fewer deviations from the prevailing norms. In many developing countries there are often numerous cultures and sub-cultures and it is often difficult to precisely determine what the societal norms are. It is incumbent upon leaders in such contexts to determine their own principles, philosophies and personal values and how to engage in the cultural aspects of the other people and communities. It is also important for leaders from other cultures and countries to examine their own beliefs to ensure that they resonate properly when doing business in other countries. Again, it is critical to distinguish the differences between principles, philosophies and personal values that are based on absolutes from those that are influenced by cultural aspects and personal perspectives. A leader has to be careful not to instinctively view situations and circumstances from his or her background and perspectives instead of a more holistic view of the prevailing values and culture(s) of the people.

As discussed in previous sections, many beliefs are based on an individual's perspectives and fit the specific requirements and expectations of society. It is unacceptable to expect business leaders in developing countries to adopt all of the norms of business leaders in the Western countries. There are many differences in cultural aspects that have to be understood and respected. Each community, country and society has its own unique social institutions and cultural aspects. Leaders have their own personal beliefs based on the norms and accepted approaches within their cultures, but they have to cognizant of those of other people and act accordingly.

Reflections

Principles, philosophies and personal values lay the foundation of leadership. They involve the fundamental beliefs that guide leaders toward proper decisions and proper actions that are rational, defendable and appropriate. Axiomatic principles by definition are universal and apply regardless of situations or circumstances. As universally accepted beliefs, norms, and standards, they are absolutes and it does not matter where one is; they always apply. For such absolutes, one cannot follow the old saying, "when in Rome do as the Romans do." However, it is also critical to realize that there are important differences in acceptable views, behaviors and practices across the world and that many principles, philosophies and personal values are influenced significantly by the norms, customs and standards of the social and political settings and the cultural aspects of the community, country and society in which the leader lives and works.

Principles, philosophies and personal values help leaders stay on course when engaged in leadership and making decisions. They provide a firm footing for being consistent and comprehensive in their duties and responsibilities to the organization, the extended enterprise, and people. Most leaders are not born with all of the attributes of great leaders, but they can acquire, develop and use the principles, philosophies and personal values as discussed in the chapter; ones that can set them ahead of their peers and contemporaries.

Leaders cannot be expected to be correct all of the time, but they can be expected to make good decisions-ones based on principles, philosophies and values. If they have a solid basis for their decisions and actions, then they are more likely to be perceived as good leaders who are making decisions based on the interests of all. Leadership is often a lonely situation, in which one must make profound decisions that affect many people and have long-term consequences. Most decisions are complicated and involve many factors, variables and considerations. There are few easy answers and in most cases it is difficult to realize the proper perspectives and to ensure that all facets have been duly considered and that the prospective outcomes are balanced, appropriate and fair.

Good leaders subordinate their own objectives and rewards to those of the organization and its employees, customers, stakeholders and other constituents. Their own success is predicated on the sustainable success of the whole, and their rewards are derived from the successes that they and their key contributors create in the market spaces and the broader business environment. Astute leaders realize that they are an important part of the whole, but they are not so arrogant to think that they are the only reason for success or that they are the only ones who should be rewarded. Instead, they are responsible for the success of others and ensure that others have the means to become successful and are recognized and rewarded for their successes.

Notes

1. www.un.org/depts/ptd/global.htm
2. http://www.fairlabor.org.

3. The FLA Workplace Code of Conduct; http://www.fairlabor. org/about_us_code_conduct_el.html.
4. www.reveonsullivan.org/principled/principles.htm. Reverend Sullivan helped formulate the principles of the UN's Global Compact.
5. European Governance: A White Paper (2001) Brussels, Belgium: Commission of the European Union.
6. David L. Rainey, *Sustainable Business Development: Inventing the Future through Strategy, Innovation and Leadership* (Cambridge, UK: Cambridge University Press, 2006, pp. 150–212)
7. Ibid.
8. Milton Friedman, *Capitalism and Freedom* (Chicago, Il: University of Chicago Press, 1962, 2002, p. 133)
9. Dominic Dodd and Ken Favaro, *The Three Tensions: Winning the Struggle to Perform without Compromise* (Hoboken, NJ: John Wiley & Sons, Inc., 2007, pp. 2–3).
10. Core competencies are the capabilities of the organization that it uniquely possesses and are difficult for others to emulate. C.K. Prahalad and Gary Hamel define core competencies as "the collective learning in organization".
11. Chris Anderson, *The Long Tail: How endless choice is creating unlimited demand* (London, UK: Random House Business Books, 2006, p. 117).
12. Ibid.
13. Ibid; adapted from Anderson's model.
14. Satish Nambisan and Mohanbir Sawhney, *The Global Brain: Your Roadmap for Inventing Faster and Smarter in a Networked World* (Upper Saddle River, NJ: Wharton School Publishing, 2008, p. 88).
15. David L. Rainey, *Sustainable Business Development: Inventing the Future through Strategy, Innovation and Leadership*, pp. 102–106)
16. Ibid, p. 219.
17. Ibid.
18. Ibid.

References

Anderson, Chris (2006). *The Long Tail: How endless choice is creating unlimited demand.* London, UK: Random House Business Books.

Dodd, Dominic and Ken Favaro (2007). *The Three Tensions: Winning the Struggle to Perform without Compromise.* Hoboken, NJ: John Wiley & Sons, Inc.

Friedman, Milton (1962). *Capitalism and Freedom.* Chicago, IL: University of Chicago Press.

Nambisan, Satish and Mohanbir Sawhney (2008) *The Global Brain: Your Roadmap for Inventing Faster and Smarter in a Networked World.* Upper Saddle River, NJ: Wharton School Publishing.

Rainey, David L. (2006). *Sustainable Business Development: Inventing the Future through Strategy, Innovation and Leadership.* Cambridge, UK: Cambridge University Press.

3

Openness, Transparency and Accountability

New Imperatives

Introduction

Openness and transparency are two nascent perspectives in the business world. They both convey the notion of being forthright, candid and straightforward about providing the underlying information and data pertaining to the products, services, operations, actions, activities and decisions of businesses. They ensure that customers, stakeholders, society, shareholders, employees and other constituents can obtain a comprehensive understanding about the relevant details of the company and its enterprise(s). They imply that business leaders are conducting their affairs in ways that are readily apparent to outside observers and that all non-confidential information and data concerning decisions, effects and impacts are made public to the extent possible and that all disclosures are made in accordance with government regulations and established standards and protocols. Openness and transparency are simple concepts that have complex implications.

Openness implies that everything pertinent to observers is obvious and clear, that nothing is concealed or obfuscated, and that business leaders behave and operate as if everything they decide and do is going to be made public. Simply put, frankness and truthfulness abound. Moreover, openness means taking proactive steps to provide disclosures to the public on pertinent non-confidential information and data including positive and negative aspects. It necessitates honesty and candor from the most insignificant issues to the most troubling problems and from the least important contributions to the most exciting breakthroughs. Openness involves being honest, putting the truth forward every time, disclosing the details properly on a real time basis, and

The Pursuit of Sustainable Leadership, pages 53–82

telling all sides of every story. It takes courage to be open and straightforward, especially in situations in which the disclosures may cause difficulties in the short term. But, such courage is often rewarded since being open and truthful builds trust inside and outside the organization. Trust is one of the most important ingredients in business transactions, exchange and relationships for enduring success. Openness begets trust; trust begets building relationships; and, relationships lead to success.

In the business world, ***transparency*** implies shining light through everything that is germane to external observers and internal participants. Transparency should be coupled with assurance that such scrutiny results in positive perceptions and realities. It is analogous to what transparency means in the physical world; the observer has more than an external view of an object; he or she can discern the inner structures, their interconnections and individual characteristics.

Accountability is a complementary perspective. It involves being answerable for decisions and actions and reporting accurately to shareholders, employees, customers, stakeholders, and the public. Strategic leaders are the agents of the company who have fiduciary responsibilities to the shareholders, investors and other parties such as government agencies and are accountable for the affairs, transactions and reports of their corporations. Strategic leaders have a duty to protect and preserve the well being and the assets of their corporation and its businesses. These are fundamental responsibilities of business leaders that are absolute obligations and are typically prescribed in corporate by-laws and government regulations. Accountability is one of the most important responsibilities that all leaders have from the highest level down to the functional managers.

Openness, transparency and accountability often reflect different spectra of the roles and responsibilities of leadership. Openness and transparency are typically voluntary with wide discretion in terms of philosophical underpinnings, policies, and practices. On the other hand, accountability is usually mandated by internal policies and external forces that prescribe what and how things are done. However, they are not mutually exclusive options. They co-exist and complement each other. Openness and transparency with respect to disclosures of information facilitate accountability associated with financial reports and other instruments like prospectus for new share offerings since trust and believability become better established through the voluntary actions.

In the grand scheme of leadership, openness and transparency usually involve intangibles that are guided by ethics, values, wisdom and judgment. Accountability is based on the more tangible requirements such as making financial disclosures and reports, obtaining approvals from the board of directors and/or corporate officers for proposals and recommendations, and ensuring the health, safety and well being of people. While accountability does include some intangible aspects based on judgments like disclosing the negative side of products and service, it typically involves requirements that are easy to understand; one that are usually based on known mandates and standards. For instances, business leaders generally know the laws and regulations that they have to comply with and the industry standards that specify product and process characteristics.

Failure to practice openness and transparency may lead to distrust and questions about the veracity of statements and claims made by strategic leaders and their organizations. While such difficulties do not immediately result in concerns, responses, and government sanctions, such situations may lead to more restrictive requirements in the long term. For example, the failures and misdeeds of corporations like Enron, WorldCom and many others resulted in the enactment of Sarbanes-Oxley Act of 2002 in the US (SOA), which places more stringent financial reporting requirements on all US companies and their senior leaders. SOA even applies to global corporations headquartered outside the US that have they shares traded on the US stock exchanges. The failures of a few business leaders led to more stringent and costly requirements for everyone.

Openness and transparency have become more important considerations over the last decade, since the world of information and data has significantly changed with the dramatic expansion of the internet. Now, anyone with the assistance of Google, Yahoo, and the other search engines has access to much of the world's information and data. It is becoming more and more difficult, if not impossible, to keep certain facts from the public. Even so-called secrets eventually become broadly known. And, the trend toward more information and data being made available on a global basis is expected to continue. Think about the embarrassments caused by Wiki leaks!

Over the last several decades, business leaders, especially those leading large corporations, have lost much of their superior positions in controlling business transactions and the resulting details. In the past, strategic leaders were able to suppress a lot of the information and data. They had big advantages over customers, stakeholders and the public because they had access to details like product costs, inventory levels, margins, etc. and could make informed decisions that outsiders could not. Today, the public often knows about the details and even disadvantaged people have the ability to learn what a product costs, how the costs are determined and what the variables are.

Ultimately, business leaders have to decide to what extent they embrace openness and transparency. They may base their decisions on the philosophical underpinnings that openness, transparency, honesty and integrity are the best approaches for achieving long-term success. They may lead change, adopt openness and transparency as fundamental ways of doing business, and develop a corporate culture that encourages openness and transparency across the business enterprise. They may persuade their people to be truthful and honest in every endeavor and hire and develop employees who believe in and promote such beliefs. They can reward employees who behave responsibly and eschew false promises, deception and unacceptable behaviors.

Good business leaders are open to scrutiny and conduct their affairs in the sunshine. They make decisions as if the whole world knows how decisions are made and what the implications are. They are not fearful of disclosures, because they have made fair and appropriate choices for the benefits of the shareholders, employees, customers, stakeholders and society. They act as true fiduciaries serving others first and themselves last. They establish policies and use best practices that support openness, transparency and accountability. They are proactive and ensure that appropriate solutions are developed and implemented before being forced to do so by outside entities, especially regulatory agencies and pressure groups. They address difficulties and problems as soon as there is an inkling of difficulties or improprieties. Most importantly, they are honest, trustworthy and sincere. In very simple terms, openness and transparency start with philosophical perspectives of being open, forthright and truthful in every regard. Accountability includes accepting the full responsibilities for one's decisions and actions and providing evidence and proof that the requirements and expectations of customers, stakeholders, employees, shareholders and society are being fulfilled. It involves the never-ending efforts to develop the best solutions, deliver appropriate and valuable outcomes and to achieve sustainable success.

This chapter includes the following main topics:

- Understanding the driving forces pertaining to openness and transparency.
- Developing and implementing the means and mechanisms for openness and transparency.
- Reinforcing accountability, doing what is right, and achieving business objectives.

The Driving Forces of Change toward Openness and Transparency

External context pertaining to openness

Context is always a good starting point when studying any business phenomenon. From the perspective of openness, context involves the broader social, political, ethical, economic, technological, environmental, and market forces that impinge upon decision makers as they lead their organizations through the multiple mazes of opportunities, challenges, risks, vulnerabilities, requirements, mandates, needs and expectations. Table 3.1 lists a number of selected driving forces pertain to openness and transparency.

Topics selected illustrate some of the more important perspectives. The discussions on these topics could fill an entire book. There are few respites in a fast-paced world and little time to deal with the existing driving forces before new driving ones emerge. While some business leaders view this like being on a treadmill that is going faster and faster as time marches on with no relief and few real gains, changes do provide enormous opportunities and prospects for obtaining significant advantages for succeeding and sustaining success. Moreover, ongoing changes provide new opportunities to excel, and those who are capable and willing can gain advantages through proactive means and mechanisms to exceed the needs, expectations, mandates, and requirements and to outperform their competitors and peers.

The ***proliferation of information and data*** is one of the most profound changes of the last two decades. The internet gives people on a global basis access to details they need for making better informed purchasing decisions about products and services

TABLE 3.1 Selected driving forces pertaining to openness[1]

Economic and Market	Social and Political
• ***People***—needs and expectations • ***Awareness***—connectedness • ***Solutions***—appropriate, safe and effective • ***Risk mitigation***—protection and safety • ***Disclosures***—relevant information and data	• ***Government***—mandates and rules • ***Communities***—right to know and reporting • ***Political forces***—stability and fulfillment • ***Laws and regulations***—compliance • ***Standards***—protect people's well being
Global Driving Forces Proliferation of information and data Information & communications technologies (ICT) A more connected world Political pressures and forces and laws and regulations Technological changes	
Technological	**Environmental and Ethical**
• ***Change***—increasing rate of changes • ***Means***—innovations and diffusion • ***Mechanisms***—internet and ICT • ***Inventions***—clean technologies	• ***Natural world***—preservation and protection • ***Burdens***—eliminate wastes • ***Ethics***—right conduct and standards • ***Ethical aspects***—standards of behavior

and for determining the strengths and weaknesses of the business policies, products, services, processes and practices and those of the suppliers, competitors and customers. This includes information about the actions of stakeholders and constituents who support or oppose the decisions of large companies and small and medium size enterprises (SMEs). Not only are such details readily available, they can be distributed at light speed to millions of like minded people.

ICT make it possible for people to be connected and to exchange views and concerns in ways that are fast and inexpensive. Interconnectivity allows disparate groups of people in different locations with different agendas to collaborate whenever the occasions arise. For instance, proponents of a given action or opponents of a proposal can send emails at little cost to thousands of people who may do the same thing multiplying the effect hundreds and even thousands of times. Thus, a few individuals or small group of concerned people can expand into a large force of millions when an issue or concern emerges. For example, the election campaign for President Barack Obama capitalized on the use of the internet, magnifying communications in a way that had not been used for elections. In a digital world the cost of sharing information is minuscule, allowing widespread distribution of information and data.

A more connected world means that the rate of the diffusion of information has increased and it is expected to increase even further. The time lag time between situations and events and the rise of serious issues or even crises continues to decline. The time horizon is also shrinking for strategic leaders who have to deal with concerns that can reach a large audience in no time. Situations may escalate out of control before actions are taken to mitigate outcomes. Think about how quickly the oil spill in the

Gulf of Mexico during 2010 became a global issue and how ill-prepared BP's strategic leaders were in handling the repercussions. It may be too late by the time strategic leaders formulate and implement responses. Moreover, there are many global concerns like corruption and climate change that every leader is forced to have positions on and deal with regardless of his or her business situation. The right answer is to act proactively and to be on the cutting edge of openness and transparency.

As people become better educated and more knowledgeable, they expect even more information and disclosures. They want to be informed so that they can make good choices pertaining to their situations. They want to know the positive and negative aspects of the products and services they buy. They have more options than people had in the past and they can use their power to force even more disclosures not just about the products and services, but how the products were manufactured, what the health, safety and well being implications are and what was designed and built into the products and services. For example, people in the developed countries are very concerned about the health and safety effects of the materials used in products manufactured in China and elsewhere.

Political pressures play significant roles in forcing more openness. Politicians often respond to the external driving forces when pressured by their constituents even when they really do not want to get embroiled in complex problems. They often try to avoid damaging their political futures by taking the wrong side in protracted debates and conflicts. For instance, many politicians are often reluctant to take actions against corporations and business leaders who are supporting their political campaigns and agendas or those who could influence public opinion against the politicians. However, political leaders are often pressured by the stakeholders, constituents and citizens to affect outcomes that the politicians might not want to deal with. For instances, blunders by a small number of strategic leaders involving corruption and bribery make it more likely that governments will enact even more regulations and controls to curb illegal or unethical actions through stringent protocols, rules, audits, and reporting requirements.

Political forces are always complex and difficult to judge. However, in today's world the political forces drive regulatory mandates that business leaders and their organizations have to comply with. Moreover, public policy issues are more open to public pressure and processes than they were a quarter century ago. "Community right-to-know" legislation has given more power and influence to individuals and social organizations in the developed countries when they seek information from "big businesses" and SMEs concerning their impacts on the external world. This influence affects the impacted communities and how the public sector organizations and government agencies manage the public's affairs. For instance, in the US the Congress passed The Emergency Planning Community Right-To-Know Act in 1986 (EPCRA).[2] EPCRA requires the states to establish protocols for obtaining and disseminating information pertaining to hazardous chemicals used at public and private facilities such as manufacturing plants. It involves community right-to-know reporting, emergency release notification, and emergency planning.[3] In the context of openness, transparency, and accountability, such legislation is pivotal, since it establishes the right of the public to obtain information and disclosures from companies and SMEs. Strategic leaders cannot hold back such details under the veil of privacy. Such legislation establishes the precedent that if business leaders do not inform the public, the public has to the right to acquire the information it needs to protect its interests.

Under the ***laws and regulations*** of most developed countries, corporations are sanctioned by the government and society. Strategic leaders have responsibilities to civil society, customers, stakeholders, employees and shareholders. These include compliance with laws and regulations, fulfillment of social and economic imperatives, contributions to the well being of humankind and the natural world, and assurance of proper governance. In certain developed countries, especially in the European Union (EU), businesses may be granted a "license to operate" based on the premise that they are required to act responsibly and in the best interest of society. The notion of a "license to operate" refers to the legal standing of corporations as regulated by the government in their home country and wherever their operations are located and to their overarching responsibilities to protect and preserve the well being of people and the natural environment.[4] In most situations duly organized corporations have to obtain a right to exist and/or be registered to operate by each of the countries, states or provinces where they do business in order to be recognized as legal entities. Moreover, corporations and their business units may be required to obtain permits, licenses, certifications, and other legal instruments that regulate, control or monitor operations and sales, and to report on their releases and certain effects and impacts. "License to operate" implies that companies may lose their right to operate if they fail to comply and conform with the laws, regulations, rules and standards.

Laws and regulations prescribe what businesses must do in fulfilling their responsibilities with regard to social, economic and environmental effects and impacts. They also prescribe what business leaders have to disclose and report and how they have to do it. The trend over the last several decades has been toward more required disclosures with more details. Traditionally, many business leaders opposed regulations and other requirements that limited their degrees of freedom. They supposedly liked laissez faire. However, not all business leaders oppose laws and regulations that impose requirements on businesses. Certain business leaders would rather have governments mandate specifications because government mandates level the playing field and everyone involved has to adhere to the same requirements. Since the governments prescribe the mandates, the business leaders do not have to be concerned about being "too open, overly candid or extremely innovative" relative to their competitors; thus, inviting the possibility of disadvantages in the marketplace like having higher costs because of the disclosures. On the other hand, if everyone is forced to adhere to the same rules and standards, there are no advantages in being the leader and preempting the others in the markets. If business leaders believe that trust and honesty are critical factors for success in the markets and with customers, then they should seek the advantages of being ahead of the pack in disclosing non-confidential information and putting the laggards into a possible credibility gap. Being open and honest is an effective competitive advantage that cannot be duplicated unless the competitors take a similar stance and have a good track record of accomplishments.

People today, especially the younger generations that grew up using the internet, expect to obtain information quickly and easily. They tend to be more resilient in their belief that they need and deserve all the information necessary for making good purchase decisions, for supporting their life style considerations, and for all of the other critical choices in their lives. Such people also want to feel good about the products and services that they buy, use and enjoy. People expect that the information and data related to business decisions are shared with the broader communities under the concept of "community right to know." Again, it is impossible to determine in advance what all of the profound issues and concerns will be; therefore, such disclosures tend to mitigate problems upfront. Many difficulties may not be apparent until some event triggers a concern. For instance, people buying toys in the US were not aware of the lead paint being used by some Chinese companies until the disclosures hit the national press; then it quickly became a key issue.

Technological change is also a critical part of the transition to a richer future. Innovative technologies generally have fewer inherent defects and burdens and are cleaners from social, economic, environmental, and market perspectives. The development of cleaner technologies provides opportunities to eliminate defects and burdens of the past and to create new value streams without the negatives of previous technologies. Such new technologies may be developed using life cycle assessment as the mechanisms to anticipate problems during design and development and eliminate them before production and marketing. Moreover, the information and analysis gleaned during life cycle assessment provide the requisite information that people seek. The disclosure of such details can give the developers of the best designs with strategic advantages. Producers from various industries may combine their capabilities to create innovative offerings that enhance the value proposition and meet customer and stakeholder expectations though the elimination of negative aspects. While perfection is still a distant dream, technological changes are moving our world toward a more open and fruitful reality.

Ethics are open-ended principles pertaining to right conduct and the generally accepted rules and standards of behavior in the society, in which one exists and operates. They are difficult to define precisely because they depend on the norms and accepted beliefs of a given society. The ethical dimension involves non-traditional, more intangible perspectives of the business environment that focus on the principles and standards of proper behavior and practices of business leaders regardless of the political or regulatory mandates. It invokes a duty by business leaders to do what is ethically right based on their knowledge, experiences and practices whether required to do so, not just based on the laws and regulations of a given country. For instance, if European business leaders know that they have to process hazardous wastes according to stringent standards and to track and be accountable for such wastes from cradle-to-grave in the EU, then it is incumbent upon them to follow best practices wherever they operate regardless of the lack of regulatory requirements to do so. An ethical duty involves using all of the knowledge, experience and prevailing best practices from similar situations and ensuring that the negative effects and impacts of businesses and operations are minimized. Business leaders are expected to use the most stringent policies and mandates regardless of local regulations.

Views pertaining to opaqueness and openness

Business leaders have struggled over the decades with the procedures and details pertaining to strategic and financial disclosures and market communications. On one side, they wanted to inform their publics about the positive aspects of their enterprises. In most developed countries, publicly-traded stock corporations are required by one or more government agencies to formally disclose information, especially information and data pertaining to financial performance and corporate well being. While most business leaders enjoy disclosing the positive aspects, many are reticent to discuss the weaknesses, failures and less flattering details, if not required to do so. There are always tensions in making decisions about disclosures. The most prevalent reasons for limiting disclosures include the concern about competition and the fear of giving away vital company secrets. Moreover, there are many corporate secrets such as those concerning strategic innovations and mergers and acquisitions that are critical for long-term success that can be damaged by premature disclosures. Strategic leaders may face legal difficulties and shareholder wrath, if they do not follow proper protocols. Premature disclosures to a limited number of shareholders or stakeholders can lead to concerns about insider trading. These concerns are legitimate; however, most strategic leaders do manage them properly. Many strategic leaders feared that providing certain details about their operations could open them up to even more scrutiny and provide antagonists with ammunition to use against the company. Moreover, the disclosures themselves may be challenged for accuracy and propriety, which may lead to more difficulties.

Strategic leaders may believe that it is especially difficult being open and transparent when handling the less desirable approaches and problems of the past. Opaqueness and disclosing only the required information seems to be the safer road, when one is more likely to be attacked for what was said than for what was not said. Opaqueness is prevalent because strategic leaders fear opening a "Pandora's Box." Many companies have hidden difficulties, defects and issues that are legacy problems that have not been fully disclosed. In many cases, they are no longer relevant or are seemingly not very important in today's context. However, in some situations a number of the difficulties fester for years until one or more spiral out of control into a crisis. Failing to handle difficulties and limiting disclosures are often dangerous games, because if a situation changes unfavorably the consequences can be disastrous. For example, the executives at WorldCom might have avoided some of the causes of its bankruptcy had strategic leaders simply disclosed the truth and rectified their situation sooner.

Market communications and traditional company-related publicity are usually intended to foster awareness, acceptance, and goodwill among many other objectives. Again, the tendency is to disclose only the positive aspects. But, occasionally such approaches backfire in the long term, if the information and data are not truthful or candid. Even in cases where the information and data provided to customers and stakeholders are accurate, the disclosures may not be totally honest. This is particularly the situation when strategic leaders engage in single-sided communications. They tell only the positive side of the story that may deceive people into believing that there are no negative factors to be concerned about.

Many marketing techniques like single-sided advertising and sales promotions often lead people to think that products and services have many applications or have only positive attributes. Such approaches may work well in the short term until reality convinces customers otherwise. By then the damage is done and it is often too late to mitigate the effects of the misstatements. In many case the statements themselves are correct, but are nevertheless deceptive because they fail to tell the whole truth.

Opaqueness is not just shielding people from information and data. It can also involve selectively telling the truth. Indeed, deception seems to do its worst when the perpetrators mix selected untruths with verifiable truths. It makes sorting out the falsehoods more difficult. Opaqueness may also lead to miscommunications through omissions. Strategic leaders may fail to provide the essential elements of what is conveyed in their communications resulting in ill-informed and misinformed people. Whether intentional or not, the resulting problems often cause the businesses as well as their strategic leaders pain and suffering in the future. For instance, some baby formula producers in the past failed to provide mothers in developing countries with the details they needed about water quality and cleanliness and some of mothers prepared the milk using contaminated water. This created problems for the mothers and the companies involved.

Openness is one way to limit the potential mistakes in improper communication. By systematically providing the appropriate disclosures, people can make good decisions about products and services, the companies they invest in, and the actions they take concerning the businesses and their leaders. Openness is not an "either-or" approach. Strategic leaders do not have to go from one extreme to the other. They do not have to adopt a "disclose everything" attitude to enjoy the benefits of openness. Strategic leaders can act responsibly and ethically without sacrificing the strategic position(s) of the company or the bottom line. Indeed, by behaving ethically and proactively, strategic leaders build trust and goodwill that resonates positively with customers, stakeholders and other constituents, thus supporting the strategies and action plans for the future. By doing what is proper and good, they contribute to doing well. They enhance their strategic and financial positions. Remember financial results are derivatives of doing well in the markets and broader social and economic communities of the world.

Strategic leaders who systematically face reality understand the value of openness and making disclosures on a real time basis. They know that most facts and situations eventually become known to the public and that in an era of mass communication and given the speed at which information spreads, the best philosophy for managing the proliferation of external information and data pertaining to the corporation is to simply stay ahead of the flow. It is much more difficult for external opponents to make a news-worthy story out of a company's problems or difficulties, if the strategic leaders have already disclosed the details of the situations and discussed what they are doing about them. Openness disarms the naysayers. On the other hand, opaqueness often compels outsiders to dig deeper into situations. It may cause them to become more dedicated and resolved in finding the truth whatever it may be. Moreover, there are many skeptics and cynics who do not rest until information and data is made public through one means or another, especially if they believe there is wrongdoing.

The power of knowledge and information

For most of the business history, information and data have translated into power. The possessor of knowledge, information and data had overwhelming advantages over others. During the nineteenth century, fortunes were made in business transactions and in the stock markets by those knowing about changing situations before the details became publicly available. For instance, railroad barons acquired huge sections of land adjacent to a proposed new rail line knowing that the land would dramatically increase in value after railroad tracks were laid. In the early twentieth century, business leaders were able to keep most of the vital information about their businesses confidential from both the public and employees. Few people knew about the details of production, marketing and cost structures. Customers were usually disadvantaged because they did know about the defects associated with the products they bought and word of mouth was too slow to make a big impact. Lower level managers and employees were unable to make critical decisions because the requisite information and data was controlled at the top. Stakeholders were often adversely impacted by corporate decisions and operations, but had few details to support their agendas and claims. The media and the press did have access to some information and data, but the processes used to obtain the inside stories were very slow and arduous, and usually did not occur on a real time basis. Occasionally, the real truth would be made public, but typically such disclosures had little impact on the prevailing situations. For instance, Ralph Nader exposed the safety defects in certain American-built compact cars of the early 1960s. He had to be persistent in finding the truth due to the many barriers to the requisite information. While there were many variations to this theme and some strategic leaders during the period acted responsibly, power generally was held by those that had the information and data. And, the few challenges by outsiders usually had little force. Corporations and strategic leaders also had great influences over outside perceptions. They painted the pictures and swayed the opinions. However, the information age has turned this reality one hundred eighty degrees. Now, information and data is broadly distributed and much of the information and data emanates from outsiders and from the bottom up. People have the means to access and disseminate incredible amounts of information and data across long distances at little cost.

Power is moving from the firm grasp of the elites (government officials and business leaders for the most part) at the top to be more broadly distributed involving multiple sectors of power. For instance, an individual can author articles, reports, opinions, and the like and share them with large numbers of people worldwide. Some observers (academics) view this as a trend that has been unfolding slowly for centuries and it has. For instance, in the Western countries at the beginning the second millennium (circa 1000) kings and aristocrats held the crux of power, then power transferred to the nation states and democracies with duly elected governments that became the centers of power; power theoretically shifted from the few (high-born aristocrats) to the many (citizens and elected leaders). In many countries power is still concentrated in the hands of elites, a relatively small group with true political and economic power. But, it is shifting to a broader base even in developing countries controlled by dictators or the ruling clique.

The rise of the global corporation in the twentieth century caused another big shift from centralized political power to a quasi-sharing (informal and unstructured) of power between elected government officials and corporate executives. During early part of the twentieth century the social, economic and political elites still enjoyed most of the power in real terms. However, as the number of global corporations increased and the technologies used by businesses improved, economic power became more widely distributed in the business world as well. Start-up companies like Walmart (founded in 1962) and Microsoft (founded in 1975) grew quickly and gained significant economic and market power and many old-line companies like General Motors, Ford and DuPont had to welcome new players that included companies from all regions of the world. Companies like Toyota Motor Company and Unilever joined the ranks of the powerful. The few became the many and the trends continue as companies like LG and Samsung join the ranks of the powerful.

Today, the situation continues to change as people and companies throughout the world gain power through information that only the elite would have had a decade or two ago. Power is shifting toward the masses and individuals as well. Many more people have the means and mechanisms to control their own destinies and create their own realities. Thomas Friedman in his book, *The World Is Flat,* provides insightful views of the new world and the implications of globalization.[5] He suggests that the social structures have changed and that people have gained incredible power and influence. And, social networking through outlets like Facebook and MySpace has opened up the means and mechanisms for global communications to broader and higher levels.

In reality, power has also shifted from the old linear patterns of previous times where one entity would enjoy power with an eventual replacement by a second and then a third entity to a new mosaic of multiple players enjoying power simultaneously. For instance, the United Kingdom was the global military and economic power of the ninetieth century being replaced by the United States in the twentieth century. Today, some scholars suggest that China will assume such leadership toward the middle of the twenty-first century. However, such thinking is linear. It assumes that previous patterns will continue. Other views include that "big businesses" will assume the power positions and become the global leaders of political and economic power. Bruce Piasecki in *World, Inc.* argues that businesses are now more powerful than governments.[6] However, a nonlinear view suggests that there will be numerous spheres of power and power will be shared between private and the public sectors; organizations and individuals, the big and the small, the new and the old, etc.

This broader perspective envisions a business world in which power is neither shifting in linear or distributed patterns among a few entities or players, but one that is becoming more multifaceted with many spheres of power and influence. While it is idealistic to believe that power could be balanced or shared evenly, it is realistic to think in terms of a more sustainable world in which neither political nor economic interests and/or business entities usurp all of the power, but one in which the social, economic and political forces and other legitimate interests can co-exist and prosper. A more holistic reflection on the conditions and trends of the early twenty-first century might indicate that governments, businesses, and people in general have improved their positions over the last decade or two, and that it is now more likely that the overarching framework will include the interests of all of the dimensions.

This is particularly important, since it is unlikely that government officials, business leaders, heads of stakeholders groups, social leaders, or individuals can solve all of the protracted problems and difficulties or lead change alone. It is collective intelligence and wisdom of many different people and their perspectives that discover, develop, and deploy the best possible solutions. It is broad, multidisciplinary thinking that usually arrives at sustainable solutions and sustainable success. Instead of one dominant form replacing another, the future paradigm may be a more holistic perspective, in which many contribute to success and ongoing progress and prosperity.

The role of stakeholders and their expectations

In a more interconnected world, stakeholders have become a viable force of change. Stakeholders are not new in the business world, but they are clearly more influential and powerful. Without the benefits of such low costs means of obtaining and using ICT and the reach of the internet, most stakeholders would be disparate groups trying to make a difference, but most likely unable to achieve critical mass and create an agenda and awareness that people understand, accept and respond to. Today, stakeholder organizations and even individuals can reach far-flung audiences and tell their version of the situations while promoting views, philosophies, perspectives and positions that may run counter to the strategies, goals, and approaches of companies and SMEs. While not all such organizations or individuals are opposed to the actions of corporations, many have specific agendas that they are passionate about and spend money and energy to obtain more attention and action. Innovative companies such as Facebook and Twitter and innovative technologies like 4G cell phones with texting have become real-time news agents and emerging forces to counter conventional media. In the past, people using alternatives to conventional media might have been able to establish a local soapbox, but they would have found it difficult to play on a national stage or in the theater of the world. But interactive networks, widespread communications and the internet provide even the smallest and least capable stakeholder organization or individual with the platforms to engage in open dialogue and interactions with anyone in the world who wants to participate. While stakeholder organizations and individuals obtain a wide spectrum of results and not all are successful, the dramatic increase in the number of such entities and their efforts over the last decade make them forces to be reckoned with.

Stakeholders are a reality of modern business life and they have to be engaged and satisfied just like customers and supply networks. Stakeholders are significant forces that can be even more potent than competitors. They may wage different struggles and may not appear as credible in their early stages of development, but they are often more committed and dedicated to their objectives than many typical competitors. Competitors often have similar objectives like being successful in a market segment and assuring the well being of the industry. On the positive side, stakeholders may offer the means and/or mechanisms to obtain a differentiated advantage. Listening to stakeholders, adhering to their concerns and taking positive steps to make improvements may be some of the best ways to leap ahead of competition.

Dealing with stakeholders tends to be a messy affair. While most business leaders like managing certain aspects of market spaces, internal operations, business transactions and the like, it is often impossible to truly manage stakeholders in the traditional sense. Stakeholders are usually a diverse set of entities and individuals with very different agendas and objectives. There may be very few commonalities between them, and there may be a wide range of driving forces that are critical to only one or several stakeholders, yet important for business leaders to handle and pay attention to. Unlike managing customer expectations and fulfilling customer needs and requirements through a well-established and precisely defined and designed portfolios of products, services and processes, stakeholder expectations, requirements, and mandates (as in the case of government regulations) often have to be orchestrated in the context of the specific situation(s) and on a piecemeal basis.

The initial steps include identifying the key stakeholders and understanding their most important agendas. This is followed by determining the linkages between the stakeholders, if there are any, and mapping out the interconnections. The next step is to ascertain their critical issues and the timeframes involved. For instance, some stakeholder groups press for immediate solutions to their concerns through government legislation. Others may be more patient and take a long-term view for obtaining the ultimate solution. For example, Greenpeace wants governments to ban whaling altogether, while other groups use consumer advertising to highlight the dangers associated with the potential extinction of several species of whales. Once there is an overall understanding of the stakeholders and their perspectives, the next step is to determine the common elements from the corporation's point of view and examine them in detail to find common ground on the most important concerns and issues. The concept is to create overarching solutions for stakeholders that are important or even critical to large number of stakeholders, and then develop tailored solutions for the specific stakeholder agendas and requirements. Obviously, business leaders cannot resolve all of the stakeholder issues and concerns; moreover, there are practical, scientific and economic limits to what can be achieved, especially in the short term. For instance, there are many stakeholder groups that have issues with automobiles; some that focus on climate change and fuel availability and others that focus on emissions that affect air quality. While many business leaders in the automobile industry want better solutions, they know that improved designs take time and money and that a wholesale change to new technologies could destabilize the economic underpinnings of the industry; it takes significant amounts of time and money for radical innovations.

Strategic leaders have a duty to their shareholders and society to make the best decisions possible based on a holistic perspective of the business environment. They must satisfy the economic needs of customers and fulfill the financial and wealth creation goals of shareholders. However, they must also ensure that the broader social and environmental issues and concerns are managed as well. While it is impossible to cover all aspects of stakeholder perspectives in this section, it is important to understand that business leaders can manage many of the stakeholder aspects though openness, transparency and accountability. While they may not directly resolve the causes and effects of many of the concerns and issues, strategic leaders can mitigate the impacts and consequences through these concepts and the underpinnings of leadership, i.e., honesty, integrity and trustworthiness. The theoretical view is that stakeholders and people in general are more willing to accept the difficulties and challenges and have patience in the developments of better solutions, if the business leaders are open, honest and truthful. People are usually more forgiving and willing to work with businesses, if the leaders are doing their best for customers, stakeholders, employees and shareholders and that people are informed about the details and have a voice in the solutions.

Openness and Transparency in Business Settings

Openness and transparency for reinforcing integrity

Openness and transparency are simple, yet far-reaching concepts that necessitate inclusiveness and connectedness. They are founded on candor and telling the whole truth. Most companies and their strategic leaders do not intentionally tell lies and falsehoods, but they may engage in narrow perspectives and limited communications. Thus, they may tend to mislead people because they hold back details, provide only part of the story, and/or they exclude vast numbers of people in the disclosures. While their communications are generally truthful in the strict sense of the definition and are usually factual, they may misinform people by limiting the scope of the disclosures and by avoiding disclosures concerning the negative effects, implications and impacts.

Strategic leaders today have to take positive steps to overcome the "old school" mentality and establish an all-encompassing way of reaching out to people by ensuring that they are transparent. In *The Transparent Leader*, Herb Baum cites three principles that a transparent company must have:[7]

- A leader who believes in telling the whole truth
- A values-based corporate culture
- Employees who are "people people" (service-oriented/team players)

Telling the whole unadulterated truth is possibly the first and foremost principle that business leaders can subscribe to that enhances their ability to be successful and to build trust with people in the organization and in the external business world. It is a leadership principle that is easy to observe and obtain, since telling the whole truth is not inborn, but a principle and/or philosophy one adopts. It is easy to acquire and takes simple skills and talents to follow. Every person who is or aspires to be a leader can engage in telling the whole truth. As simple as it sounds, some business leaders of today may have difficulties following such thinking. They may believe that such an approach goes too far. For instance, marketers may promote the great applications that their products can be used for, but often do not warn people about the potential limitations unless mandated to do so. For example, beer companies try to convince beer drinkers about the great taste and wonderful experience when consuming their products. While some of the beer advertisers suggest that consumers should drink responsibly, they usually do not inform people about such dangers as developing liver disease after years of excessive drinking or the potential of becoming an alcoholic. Telling the whole truth also involves disclosing the all relevant aspects as soon as they become available and can be validated for accuracy and suitability. While there are many leaders who reluctantly provide information and data only after long struggles with customers and stakeholders or when they are forced to do so by government agencies or the courts, being truthful implies proactive disclosures so that people can make informed decisions and avoid or mitigate the negative sides of any situation to extent possible. Of course, properly informed people can discern whether to use the products and services or engage in the processes and activities. For instance, overweight people might avoid certain foods and drinks, if they are fully aware of the high caloric value of certain products. While the company may lose some sales and revenues, it might also reduce being criticized for contributing to obesity by stakeholder groups.

Transparency involves having personal and professional values that serve as guides for decision making. The precepts discussed in Chapter 1 have to be alive within the leadership and organization. A values-based culture is more than words and slogans. It is a deep-seated respect for the underlying principles and beliefs of the organization and ones used in day-to-day operations and in long-term strategy formulation and implementation as well. For example, Johnson & Johnson for many years used its Credo as guidelines for decision making.[8] The Credo spells out the values and principles of the company and provides employees at all levels with the philosophical underpinnings that the company believes in and wants to maintain above all else.

Openness and transparency involves living the truth, being totally honest, and having integrity across the entire company and its enterprises. They must be real and valid in the hearts and minds of the leaders and the employees. And, integrity necessitates providing the best solutions possible, ones that are credible, reliable and suitable for intended applications. It implies going beyond making full disclosures about the products and services, the operations, and the related decisions by providing the requisite details for people to use the products and services safely and successfully over the long term.

In their book, *The Naked Corporation,* Don Tapscott and David Ticoll discuss the Values-Value Ladder. They suggest that business integrity enables trust that strengthens relationships which produce value.[9] Their flow diagram indicates that transparency feeds integrity, validates trust, informs relationships, and evidences value, all in support of customers, employees, partners, communities, and shareholders. They link transparency to business success. Their insightful work focuses on using corporate values as the means for obtaining trust throughout the internal and external constituents to build solid relationships and create enduring value. Tapscott and Ticoll provide insights and understanding of how honesty, integrity, trust and relationships create value.

Openness and transparency are interconnected principles that link honesty, trust, relationships and success in an ongoing, self-reinforcing cycle. It actually involves a continuum that feeds on itself when successful. Figure 3.1 provides a variation to the basic theme and key elements of transparency and openness of a self-sustaining continuum. First and foremost, truthfulness establishes the foundation of openness and transparency and provides the continuity across space and time. It is singularity. Truthfulness as discussed is the unabashed telling of whole truth without modification or exception. It underpins candor and integrity. Truthfulness, candor, and integrity collectively tie the basic philosophies, principles, values, beliefs, ethics, behaviors and respect for people that form the foundation of leadership with the critical perspectives

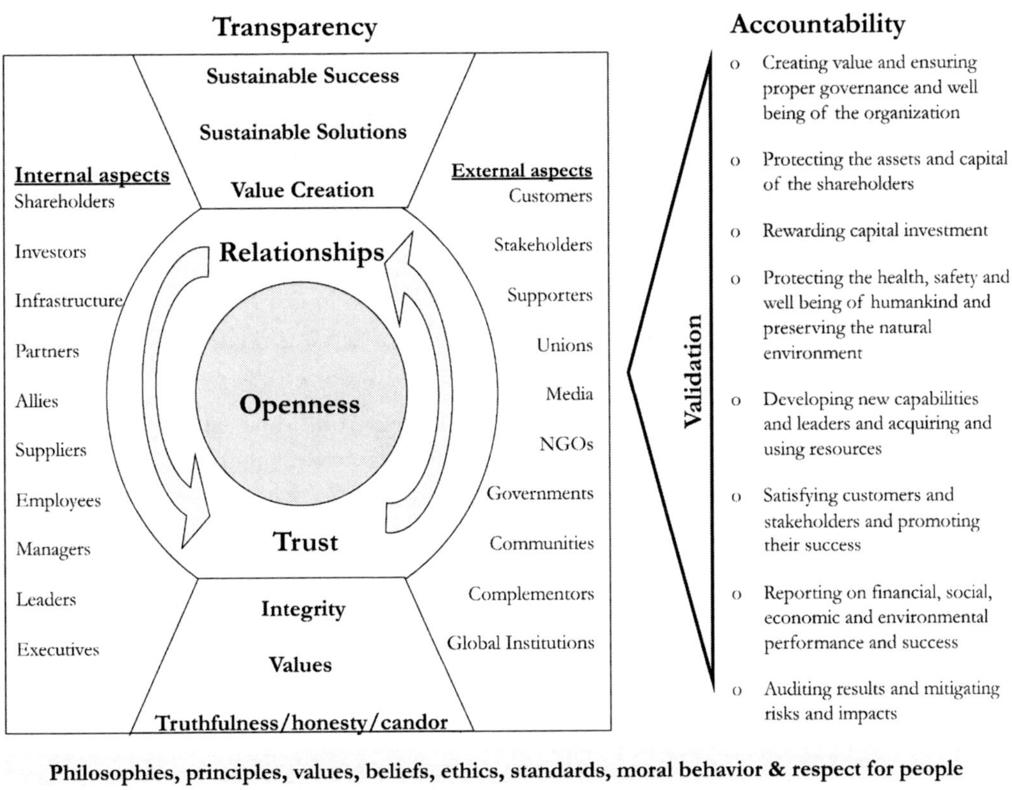

Figure 3.1 Interconnections of openness, transparency and accountability.

focusing on creating value, developing solutions, and sustaining success. Moreover, they help to ensure that the leadership and management of the organization remain solid over time so that the systems and structures are supported by an unshakeable foundation. It is upon that foundation that trust is built for both the internal aspects and the external ones.

All players and entities including customers, stakeholders, supporters, providers of complementary products and services, communities, governments, employees, partners, allies, suppliers, shareholders and others listed in Figure 3.1 must trust each other when engaging each other, working together, building relationships and/or making decisions. People make decisions based on trust and their understanding of the truth. For instance, people who travel via airplanes trust the carrier, the aircraft manufacturer, the pilots, the air traffic controllers and thousands of support personnel across the entire system. It would be folly to get on an airplane that is not certified or fully checked out to ensure that it is safe to operate and that the provider has a good safety record. The business world is fundamentally based on trust. Trust underpins everything that follows, especially establishing and building relationships.

Value creation and sustainable success depend on creating, building and reinforcing relationships. Business success requires positive and enduring relationships with all of the internal and external entities and individuals. While some businesses can sell defective products or faulty services once or twice to customers or can achieve success in the short term, such failures damage or obliterate trust and relationships are broken or destroyed. In simple terms trust builds and supports solid relationships, which in turn support sustainable success. But, it is not a linear process in which trust leads to relationships and relationships lead to ongoing value creation and sustainable success. It is a continuum. The "truthfulness-trust-relationship-value creation" linkage is an ongoing spiral that has to be reinforced every day, every week, every month and every year. It requires continuous attention and efforts though openness and transparency to ensure that success continues. Trust via truthfulness, candor and integrity supports relationships and the ongoing development and reinforcing relationships enhances trust. And, it is an ongoing cycle with almost instantaneous loops.

The values of leaders and the organizations are pivotal in ensuring success. The foundation is built on values that must be unshakeable and maintained as truisms over time and generations of leaders, managers and employees. They must be reinvigorated on an ongoing basis, just like trust, and they must be translated into the new realities of the future. Corporate values and those of the leadership provide the substance, which supports the entire organization. An embedded organizational culture of high standards, values and beliefs creates an air of openness, since people in such situations are not hurt by the truth and its implications. They have nothing to hide since everything is in the open. They welcome scrutiny because it shines the light on favorable outcomes.

People are the essence of business. They are empowered when they have the facts and the truth about the why, the what, and the how. Armed with the truth, they become a significant part of value creation and key contributors to sustainable success. Great leaders and great people make the difference between success and failure.

Accountability and its underlying aspects are discussed in the final section of this chapter.

Openness and transparency across the extended enterprise

Openness and transparency are critical constructs for the entire extended enterprise, not just the corporation and its organization. They transcend the corporation. They have to be embraced and enjoined by all of the entities that support the corporation and its enterprises, if sustainable success is to be achieved and maintained. Great care has to be used to assure that problems and difficulties are not eliminated from the corporation's operations and processes and simply moved upstream to supply networks giving the appearance of creating solutions when in reality the problems and difficulties are masked because they are in someone else's domain or because they have been commingled with many others to make it impossible to ascertain who is responsible.

Openness and transparency apply to relationships, agreements, actions and transactions between the corporations and their suppliers, partners, and with customers, stakeholders and other constituents to ensure that all affairs including problems and difficulties are managed properly and appropriately. Today, one of major concerns of employees, customers and stakeholders alike is that the principals, especially strategic leaders of major corporations, simply transfer (outsource) their most deleterious operations and processes to outside entities that are not as capable of providing the requisite solutions. Such principals might claim their overall operations and processes have been improved because they removed some of the most troubling aspects. While such claims might be true statements, the reality of the situation could be very different. For example, a major corporation spun off its chemical division in the 1990s to avoid having to count the large quantities of hazardous waste generated in the chemical processes in its toxic release inventory required under SARA Title III, Emergency Planning and Community Right-to-Know Act of 1986."[10] Section 313 of EPCRA required that companies generating hazardous must provide a toxic release inventory to the Environmental Protection Agency. While such companies might claim a reduction in their waste streams, in reality no improvements would have been made if the same processing continued after the change. The only result would have been the transfer of negative aspects from the principal(s) to the supply networks. In certain situations the end result could be even worse, if the supply networks are less capable than the principals. One of the major concerns about such outsourcing is the lack of control or the loss of control over the negative aspects. Moreover, if strategic leaders are not diligent and honest, claims of improvements may be made when no such improvements exist overall. If the surrogate(s) is less capable in affecting solutions than the principal(s), then the changes result in worse situations and outcomes, not better ones.

Life cycle thinking and assessment are perspectives and methods to overcome such potential deceptions or oversights. Life cycle thinking and assessment use systematic methods to analyze and evaluate the resources used, the outcomes produced, and the environmental degradations and burdens generated during the design, development, production and deployment of products and services from cradle to grave. This includes analyzing the upstream processes of the supply networks and the downstream applications of customers and stakeholders. Life cycle assessment (LCA) is a multi-stage input-output model that examines all of the inputs and outputs and their impacts, including materials, products, wastes, and emissions. It includes an inventory of the resources and energy inputs for products and processes, and the outputs from each stage of the product life cycle. LCA includes an impact assessment examining the potential impacts and their consequences on ecosystems and human health, and an improvement assessment, detailing the strategies and methods used to mitigate the negatives. The goal is to improve the positive and reduce the negative implications and impacts.

Life cycle thinking and LCA enhance transparency and openness, if done properly with the objectives of making improvements and sharing the results with the appropriate entities. While they can be complicated and require significant efforts, time and money to orchestrate, they provide greater knowledge and better dissemination of the truth. Firstly, they include all positive and negative aspects from the beginning to the end and across the whole extended enterprise. Impacts are identified, disclosed and dealt with regardless of where they are in the extended enterprise. Secondly, they go beyond the known truths and attempt to discover hidden problems and difficulties. While it is impossible to require strategic leaders to solve problems that they are unaware of, there are situations in which business leaders turn a "blind eye" to suspected problems or issues. While it is difficult to specify exactly how far strategic leaders have to go to ensure that their products, services, operations, and processes are the kind and quality people expect, responsible strategic leaders have a duty to do their very best when developing, producing, delivering and managing sustainable solutions.

The business case for openness and transparency

Openness and transparency involve complex requirements to assure that people have the information and data to ascertain the truth and know the underpinnings of decisions, operations, processes, products and services. The most compelling reason for openness and transparency is to build trust and lasting relationships that create value for external entities and strategic, market and financial successes for the corporation. Openness and transparency reduce the risks of having issues and concerns spin out of control and become crises that cost money and reduce customer and stakeholder satisfaction. They also reduce the potential for corruption and malfeasance, since information and data are available to outsiders who can review the situations and decisions.

Simply put, openness and transparency protect and preserve the trust that has been established over time. Of all of the intangibles that companies and business leaders enjoy, trust is one of the most powerful yet fragile assets of the corporation. Like reputation, trust takes arduous efforts to build, solid performance to maintain, creativity and leadership to enhance, but it can be easily lost through the poor decisions and actions of a few leaders, managers or even employees.

Openness and transparency provide shareholders with the details that they need for making good investment decisions. They also provide shareholders with the confidence that strategic leaders are acting on their behalf and can be trusted to protect the assets and well being of the corporation and the investors' interests. They reassure employees that decision makers are performing their duties and responsibilities in the best interest of all and not their own self-interests.

Businesses and operations that are conducted in the open provide leaders and managers across the extended enterprise with the knowledge that they are being treated appropriately and with respect. Openness and transparency are not a panacea for all problems, issues, concerns, etc., but as mechanisms they are both proactive in establishing the high ground and precautionary in avoiding difficulties. They fit into the premises of six-sigma quality thinking, which state that it is less expensive to eliminate the causes of defects and burdens than to deal with their impacts and consequences and spend money to fix the resulting damage.

The public demands more and more information and data from corporations and businesses each year. The internet gives people access to vast quantity of information and details about the corporations and their involvements. Some is accurate and favorable and some is not favorable. But if one was to examine the inaccurate information and data available, it is most likely to be unfavorable because someone or some organization has taken issue with the corporation. It is virtually impossible to counter all of the misleading statements and views even if business leaders have the time and money. Openness and transparency address such challenges from the opposite direction. Rather than defending against inaccuracies, strategic leaders simply preempt counter views by providing the best evidence someone would want to have; the information and data from the primary source. Openness and transparency disarm the detractors and nullifies most of their clout, since the negative side has already been disclosed, if there is one. This is especially the case, if the company has history of being open and transparent.

Lastly, failures to provide proper disclosures are often taken as signs of potential difficulties. Inactions and the lack of disclosures often appear as cover-ups, which compel stakeholders to dig even harder and deeper. It is often easier to lay the truth out and face up to the issues. The lack of propriety or the hints of a cover-up are often viewed as more serious than original problems. Remember President Nixon! His problems got worse and worse as he tried to keep the lid on disclosures.

Accountability and Doing What is Right

Overarching perceptions about accountability

Leadership involves being responsible and accountable for all that happens or fails to happen. It also involves being honest, engaging in moral behaviors, managing and performing in proper ways and achieving expected results without being under direct supervision or control. Leadership requires a mindset that the leader is ultimately the person who is answerable for the actions, activities, behaviors, outcomes, and overall performance of the organization and the enterprise. Strategic leaders are responsible for the strategic direction, strategy formulation and implementation, proper execution, organizational well being, attainment of the desired performance and sustainable success. They orchestrate the development of the organizational capabilities, the acquisition and allocation of assets and resources, the creation of value, the crafting, production and deployment of the solutions, and the integration of the enterprise. While strategic leaders often focus on the near-term aspects such as operational efficiency and effectiveness, financial performance and oversight, it is critical that they provide stability and safeguard the long-term viability of the enterprise. They have to improve the business prospects through new market and business opportunities as they are discovered or become available, deal with new competitors as they emerge, and ensure that the best solutions are provided to the existing and potential customers in increasingly diverse situations and more complicated business environment.

Additional responsibilities of strategic leaders include discovering new means and mechanisms for achieving success, improving various facets of the business enterprise and the social and environmental underpinnings, mitigating challenges and vulnerabilities, and preparing and developing employees and potential leaders of tomorrow to assume roles in a more capable and enlightened organization. Strategic leaders can reinvent their corporations by understanding the external business world and inspiring a proactive mindset within the organization and its extended enterprises. The requisite strategies and actions to realize one's potential must be framed in the realities of today's world and based on a vision for tomorrow. They must be inclusive and not limited to the direct beneficiaries of the corporations or its strategic leaders. Strategic leaders are accountable for everything from the highest level dictates of the board of directors to the most mundane operation. While actions, activities, work flows and the direct accountability for their execution can be delegated to lower level managers, supervisors and employees, the primary responsibilities still remain with strategic leaders who provide oversight to ensure that everything is executed properly.

Accountability implies that regardless of the circumstances and the people involved, strategic leaders are answerable to shareholders, boards of directors, higher level leaders (if there are ones), their peers, subordinates, customers, stakeholders, and society in general to the extent of the effects and impacts of their decisions, actions, inactions, and failures. Based on the concept of accountability, strategic leaders with the authority and flexibility to make decisions can take actions without always having to ask for permission and to proceed with routine matters and those that have been previously approved from a strategic perspective. Accountability is an extremely broad and far-reaching construct that extends from proper governance to auditing past performance and results and reporting salient information and data to shareholders, board members and appropriate corporate leaders and external constituents. Accountability includes the means and mechanisms for creating value, protecting the well being and assets of the organization, preserving the health, safety and well being of all that are affected by the corporation and satisfying all of the constituents from customers and stakeholders to shareholders and employees.

Accountability is both a dynamic and passive construct. It is dynamic in the sense that it facilitates making good decisions and taking positive actions. It is about leading and being proactive. The passive side suggests that leaders should always act as if someone is watching and documenting their decisions and actions because at anytime everything can be scrutinized by outside entities and/or board members. While such a notion has both positive and negative implications, the philosophical perspective is intended to be positive. Strategic leaders act in a prudent and forthright manner because they believe that it is the most effective way to achieve success. They avoid misleading communications and wrongdoing because they realize that such dealings eventually become public and the revelations will cause incalculable damage to the corporation and to the individuals involved. Full disclosures of the details reinforce the accountability of strategic leaders, because they know that they will be scrutinized and that there will be no hidden elements.

Proper governance through accountability

The governance structure includes the board of directors' and corporate officers' fulfillment of their fiduciary responsibilities to protect intellectual capital, corporate assets, and the interests of shareholders, society, customers, stakeholders, employees, partners, and all constituents. It also involves the organizational structure and leadership of the corporation, especially strategic management and the management systems for managing any potential outcomes whether they are normal expectations or the most unlikely scenarios.

The governance of a corporation or any business organization is a vital concern to everyone directly or indirectly involved. Traditionally, governance meant the proper and legal conduct of the affairs of the corporation and assurances to internal and external parties that the corporate, strategic and operational systems and structures were properly designed, maintained and controlled. Under the concept, executives and strategic leaders ensure that systems, processes, and actions are functioning properly, that all compliance requirements are understood and met, and that value systems are appropriate, effective and delivering results. Governance also means managing change, being inclusive and innovative, and protecting the well being of the corporation.

Proper governance has at least four critical components to it. The first involves the legal framework of the corporation that is established through the laws under which the corporation or business is organized. For most corporations various forms of government provisions set the rules and regulations under "corporate law." They are the means and mechanisms for duly organizing business entities. For instance, in the US the states enjoy the role of establishing corporations and other forms of businesses under the laws enacted by the state government. Historically many corporations were set up under the laws of the State of Delaware because it had very favorable provisions that made compliance relatively easy.

The second involves the legal requirements as established by various governments and independent entities that regulate one or more aspects of corporations. This involves all of the laws enacted and regulations promulgated pertaining to how business is to be conducted, the rules that have to be followed, the mechanisms for managing and controlling the interactions between entities (commercial codes and trade laws), reporting requirements for informing shareholders, investment communities, and important constituents, and a plethora of other aspects. Business leaders generally understand the needs for laws and regulations and often want government entities to establish stable conditions through regulatory constraints and mechanisms so that all businesses can fairly achieve their objectives with minimal risks from deviant behaviors of criminals and wrongdoers. Astute business leaders know that deviant behavior by a few of their peers whether criminal or not affect all businesses and put pressure on government officials to take actions to solve the problems.

The third involves standards and expectations in dealing with external norms and pressures. These include the broad fiduciary duties and the responsibility to society, customers, stakeholders, and other constituents to act and behave fairly, honestly and appropriately in protecting and preserving economic stability, promoting social well being, and providing environmental safeguards.. Business leaders are expected to be responsible and ethical. They are also expected to handle any difficulties they create and to mitigate any impacts and risks they impose on customers, stakeholders, and society. Doing so is fundamental to the basic trust component of public acceptance. Corporations can maintain that trust through openness transparency, and accountability.

The fourth involves protecting the well being of the organization and ensuring that the people therein are enhanced, developed and rewarded for their contributions. Accountability to the people of the organization and the enterprise is the key to creating a work environment that is conducive, and encourages superb contributions and personal development. Strategic leaders not only can expect good performance from each individual, but each person can expect that the leaders provide all of the proper ingredients for achieving success.

Accountability within the corporation and the enterprise is a two-way street that has road blocks in some organizations when employees try to obtain information and feedback from the strategic leaders. Leaders provide annual reviews for the employees, but are not often accountable to the employees for their contributions as leaders or lack thereof. In too many organizations lower level managers and contributors are blamed for the failures of the higher level management. Accountability also involves taking responsibility for all of the successes and failures and ensuring that improvements are made. It is not the intent herein to provide all of the details of the governance of businesses but to highlight some of the critical areas pertaining to accountability.

Using openness and accountability to eradicate the negative side

The business world has many great strategic leaders who want to make a difference in enhancing the well being of all people and the natural world. Fortunately, the great majority of the leaders are positive and they do their best to exhibit excellent behaviors. Unfortunately, there are also a small number of leaders who live on the negative side, promoting their own selfish agendas. There are also dishonest people who try to gain unfair advantages over others and to usurp power and influence to further their own positions. From a business perspective, the negative side includes strategic leaders and practitioners engaging in illegal, unethical, unfair, and inappropriate actions and behaviors. The actions of some of these leaders involve blatant disregard for honesty and candor and illicit means and mechanisms. Generally, such aspects are illegal and fall under the category of criminal actions.

Dishonesty, corruption and bribery, whether they are illegal or not in a given country, rob companies, customers, and people in general of their full measure of value creation by siphoning off some portion of the gains and outcomes for illicit purposes. Corruption, embezzlement and theft distort economic considerations and make it more costly to obtain products and services at fair and affordable prices. They cause hardship on economically disadvantaged people who need to acquire products and services and to fully participate in social and economic systems and structures, i.e., have fair employment opportunities. The threats of wrongdoing and miscues are always present even among respected leaders. One way to thwart such possibilities is to have safeguards in place based on openness and accountability. Ongoing disclosures from the company or from insiders who are called "whistleblowers" make it less likely that business leaders and other decision makers will engage in improper behaviors if they know that all transactions, activities, etc. will be made public.

The perspectives herein focus more on the inadvertent or circumstantial mistakes and blunders rather than the well thought-out criminal actions and behaviors involving corporate corruption. Openness and accountability provide ways and support apparatus to avoid making wrong decisions when engaged in complicated situations that have conflicting agenda and objectives. Moreover, openness and accountability in conjunction with precepts and principles like integrity and fairness provide the foundations for making good decisions regardless the challenges involved.[11] Openness, transparency and accountability are dual-sided in the sense that they make leaders think about creating good, making good (proper) decisions and avoiding improper behaviors. They cause certain leaders to avoid engaging in the negative side because there is a high probably that inappropriate decisions and deeds will become public knowledge. In a world of easy access to information and data, it is becoming more and more difficult to take improper or illegal actions that can be covered-up or "swept under the table."

Transparency International is non-profit service organization that promotes openness and transparency and tracks corruption on a worldwide basis. It publishes an annual report pertaining to global corruption. Its Corruption Perception Index highlights corruption within countries and provides an understanding of levels of corruptions from one country to another.[12] The overall objective is to shed so much light on wrongdoing that it is impossible to perpetrate it without getting caught. It encourages right behaviors so that concerns like corruption and bribery disappear.

Corporate reporting and passive approaches

Corporate reporting originated in the financial arena where laws, regulations, directives, and the protocols of the responsible government agencies mandated annual financial reports. In the US, the Securities and Exchange Commission (SEC) requires detailed financial reports that follow explicit specifications. In the EU, several countries require corporations to prepare annual reports on their social, economic and environmental actions and implications and disclose the impacts associated with their operations. Specifically, corporations are required to provide social and environmental and/or sustainability reports. This is part of the general trend toward more reporting, disclosures, and openness.

Environmental reporting was born out of the necessity for corporations to inform the public about their operations and programs and the positive gains and negative impacts. Specific problems often became sensational newspaper headlines with national and international media attention. The stories of the Exxon Valdez oil spill and the Royal Dutch Shell's Brent Spar incident are just two examples. On the positive side, corporations with proactive social and environmental strategies and good track records use such reporting to enhance their corporate reputations and build trust with customers and stakeholders. Companies like DuPont, Proctor & Gamble, Nestlé and Ciba-Geigy (Ciba-Geigy is now part of Novartis) led the way in publishing comprehensive environmental reports. For example, CIBA's 1992 Corporate Environmental report was 28 pages long and included comments by corporate executives, a discussion of the company's progress toward sustainability, and sections on resources, wastes, products, and safety. CIBA's proactive management recognized the importance of becoming more sustainable and establishing a track record for anyone to examine.

Openness, transparency and accountability led the way to dramatic improvements. Many major corporations also recognized the importance of environmental reporting after they had significant compliance or public relations difficulties. For instance, Dow Chemical Corporation (Dow) and United Technologies Corporation (UTC) became advocates for environmental leadership and corporate reporting, turning their environmental problems into opportunities to excel. During the late 1980s, Frank Popoff, Dow's chief executive officer (CEO) at the time, turned a laggard into a leader by moving Dow from denial to dialogue. It became an advocate for public reporting and broader corporate disclosures. It was a key contributor to reporting guidelines developed by the Public Environmental Reporting Initiative (PERI) during the early 1990s.[13] PERI guidelines were intended to be a voluntary reporting framework that would facilitate comparative analysis.[14] The context was narrowly focused on environmental performance with links to the operating systems. PERI was relatively simple, yet it formed the basis for today's more sophisticated corporate reporting that has evolved to include social, economic and environmental considerations. George David, UTC's former CEO, became an early advocate of sustainability reporting.

In 1997, the Coalition for Environmentally Responsible Economies (CERES) with participation of the United Nations and a number of non-governmental organizations, global corporations, consultancies and universities created the Global Reporting Initiative (GRI) to formulate and implement a "common framework for enterprise-level reporting on the linked aspects of sustainability: the environment, the economic, and the social."[15] The enterprise-level scope and the inclusiveness of the social, economic, and environmental considerations represented critical changes in the thinking about what corporate reporting should include. GRI expanded environmental reporting to encompass the whole of the corporation, not just the operations, and to include external factors indirectly linked to the corporation. Traditionally, such reports included only information directly related to the company's operations, processes and products, i.e., the direct responsibilities and compliance. GRI moved environmental reporting from simple management reporting to a more balanced accounting of the social, economic and environmental performance of the enterprise and the corporation's progress toward sustainable development. GRI's Sustainability Reporting Guidelines 2002 provides a comprehensive understanding of the principles and recommended report content. [16]

The overarching elements of accountability include transparency, inclusiveness and auditability. Corporations are expected to fully disclose their positive contributions and negative effects and impacts and to openly provide customers and stakeholders with the information needed for making informed decisions and for building trustful relationships with the corporation. In the complex business world of today with broader responsibilities and more intense requirements, customers and stakeholders want to understand the capabilities and integrity of corporations. Their "need to know" involves much more than just buying products and services.

Inclusiveness helps corporations meet that need. It involves engaging diverse groups of customers, stakeholders and constituents in understanding the full scope of operations, products, and services, as well as the social, economic and environmental considerations. It also means reporting with performance indicators that cover the spectrum of social, economic and environmental operations and their impacts across geography and time.

Auditability refers to the ease with which external organizations can scrutinize reported information to discern the credibility and accuracy of the information and reports. It involves the ability of customer and stakeholder groups to independently verify the details. Inclusiveness and auditability are complementary. Reporting has to be as comprehensive as possible and include information and assessments that can be verified by third parties. For example, companies using less sophisticated reporting guidelines are often selective in what they report. Certain corporations report on metrics and indicators that they wish to track instead of using a broad set of criteria that customers and stakeholders might want to know. Such corporations skew the reporting to the most favorable outcomes. For instance, a company engaged in nuclear power might focus on its contributions to limiting greenhouse gases, especially carbon dioxide, but it might fail to discuss its issues regarding nuclear wastes or radioactive emissions. The limited scope of the reporting mechanisms can mislead people to think that the corporation is meeting expectations when in reality it has highlighted only the most favorable implications and outcomes.

Accountability gives business leaders the flexibility to perform and the mechanisms to ensure proper performance. Leaders must know that their decisions and actions are subject to scrutiny and that they are accountable.

Reflections

Openness and transparency are critical factors that promote accountability and good decision making. They encourage strategic leaders to think about the underlying perspectives of their decisions and their strategic logic. Truthfulness underpins all decisions and disclosures and is the source of building trust in the business environment. It creates the means to build solid relationships with people across the enterprise and within the organization. Truthfulness, candor and integrity are among the most valuable means and mechanisms used by business leaders in creating value and achieving sustainable success.

Even leaders who are not well-endowed with innate leadership qualities like charisma and excellent intuition can develop into great strategic leaders by acquiring knowledge and adopting powerful approaches like telling the whole truth, being open and transparent, and promoting full accountability. These are profound yet simple ways to become a successful leader; ones that serve the incumbent well regardless of the situation or circumstance. They are fundamentals that are timeless and hopefully will be in vogue decades from now.

Truthfulness, in particular, is an essential element of leadership that differentiates the strong from the weak. Strong leaders tell the truth and encourage others to do so. They depend on the truth to resonate their vision, dreams and aspirations. The truth helps them in creating trust and building enduring relationships. The opposite is true of untruthfulness. While it is easy to lie, to mislead and to deceive, the perpetrator usually gains only short-term advantages, since it is difficult to maintain lies and deceptions. The small gains obtained due to the falsehoods are decimated by the loss of trust and the consequences that they have on relationships with people and the negative effects on sustainable success. Mahatma Gandhi was cited as saying "***There is no happiness like the truth, no misery like untruth.***"[17] He was exactly right. Truths create and untruths destroy. Worse yet, it takes considerable time and efforts to develop trust and build solid relationships and only moments of untruthfulness to dissolve the goodwill and positive dispositions.

Accountability involves being responsible for one's decisions and actions and ensuring that they are substantiated through validations and verifications. While truthful leaders usually depend on the trust and goodwill that they establish over the course of time, they must continuously reinforce the trust with solid evidence. Full disclosures of information and data and ongoing reporting to the plethora of interested and supporting parties, entities, and individuals perpetuates value creation and sustainable success for all.

Leadership involves having effective and comprehensive perspectives of the business world and all of the people in it. However, it is virtually impossible to identify and map out all of the characteristics and behaviors that individuals should exhibit. Yet with all of the complexities involved, many of the underpinnings (fundamentals) are relatively simple. Truthfulness is one of the foremost in importance and the easiest to achieve. It just takes a commitment to telling the truth.

Openness and transparency are corollaries to truthfulness. They reinforce the benefits of truthfulness and are truly proactive approaches for staying ahead of expectations in the business environment and markets therein. Leaders that provide critical information and data before required or forced to do so gain the confidence, respect and trust of the people within the organization and across the business world. Openness, transparency, and accountability are some of the simplest prescriptions for achieving sustainable success, yet they are among the most profound.

Notes

1. David L. Rainey, *Sustainable Business Development: Inventing the Future through Strategy, Innovation and Leadership* (Cambridge, UK: Cambridge University Press, 2006, p. 229). The graphic is adapted from the discussions in the reference.
2. Thomas F. P. Sullivan, *Environmental Law Handbook, Fourteenth Edition* (Rockville, MD: Government Institutes, Inc., 1997, pp. 481–509).
3. Ibid, p. 481.
4. Global Environmental Management Institute, *"Environment: Value to Business"*, Washington, D.C., 1998, p13. The concept of the 'License to Operate' involves the public trust to operate in safe and responsible manner. It involves responsibilities to act in a safe and prudent manner that does not jeopardize society, customers, employees, and related entities. It is based on the legal responsibilities to comply with laws, regulations, and directives and the ethical responsibilities to ensure that outcomes are positive and do not involve unreasonable risks.
5. Thomas L. Friedman, *The World Is Flat: A Brief History of the Twenty-first Century* (New York, NY: Farrar, Straus and Giroux, 2005).
6. Bruce Piasecki, *World Inc* (Naperville, IL: Sourcebook, Inc., 2007).
7. Herb Baum, *The Transparent Leader: How to Build a Great Company Through Straight Talk, Openness and Accountability* (New York, NY: HarperCollins, 2004, p. 6).
8. Johnson & Johnson's Credo is its stakeholder strategy. The Credo is as follows:

    We believe our first responsibility is to the doctors and nurse, and patients, to mothers and all others who use our products and services. In meeting their needs everything we do must be of high quality. We must constantly strive to reduce our costs in order to maintain reasonable prices. Customers' orders must be serviced promptly and accurately. Our suppliers and distributors must have an opportunity to make a fair profit.

    We are responsible to or employees: the men and women who work with us throughout the world. Everyone must be considered as an individual. We must respect their dignity and recognize their merit. They must have a sense of security in their jobs. Compensation must be fair and adequate, and working conditions clean, orderly and safe. Employees must feel free to make suggestions and complaints. There must be equal opportunity for employment, development, and advancement for those qualified. We must provide competent management and their actions must be just and ethical.

    We are responsible to the communities in which we live and work and to the world community as well.

    We must be good citizens –support good works and charities and bear our fair share of taxes. We must encourage civic improvements and better health and education.

> ***We must maintain in good order the property we are privileged to use, protecting the environment and natural resources.***
>
> ***Our final responsibility is to our shareholders.*** Business must make a sound profit. We must experiment with new ideas. Research must be carried on, innovative programs developed, and mistakes paid for. New equipment must be purchased, new facilities provided, and new products launched. Reserves must be created to provide for adverse times.
>
> ***When operate according to these principles, the stockholders should realize a fair return.***

9. Don Tapscott and David Ticoll, *The Naked Corporation: How the Age of Transparency Will Revolutionize Business* (New York, NY: Free Press, 2003, p. 74)
10. SARA Title III is part of the Superfund Amendment and Reauthorization Act of 1986.
11. Good decisions are ones that are based on the overarching principles of leadership and management.
12. Transparency International, *Global Corruption Report 2006* (London, UK: Pluto Press, 2006, pp. 298–303).
13. PERI included a number of major corporations and several stakeholder organizations. They included the Business Council for Sustainable Development, International Institute for Sustainable Development, Deloitte & Touché, the Coalition for Environmentally Responsible Economics, the Council on Economic Priorities, the Investor Responsibility Research Center, and the Global Environmental Management Initiative.
14. PERI guidelines were written to accommodate the reporting requirements of the following: Chemical Manufacturers Association's Responsible Care; the U.S. EPA's Toxic Release Inventory; the European Union's Environmental Management and Audit Scheme; U.K.'s BS7750; the National Pollution Release Inventory and Accelerated Reduction Elimination of Toxics in Canada; The Ministry of International Trade and Industry guidelines in Japan; and the emissions inventory of SEDESOL in Mexico.
15. Global Reporting Initiative, March 1999, Sustainability Reporting Guidelines: Exposure Draft for Public Comment and Pilot Testing, p. 1.
16. Global Reporting Initiative, 2002, Sustainability Reporting Guidelines 2002, pp. 22–30.
17. Mahatma Gandhi, *The Words and Inspirations of Mahatma Gandhi: Peace* (Boulder, CO: Blue Mountain Press, 2007, p. 52).

References

Baum, Herb (2004). *The Transparent Leader: How to Build a Great Company Through Straight Talk, Openness and Accountability.* New York, NY: HarperCollins.

Gandhi, Mahatma (2007). *The Words and Inspirations of Mahatma Gandhi: Peace.* Boulder, CO: Blue Mountain Press.

Friedman, Thomas L. (2005). *The World Is Flat: A Brief History of the Twenty-first Century.* New York, NY: Farrar, Straus and Giroux.

Piasecki, Bruce (2007). *World Inc.* Naperville, IL: Sourcebook, Inc.

Rainey, David L. (2006). *Sustainable Business Development; Inventing the Future through Strategy, Innovation and Leadership.* Cambridge UK: Cambridge University Press.

Sullivan, Thomas F. P. (1997). *Environmental Law Handbook, Fourteenth Edition.* Rockville, MD: Government Institutes, Inc.

Tapscott, Don and David Ticoll (2003). *The Naked Corporation: How the Age of Transparency Will Revolutionize Business.* New York, NY: Free Press.

Transparency International (2006). *Global Corruption Report 2006.* London, UK: Pluto Press.

4

Qualities of Leadership and Leadership Development

Introduction

Successful leadership depends on the qualities possessed and exhibited by the leaders themselves. The qualities of leadership are difficult to articulate fully, since there is always the possibility of not identifying all of the essential ones critical for success. Moreover, since leadership is dependent on the individual and context, the significance of each of the qualities of leadership is difficult to generalize and many depend on the situations and circumstances. Leadership is not like many management constructs such as product development, finance, accounting, statistical analysis, and hundreds of others in which there are well established and generally accepted concepts, approaches, methods and techniques for defining, developing, achieving and measuring proper outcomes and success. Trying to define all of the qualities of leadership is virtually impossible to accomplish. Fortunately, leadership is an art with many variations and styles that can lead to success.

The qualities of leadership depend on context, i.e., what is happening in the business environment and who the leader is, his or her background, knowledge, experiences and personal values. Leadership is influenced by situations, circumstances and norms in a given organization and society. Certain qualities like unwavering in a commitment to the mission or achieving difficult objectives may be essential for a military leader, but questionable in situations like a new product development in which the expected outcomes are harder to precisely define and where flexibility and adaptability are important factors.

The Pursuit of Sustainable Leadership, pages 83–114

Context defines relevance and helps determine the importance of each of the qualities of leadership. For instance, leaders who are responsible for research and development programs should be creative and be able to promote creativity in others. On the other hand, leaders responsible for production have to use specificity and ensure that outcomes exceed established standards and criteria. However, in most cases it is not an "either-or" situation, but one that requires more of certain qualities than other ones. It is crucial to remember that it is rare when one of the qualities of leadership overwhelms all of the others or when an individual can succeed based on just a few qualities of leadership. For instance, President John Kennedy had incredible charisma that he exploited during elections, yet he had other outstanding qualities like personal courage and great confidence that also contributed to his political success. Moreover, it is also rare when anyone has all of the requisite qualities of leadership or exhibits them in perfect unison or balance.

The qualities of leadership may be viewed in terms of a matrix based on whether they tend to be innate or learned versus whether they tend to be tangible or intangible. The categories of qualities include the more innate qualities like charisma on one side to ones like personal knowledge and capabilities that depend more on learning on the other side. And, there are qualities that exhibit some aspects of being innate and some that are based on learning. Innate qualities are inborn and difficult to acquire through learning and experience. For instance, a leader may have inherent characteristics and abilities like having a great memory and a vivacious personality; ones that are difficult if not impossible to learn. However, the good news is that a vast majority of the qualities can be acquired or enhanced through learning and personal development.

Tangible aspects are ones that are more discernible and easier to measure; intangible qualities are esoteric, open-ended and often more difficult to precisely articulate. While many management theories require that characteristics and outcomes be measurable which favors the tangible-type qualities, when it comes to leadership qualities great care as to be taken to ensure that perspectives are not skewed to one side or the other. Both tangible and intangible qualities are important.

Leadership development is a mechanism for improving one's qualities of leadership over time and increasing one's abilities to lead and to be successful. It refers to an individual leader and his or her growth and advancements as a leader through new knowledge, learning and experiences among other aspects. Leadership development has general aspects that can be applied to all leaders and individualized elements that have to be customized. For instance, the more tangible aspects can often be conveyed and learned based on the experiences of other leaders. They are much easier to define. It is also easier to provide the means and mechanisms to enhance them. They can be acquired through education, training and on-the-job experiences. The intangible aspects often require more personal approaches like coaching and mentoring. They are often vague and difficult to understand, appreciate and improve. They require detail assessments and specific game plans for personal development. Intangible aspects have to be addressed using focused activities like building one's confidence through multiple coaching sessions and exercises.

Leadership development is not just an event or a program, but a continuum that is crucial for the success of even well-established and experienced leaders. While certain individuals have game plans for leadership development, it is important that the overall development plans be flexible and adaptable. The business world is constantly changing and the required knowledge, skills and combination of the qualities of leadership shift over time. One may have most of the critical qualities of leadership in a particular setting and be hopelessly out of sync in another. For instance, certain highly competent strategic leaders who have successfully managed operations in their home country are often ill-prepared, when asked to manage the same type of operations in another country. Such leaders often do not realize that context has changed and what is acceptable or preferable in one setting may be totally improper in another. For example, strategic leaders at Walmart had difficulties expanding its retail operations outside the US. The company did not enjoy success in developing its retail operations in Germany. There are many reasons why its leaders failed, but one of the main reasons may be that they were not prepared to deal with the different market and cultural aspects when doing business in a European country.

Leadership is a complex construct that takes incredible knowledge, learning, diligence, fortitude and commitment to acquire the requisite perspectives, knowledge, know-how, skills and capabilities and to sustain one's development over the decades. Successful leaders continue to grow, develop and mature everyday of their lives. As with many of the business aspects, leadership is about the never-ending quest for perfection that is never fully realized.

The chapter includes the following main topics:

- Articulating the qualities of leadership
- Outlining the essential aspects of leadership development

The Qualities of Leadership

Perspectives on the qualities of leadership

The age old question pertaining to leadership revolves around whether leaders are born or developed. There is evidence on both sides of the question to support whichever premise one might wish to attempt to prove. The general answer is that both of the prevailing premises have merit. Leadership has both innate and learned qualities. Great leaders manifest certain qualities that have inherent aspects based on the person's genetic makeup as well as other characteristics that are developed over time through learning and experiences.

In simple terms, the qualities of leadership can be portrayed as those of the heart and the mind. The heart represents those qualities that are exhibited through personality, beliefs and values, and one's physical, emotional and psychological make-up. While not entirely innate, many are developed during the early years of a person's growth. They are akin to athleticism and natural physical prowess. Many of the characteristics of truly outstanding athletes are due to their nature and innate physical constitution. For instance, football players can be taught the plays, maneuvers, and proficiencies of the game, but those that excel usually have many natural talents like great speed, exceptional dexterity, great instincts and outstanding stamina. Many of the aspects that pertain to the heart involve the underlying makeup of the individual leader. These qualities are much more difficult to deal with. For instance, the ability to inspire people and to enjoin them in the quest for success is often related to charisma or one's affinity to connect with people. It comes from one's inner spirit. The question is: how does one acquire or learn the ability to inspire others to achieve greatness or to take on difficult challenges? And, how does one teach or learn charisma? These are some of the key challenges that have to be answered.

The mind represents those qualities that are acquired over time through new knowledge, education, training, and personal development. People generally become more adept as they have opportunities to lead and exhibit their leadership talents and skills. Again, not all such aspects are purely learned and certain individuals clearly have more natural abilities to learn and to translate their learning into talents, know-how, capabilities and positive results than others. Moreover, just acquiring the knowledge and abilities through learning and personal development does not mean that they can be translated into superior leadership qualities and characteristics. Regardless of a leader's nature and background, many of the principles, percepts and talents of leadership can be learned, developed and followed. This is especially true of those pertaining to the mind. For instance, all leaders can exhibit honesty and integrity. Everyone can be selfless and focus on the full spectrum of duties and responsibilities including ensuring that everyone involved is cared for and supported in their quest to be successful.

Leadership can be described as being a multifaceted and intricate construct that involves numerous perspectives and profound aspects. It involves the integration of the heart and the mind. It is based on who you are from the basics of human nature, how you have developed over time through learning and experiences, what you think and believe, and how you make decisions and act. It is not one aspect or another, but a complex array of characteristics. For example, former US President Dwight David Eisenhower was just a bright military leader with an outstanding record not unlike many of his peers prior to World War II. But, circumstances changed everything. He was selected as one of the senior leaders to prepare the plans for defeating Hitler and was instrumental in developing the integrated military system for the invasion of the continent and in building relationships among the Allies. Based on his planning skills and abilities to work with a broad array of political and military leaders, he was given the opportunity to lead the military forces for D-Day for defeating the Nazis. Eisenhower was successful because he had many leadership characteristics including being able to deal with extremely complex challenges, having the physical abilities to endure long hours and trying times, having the people skills to get other generals with high strung personalities to work together, and being willing to engage in actions with uncertainties and risks.

Leadership involves knowing, assessing, doing, adapting, inspiring, making decisions and leading among many other aspects. While many business schools can teach people about the prevailing theories, constructs, processes and practices of management, it is much more difficult and complicated to educate people about the qualities, characteristics, mindsets, attitudes, talents and behaviors associated with leadership. Since many of the qualities of leadership cannot be precisely defined and taught, it is challenging to identify all of the qualities or characteristics necessary for covering all of the situations and actions that leaders engage in. Leadership is complex and varied. Again, context is critical. For example, Winston Churchill became a great wartime political leader because he had unwavering courage and the fortitude to stand up against the overwhelming superiority of the Nazis during the Battle of Britain. His steadfastness and commitment to safeguarding his nation and democracy made him the ideal leader during those tumultuous times. Yet, soon after the war, people voted for new leadership into the Parliament and with it, a new Prime Minister, Clemet Attlee. The electorate viewed Churchill's leadership qualities in terms of the times and critical needs and requirements of winning the war. While this does not say that Churchill was not an adept leader during more peaceful times, it does suggests that his most outstanding qualities were most apparent and appreciated during difficult circumstances. Moreover, people make judgments that are imperfect and based on their perceptions rather than a rigorous comparative analysis of the candidates. Thus, leadership tends to be open-ended with many characteristics.

Leadership involves using one's natural advantages to the extent possible and developing or enhancing other attributes to augment them. Both the heart and the mind are critical for succeeding. Moreover, since not everyone is equally endowed, many individuals can overcome inherent weaknesses through personal development and investments in complementary capabilities that mitigate or eliminate some of the underlying limitations. Conventional leadership theories usually suggest focusing on your strengths and overlooking your weaknesses. Often a person's strengths support and contribute to his or her successes during the early stages of a career. But, weaknesses may ultimately and unfortunately limit one's potential in the long term. Most people have difficulty improving many of their weaknesses or limitations, especially those pertaining to natural and physical characteristics. For instance, if you are not a great public speaker or have difficulty inspiring people because of the lack of a powerful voice or presence, you can offset such challenges by learning how to construct powerful messages that resonate through other communication mechanisms. But, there are limits to the degree of improvements and such improvements may be insufficient to rectify the problems. Yet, most leaders can overcome certain inherent weaknesses by changing the ways in which they handle situations or by gaining knowledge and experience. The person may be much better in one-on-one situations than in group settings; therefore, he or she may have to spend more time engaging in direct communications and speaking speak with each person or with small groups. There are many avenues to overcome weaknesses and it is important to do so when one establishes his or her plans for achieving long-term success, especially when the person is relatively young and has the time and risk free mechanism to learn and overcome such challenges.

The actual means and mechanisms may be less relevant than the concept that leaders must take broad perspectives and achieve success through multifaceted approaches, especially ones that counteract weaknesses and negative aspects. These include using their natural abilities to the maximum, acquiring new knowledge, skills, and capabilities, and gaining experience and confidence through actions, interactions and relationships. In simple terms, leadership involves dual-sided (multi-sided) thinking and actions. One should use his or her strengths to the maximum, but at the same time he or she must also work diligently to eliminate or neutralize weaknesses and limitations.

Innate and learned qualities of leadership

The qualities of leadership are multifaceted and numerous. However, there are several that are critical in most contexts or situations. Again, such qualities can be tangible and intangible; tangible qualities involve ones that are more related to reality and intangible ones are more related to perception. Both are important aspects of leadership.

Table 4.1 provides a matrix of some of the most important tangible and intangible aspects in terms of innate and learned qualities. The matrix is not intended to be comprehensive or precise. There are many more qualities beyond those listed. Moreover, the actual positioning or importance of each of the qualities depends on context and the individual. For instance, in military situations involving conflicts and war, courage and concern for people are more crucial aspects than charisma and open-mindedness. On the other hand, political leaders generally rely on charisma and personal characteristics (appearance and physical attractiveness) more than knowledge and commitment. For example, President Kennedy enjoyed many more of the innate and intangible qualities listed than his opponent, Richard Nixon in the 1960 presidential election. Kennedy won the election even though Nixon had more experience and knowledge of the political realities and government operations.

Each is important in its own right. The more innate qualities include charisma, intuition, intelligence, open-mindedness, courage, and personal characteristics.

Charisma is the intangible side of personal characteristics involving an innate ability to attract or be attracted to people on a physical and/or emotional basis. It involves the rare quality to make positive connections with most people and to obtain their

TABLE 4.1 Selected qualities of leadership

Categories	More innate	In-between	More learned
	Person characteristics	Appearance/behaviors	Capabilities/experience
More tangible	Courage	Ethics/core beliefs	Competencies/knowledge
	Open-mindedness	Innovativeness	Cultural aspects
	Intelligence	Personal values	Concern for people
More intangible	Intuition/insightfulness	Passion/inspiration	Commitment
	Charisma	Wisdom/judgment	Confidence

support and loyalty, even devotion. Some leaders simply exude a highly energized personality and have extraordinary charm. Charisma is a quality that is hard to exactly articulate and it is even more difficult to emulate, if you do not have it. Charisma is exemplified by the old saying, "I cannot articulate it, but I know it when I see it." It is a leadership quality that is dependent on the culture, situation and circumstance. It is often based on the perspectives and interpretations of the recipients. In one society, a person may have charisma and in another one he or she may not. For instance, some dictators are viewed as great leaders by their close followers, but are often despised by other people who are not part of the elites (the inner circle of political supporters) or the indigenous population. Certain leaders exhibit great charisma when giving speeches or addressing large crowds, but the same leaders may be ineffective in one-on-one situations or when engaging in actual activities and outcomes. Their charisma is based on circumstances. For instance, publically-elected political leaders may seem to be charismatic during elections when their personalities are more free-flowing, but less effective when they are trying to govern. They are gregarious when dealing with broad concepts and meeting people in non-threatening situations, but they are less outgoing and forceful when they have to come to grip with real world problems and the associated details.

Intuition is the faculty of sensing what has to be done or even what is happening in complex situations. Intuition involves deducing an understanding of the situations and circumstances without having all of the facts or details. It also involves having the ability to develop insights and new ways of thinking and doing things without having previous experiences or fully assessing all of the implications. For example, Ken Iverson, the former CEO of Nucor Steel, realized that if he shared the increases in profits with employees due to improvements in the operating system and the contributions of their labor, his company would obtain even greater profits based on the extraordinary outcomes obtained. Before having the evidence that his approach would work, Iverson instituted an incentive system of rewarding workers with pay for performance that turned the organization into one of the most successful US-based steel companies. Moreover, he instinctively realized that he had to pay the bonuses on a biweekly basis to sustain the incentives and the outcomes.

Intelligence is the capacity to learn and understand. It involves the mental faculties to acquire new knowledge and to use it beneficially. It is the aptitude to digest facts, information, and details and ascertain what they mean and how they may be used. It involves mental capabilities to process knowledge, draw relevant conclusions and make appropriate decisions. Intelligence is a complex quality that has numerous meanings and implications. While it is possible to enhance one's learning skills, most people have inherent abilities to learn certain subjects and not others and to reach a particular degree of learning and knowledge. For instance, some leaders have outstanding abilities to plan, but are ineffective in knowing how to implement the plans. Other leaders may be very good at managing things, but very poor in leading people. While it is difficult to precisely measure one's intelligence or learning abilities, some people are more capable of learning than others, and some people learn particular subjects better than others. For example, Albert Einstein was particularly well-endowed in learning abstract subjects like theoretical physics, yet he was not inclined or able to reach the same levels of achievement in more mundane topics.

Open-mindedness is an innate quality to understand and deal with broad perspectives. It involves the ability to develop new ways of thinking about what could be done and seek out new solutions to achieve the desired outcomes. It is not easily defined and varies considerably in meaning and circumstance. It usually involves having a broad view about context and finding many alternate ways of dealing with the possibilities and realities. For instance, Fed Smith, the founder of FedEx, realized that the effectiveness of his logistical system was more important than its efficiency. He created a system of routing all packages through Memphis to reduce the complexities of the airfreight business. Open-mindedness also includes understanding situations and circumstances from the perspectives of other people; seeing the world through the eyes of others. Open-mindedness requires being responsive to the views of others and providing others opportunities to present their ideas and approaches. For example, marketing leaders in the developed countries try to find new ways to provide people with entertainment, but most people in traditional societies entertain themselves. It also involves giving contrary opinions equal opportunities to be heard and adapted.

Courage involves the mindset to face up to challenges, difficulties, uncertainties, risks and dangers. Even in situations that are not threatening, courage is important especially when making decisions that pertain to leading change or developing cutting-edge approaches, because there is always the possibility of failure. Leaders who are fearful of failure usually do not take bold steps and often rely on incremental improvements and stepwise approaches. They focus more on minimizing risks, rather than taking advantage of opportunities and trying to obtain great outcomes. Leaders have to have courage in dealing with people, making decisions, taking risks and leading companies. It may seem easy to go along with the mainstream perspectives, but it takes enormous courage to lead, especially when you are invoking a paradigm change. For instance, many US-based business leaders focus on maximizing profits, which is the typical paradigm in many related circles like the stock markets. It is relatively easy to justify certain decisions, if they are in keeping with the mainstream views. However, it takes enormous courage to adopt a new paradigm such as sustainable development and leading change based on the integration of social, economic and environmental considerations. While courage is typically an innate quality, it can be enhanced through knowledge, experience and learning. Leaders are more inclined to take actions, if they have the requisite know-how and background pertaining to the situation, especially if there are high risks. For instance, a business leader who is technologically sophisticated is more likely to engage in radical innovations, since he or she has the professional capabilities to ascertain the merits of the investments.

Personal characteristics like height and one's physical nature are predetermined for the most part, but they can be enhanced to some degree. One's health and physical makeup are particular important aspects that can be improved with good nutrition, diet and exercise. While personal characteristics can also be enhanced through certain medical procedures and cosmetic techniques, there are real limits to such improvements. Certain personal characteristics are difficult to obtain and/or improve, if one has not been enriched through natural endowments. For instance, the height of an individual often contributes to other people's perceptions of the person's leadership abilities and stature. For example, George Washington was perceived as a natural leader because at six feet two inches tall and he stood above his peers. A key to leadership is to be your real self given your personal characteristics and enhance what is really possible. For example, James Madison, the author of the Constitution and the 4th President of the US, was only five feet tall, yet he used his great intellect to offset any perceived disadvantages due to his height. He relied on his wit and knowledge. As an aside, some leaders try to be something they are not and they often come across as fake or phony.

The middle ground or in-between qualities are ones that exhibit both innate aspects and learned ones. They are the areas in which incumbents and potential leaders can make dramatic improvements. Some of the most important qualities in this category include wisdom, passion, personal values, innovativeness, ethics, and appearance/personal behaviors.

Wisdom is an intangible quality. Having and exhibiting wisdom is a virtue. It involves the ability to make good judgments and decisions; ones that are just, fair, balanced and appropriate. Wisdom also involves examining situations from multiple perspectives and making good decisions that are sustainable. Wise leaders know that unwise decisions have repercussions. For instance, a good leader realizes that if he exploits customers in the short term, he will alienate them and they may seek other options as soon as they can. Strategic leaders can improve their capacity to make wise choices by focusing on the people involved in addition to the business objectives and expected outcomes. The view is that if people are satisfied and successful, then there is a higher probability that the business objectives will be met as well. For instance, when seeking a certain level of profits, the best way to realize the objective is through delivering the best solutions and having great relationships with customers and stakeholders. Again, Iverson sharing of the economic benefits with his employees was not only wise but it lead to even greater outcomes.

Passion is the boundless enthusiasm and dedication to the organization's aims, beliefs and people. Passion is a powerful emotional feeling about what one is dedicated to and what he or she pursues regardless of the time and effort required. It involves being steadfast about what one wants to achieve and being truly engaged in obtaining the desired outcomes. Having deep-seated passion is one of the qualities that can elevate an individual above what is generally believed to be possible. Leaders with extraordinary passion often overcome many of their limitations allowing them to be successful in situations in which they lack some of the requisite skills, talents and resources. For example, during the early years (the late 1970s) of Microsoft, Bill Gates and Paul Allen achieved great success because they had a strong desire and passion to create an extraordinary enterprise. They let nothing stand in their way. Even though they had minimal resources, they persevered because they truly believed in what they were trying to accomplish. Their passion for their business reinforced their vision for creating an exciting new enterprise for personal computing. ***Inspiration*** is the ability to instill passion in other people and to get them to become engaged and to contribute. It involves projecting one's being in a way that other people desire to become part of the opportunities.

Personal values are the beliefs that guide one's decision making and actions as discussed in the previous chapters. They are often based on the individual's family background and upbringing. They may also be enhanced or even changed through learning and new knowledge. While it is difficult to stipulate exactly what the right personal values are, it is clear that leaders who have well-established and ethically-sound values and beliefs are often more capable of achieving positive outcomes because they have a solid foundation by which they are guided. Moreover, leaders with a good sense about themselves are more likely to lead people and organizations in a consistent and forthright manner.

Innovativeness is truly a mix of innate and learned qualities. Like many qualities it is extremely difficult to characterize exactly. Many of the attributes associated with innovativeness and creativity are natural ones that leaders either have or do not have. For instance, it is hard to develop creative artistic talents, if you do not possess them naturally. However, leaders can develop a mindset that facilitates innovativeness. They can enhance their abilities to be creativity and to create new approaches. While such leaders may not become the inventors of new technologies or the designers of new products, they may develop the skills and talents for leading such people and organizations. One does not have to be a great inventor to be an innovative leader. As an aside, the conductor of a philharmonic orchestra may understand the various musical instruments, while not being capable of playing any of the instruments. Nevertheless, the conductor can lead the orchestra's performances and can even develop new ways of choreographing the presentations. Learning and experiences often provide the knowledge to understand the nuances of being innovative.

Ethics in this context involves the principles, rules and standards of one's behaviors and conduct and those of his or her organizations. Ethics provide guidelines that underpin good decision making and ensure consistency over time. They are based on what the leader perceives to be important and proper in managing his or her affairs, professional decision making and actions and personal behaviors. It is difficult to be a great leader, if one has fundamental flaws in ethics and proper conduct. Being honest and trustworthy and exhibiting openness and fairness are some of the most important ethics that resonate positively within the organization and across the enterprise. They make the leader authentic in the eyes of the superiors and subordinates alike. Having integrity is an ethics-based quality that can be developed and used as a means for differentiating one's being and style from those of ones who are not as honest and ethical.

It can be argued that ethical leaders make the best decisions possible for their organizations, even if they personally suffer adverse consequences or do not obtain their due rewards. Think about Churchill who was roundly criticized for not supporting the 1938 Munich Agreement in which then Prime Minister Neville Chamberlain agreed to hand over the Sudetenland to Hitler to obtain "Peace with Honour."[1] Even though King George VI supported Chamberlain and a majority of the Parliament went along with the agreement, Churchill and his Conservative Party were steadfast in their opposition. It did not take very long to determine who was right, when Hitler attacked Poland on September 1, 1939. Moreover, during the war Churchill was adamant about carrying on the fight and not capitulating to the Nazi when the war seemed hopeless and others advocated giving up.

Appearance is clearly a mix of natural characteristics and ones that leaders can develop and improve upon over time. A leader can create a pleasant appearance that is well honed even though the person does not possess natural beauty. Improvements can be made through selection of the right clothing and personal style as well as enhancements in professionalism and stature. Moreover, appearance is based on the eyes and perceptions of the observers. A leader can fit the expectations of others without compromising his or her principles by adapting high standards of dress and decorum. For example, William Howard Taft, the 27th President of the US and Chief Justice of the Supreme Court, was a large man who always presented himself in public with style and dignity.

Personal behaviors are critical for success. Exhibiting socially sound and proper personal behaviors is an important way for gaining respect and influence in many situations. People generally follow respectable and trustworthy leaders. Moreover, leaders who exhibit proper behaviors are less vulnerable to personal attacks and criticisms. Their judgments are more likely to be accepted and valued, if they are based on well-established codes of conduct and established principles. Moreover, leaders can reduce the pressures from external stakeholder groups if they are open and inclusive in their professional decisions and personal activities.

The third main category involves those qualities that are based more on learning and experience. These are the areas that everyone has an opportunity to excel and to overcome some of the limitations of one's inborn or inherent characteristics. These qualities are easier to develop and acquire than innate ones. While there are constraints like time and money for education and training and limits to one's natural abilities to learn and understand, the "sky is the limit" when it comes to stretching one's potential through personal and professional development. They include confidence, commitment, concern for people, cultural aspects, competencies and capabilities.

Confidence is one of the most critical qualities of leadership. Great knowledge and skills are often inconsequential if leaders do not have confidence in their talents and abilities. Leaders have to believe in themselves and trust that they have the right answers when they have done their "homework." The lack of confidence often results in sub-optimized positions and outcomes, because the leaders are unable or unwilling to take bold and audacious actions. They may have the "right stuff," but they lack the self-assurance to proceed or they are timid as they move forward. Leaders with confidence believe that their solutions, strategies and actions are proper and that they have made good and wise decisions. Confidence implies being on the right track and being decisive. It also implies aggressively carrying out well conceived plans using appropriate methods and actions. Confident leaders usually enjoy more success, because they do not hesitate or stumble during implementation and execution. Of course, confidence does not imply being foolhardy and taking extremely risky actions when the evidence is clear that the approaches will not lead to success.

Commitment is a key quality that reinforces how people view the leader and whether they can depend on him or her. True leaders are committed to their efforts and the people they are associated with. Many leaders have great ideas, craft excellent strategies and develop outstanding plans, but fail to implement them properly. They waver in their commitment to stay the course until the results are obtained. They delegate the work to others, but do not provide the support and oversight necessary to achieve success. For instance, strategic leaders investing into new-to-the-world technologies often do not have the patience to continue making the necessary investments until the long-term benefits come to fruition. General Motors (GM) was a pioneer in electric vehicles, but its strategic leaders reduced their commitments to the technology when GM's early electric vehicle, EV-1, was not successful in the marketplace during the mid-1990s. On the other hand, Robert Noyce and Gordon Moore, founders of Intel in 1968, along with Andy Grove, did everything possible to stay ahead of the competition and continued making significant investments in microprocessor technologies during the 1970s and 1980s even though the returns were relatively modest. They did not achieve truly great successes until the introduction of the Pentium in March 1993.

Concern for people is one of the most critical factors for achieving success. Leaders are generally successful because other people in the organization help them achieve success. The concern for other people is clearly a duty and responsibility of all leaders. Yet, many leaders place it low on their list of priorities. It is broad-based including concerns about direct relationships with superiors, customers, stakeholders, and employees to ones pertaining to wide-ranging relationships with peers, colleagues, shareholders, and communities. It also includes the overarching concerns pertaining to humankind and society in general and the emotional sides of one's responsibilities. In a Harvard Business Review article, Daniel Goleman discusses the five components of emotional intelligence: self-awareness, self-regulation, motivation, empathy, and social skills.[2] The last two components specifically involve how leaders deal with people. Empathy connotes an understanding of other people's situations and feelings; it fits the quality of concern for people through developing human-related connections with others. A key to successful leadership is understanding reality from the perspectives of other people to the extent that one can. For instance, instead of trying to sell someone the products that are available, the proper approach from a people perspective is to address what they need and want. This is especially critical for people in developing countries. Having effective social skills provides leaders with the knowledge and know-how to engage other people in a broad array of settings. This includes knowing how to interface with people from other cultures. Leaders not only have to be concerned about people, but they must be able to take actions to gain outcomes that benefit people from their perspectives and realities. This topic is extremely broad and implies ensuring that the contributors, participants, recipients, and other people are taken care of, enriched to the extent possible and not harmed from the products, services and business activities.

Cultural aspects are critical and pertain to people as well. Cultural aspects include the beliefs, values, language, rituals, symbols, history, institutions, and ways of thinking and behaving in a society. They are the shared perspectives and norms of a group or community of people. In a given society, the cultural aspects are generally passed from generation to generation. On a global basis, and even within one's home country, culture is a key variable that is a critical consideration and a key variable that differentiates a society and provides a sense of commonality. However, as the populations change, especially in the developed countries, and they become less homogeneous, the business environment in those countries is expected to become less predictable. Leaders can improve their standing in society by ensuring that they deal with people across the spectrum of the social dimension and the cultural differences in appropriate ways and understand the cultural norms and requirements. To do so, strategic leaders must reflect on a broad range of social factors as they develop their methods for dealing with people. Leaders need to know how people behave and what they expect in various situations and ensure that their interfaces and interactions have positive outcomes and promote social well being.

Competencies are qualities that are very important in leading complex organizations. Competencies are those areas the leader is very well qualified, having superior knowledge and know-how pertaining to the subject. They are learned abilities and skills that are acquired through education, training and experience. The more one knows, the more he or she is able to lead and be effective. While there are no guarantees of success, knowledge and know-how facilitate achieving positive outcomes. Moreover, the more diverse and in-depth one's knowledge is, the more likely the leader is able to handle complicated or novel situations and to make appropriate decisions. In today's business world, knowledge and experience are critical factors in achieving success. Leaders with broad knowledge and experience are more capable of making good decisions and are less reliant on their "gut feeling" or intuition.

Leaders are expected to be competent in their roles and responsibilities and in decision making. They are expected to become competent quickly, if they are engaged in new assignments and to learn the basic aspects of their positions and duties in a short period of time, generally less than a few months. While leaders are not expected to be experts, they are expected to have a reasonable level of knowledge and know-how so that they can make proper determinations.

Capabilities are the broad skills, talents and abilities. They are usually less intense than competencies, but are nevertheless still important strengths and qualifications that one enjoys. Capabilities include the cognitive ability to obtain insights, assess options and make the most appropriate choices. On the positive side, leaders can enrich their personal situations by enhancing their personal capabilities through education, learning and experience. Learning and experience give leaders the knowledge, proper attitude and capacity to make and implement their decisions with gusto. In particular, experience gives one the ability to understand situations and to formulate approaches that are logical and sensible from the broader perspectives and realities over time. Mature and knowledgeable leaders are often more capable of thinking and acting in terms of the internal constituents and the broader context of the business world and the social and market-related aspects in concert with the ethical, technological and environmental considerations.

While there are no guarantees that having these qualities or other related qualities will produce outstanding leadership traits, building and sustaining a solid foundation of such qualities provide leaders with the belief and self-assurance that they can make good decisions and that they can lead their organizations. While it is important to use one's natural strengths and inherent advantages, there are many ways in which leaders can build additional advantages and become more successful over time. They can acquire new knowledge, skills and talents. They can become broader in their perspectives beyond being masters in a few fields; they can expand their horizons into other related fields of endeavor. In today's business environment, leaders have to be multi-specialists and generalists at the same time. Most business leaders understand and are knowledgeable about management and finance. Think about the influence and power they gain when they have a comprehensive understanding of the social and environmental dimensions or have a holistic perspective of the external environment. For instance, leaders need to know the history, culture, economic and political systems, the ecosystems, etc. of a country that they plan to do business in.

The qualities of leadership can be enhanced by increasing one's strengths and reducing, if not eliminating, the weaknesses. In the short term, improving strengths may work well in making progress toward higher levels of leadership. However, if one is not careful and diligent, weaknesses may limit one's potential and advancements in the long term. Again, the multi-sided perspectives indicate that leaders and candidates for leadership positions have to concentrate on both their positive and the negative aspects. These concepts are more fully developed in the next chapter.

Individualizing the qualities of leadership

The qualities of leadership include many more categories than those identified in Table 4.1. As discussed in the previous section, the basis for determining the relevance and importance of the qualities of leadership depends on the situations and circumstances. For each of the qualities there is often a range of possible definitions and specifications. For instance, what does the notion of confidence actual mean in a business setting? Generally, it implies a feeling of being certain and self-assured in a situation or with a topic. While the qualities of leadership are intended to imply the positive side, there are always the potential for individual leaders and practitioners to misinterpret or misapply them. For instance, confidence should be based on knowledge and learning, not arrogance or self-righteousness. Arrogant leaders alienate people and limit their potential for success. Moreover, if people believe the leader is self-centered or self-serving, they are less likely to make significant contributions or they pay more attention to protecting themselves against blame and criticism that the arrogant leaders often tend to use.

Qualities of leadership focus on the attributes of the leader and how they are characterized from the individual's perspectives. While there are significant limits to what one can do to remold one's natural being, each individual has within himself or herself the self-determination to become more than what he or she is. Self-improvement is an ongoing way to becoming more successful. Leaders and would be leaders can choose what the qualities actually mean in their positions and/or situations. Leaders choose their virtues. They must be carefully selected and should be based on logic and norms. Moreover, individuals should avoid extremes. According to Aristotle, virtues should be determined by reason and follow the "principle of the golden mean between two extremes."[3] This implies that the choices should not be skewed toward the extremes of the choices (qualities). For instance, leaders must have courage when making decisions and they must stand behind those decisions during implementation and execution. However, too much courage may lead to recklessness, if one takes it to an extreme; too little courage may lead to indecision or wavering during execution. The learned qualities are dynamic and there are fewer absolutes. It is impossible to state exactly what the requisite capabilities are for a given situation. Moreover, the appropriateness of capabilities and even competencies change as the business environment changes. As the business world becomes more turbulent and complex, it is incumbent on leaders to keep pace with the changes or even leap ahead of change through learning and experience.

Determining the requisite learned qualities is an ongoing necessity of leadership. A leader's personal capabilities and competencies are also a function of his or her reality. As one's reality changes a leader has to assure that his or her capabilities and competencies are still relevant and necessary and/or what are the new ones that are required for the position(s) and situations. For instance, if a leader is given a new assignment, the roles and responsibilities of that assignment may require certain knowledge and capabilities. The individual should ensure that he or she has the necessary qualities and qualifications to meet the challenges. If he or she does not have all of the necessary qualities, then he or she should engage in learning and take every action to acquire the capabilities, competencies, knowledge, and information, etc. as soon as possible. Moreover, it is crucial that the individual customizes the qualities of leadership on an ongoing basis to fit his or her own changing situations and circumstances. For instance, after the attack on Pearl Harbor on December 7, 1941, President Franklin D. Roosevelt (FDR) had to quickly shift from managing the federal government, focusing on the national economy, and trying to end the Depression to being a proactive commander-in-chief and leading the US military forces to counter the aggression of the country's enemies. FDR had very little time to make the adjustments and could not make excuses about not being prepared to manage such changes or needing more time to develop new competencies and capabilities. He was simply thrust into the situation by external circumstances and he had to respond immediately. While his knowledge and competencies associated with economics and political forces were of great assistance to him, he had to learn quickly new subjects pertaining to the military and war. FDR's situation is an extreme case of making transitions from using one's natural qualities to developing a different array of qualities; however, it provides a great example of what leaders may have to deal with in a rapidly changing and turbulent business world.

Strategic leaders often have to reshape their thinking and modify their perspectives as the world changes. For instance, strategic leaders at GM generally thought in terms of being the industry leader for most of twentieth century. As Toyota made great gains in market share and industry success, GM's leaders had to adjust their view of reality and adapt a new mindset about how to regain GM's strategic position and prominence. Moreover, the strategic leaders of GM today have to think about how to focus on how the company has change to compete on a global basis with rapidly emerging markets in China and India and the more limited existing markets in North America.

Leaders should never be satisfied that they have exactly the right qualities and methods to lead in a dynamic world. It is arrogant to think that one has the precise combination of leadership qualities that can be expected to match all situations and circumstances. The forces of change in the business environment quickly make any such sense of nirvana a fleeting fancy. If a leader believes that he or she has obtained the perfect combination of leadership qualities, there may be a tendency to prevent changes from occurring because such changes are viewed as threats to one's leadership position. For example, Henry Ford resisted changing the Model T, because he did not want to sub-optimize his perceived sense of perfection. But, technological advancements by the competition forced changes anyway; principally the "the closed-couple" design and the more advanced and powerful car, the Chevrolet.

Leaders have to be proactive in making ongoing improvements and focusing on personal development because leadership involves the never-ending quest of excellence; a quest that provides enormous personal opportunities for those who accept the challenges and endeavor to make great strides in becoming a true strategic leader. The pursuit of sustainable leadership involves examining all of the qualities of leadership and becoming more sophisticated in one's repertoire.

Leadership Development

Overarching perspectives on leadership development

Leadership involves inspiring people, setting the overarching direction, ensuring governance, providing energy, providing guidance and oversight, ensuring that progress and outcomes are on the proper track among numerous other aspects. While leadership actually involves many more facets than just these aspects; inspiration, direction, guidance, support, progress and oversight are good descriptive words that imply countless aspects of leadership. However, they are subjects that are difficult to precisely articulate.

Leadership development involves a broad array of the ways to enhance one's qualities of leadership and the associated repertoire of skills and know-how. There are no "magic formulas." Furthermore, there are no quick weekend leadership development programs that provide the crucial ingredients for obtaining quantum leaps or instantaneous outcomes. Rather leadership development involves hard work and dedication for improving all of the qualities that one can improve. It also involves recognition that it is not a level playing field. Not all qualities can be improved equally. Leadership development involves non-linear means and mechanisms for achieving the desired results. It is easy to teach young and/or unsophisticated leaders the fundamentals (the basics) of leadership and what leaders are expected to do. The requirements for making improvements are often obvious and efforts usually translate into immediate benefits. Such efforts usually concentrate on skills, know-how and capabilities. As the individual becomes more astute and knowledgeable about leadership and gains more real-world experience, it becomes more and more difficult to realize ongoing gains and advancements. Furthermore, the more innate qualities are extremely difficult, if not impossible to improve in most cases, and the learned qualities usually require considerable time and continuous efforts to make significant progress. And, the gains may not be readily apparent in the short term and they are often manifested after multiple endeavors are made and the results converge over time. Yet, it is in the long term or in one's more mature years that leadership development becomes more essential, especially if one wants to continue grow and develop and to become a more capable and sophisticated leader.

The success of leadership development is often related to the individual's perception of the needs for ongoing development in light of his or her underlying qualities, skills and abilities. The novice typically has a good understanding of his or her strengths and weaknesses and is usually willing to make the investment to attain the necessary improvements. The rewards (improvements, advancements and promotions) reinforce the willingness to make the ongoing developments, i.e., the gains usually more than offset the costs (time, effort and money). On the other hand, as the leader matures, becomes more sophisticated and obtains high-levels of management, there is a tendency to avoid further development because the individual believes that he or she has the requisite qualities and talents for success. Such leaders often have the perspectives that time is on their side and their successes will come. Moreover, for the more mature leaders ongoing efforts into leadership development do not always seemingly provide appropriate returns. They may perceive that the costs outweigh the benefits. Such perceptions lead to frustration and they stop making the investments because they do not appreciate the long-term benefits often involve time lags, i.e., the big gains manifest themselves years later.

Leadership development is not the same as management development. Leadership development involves understanding and improving oneself and learning how to effectively instill and inspire the vision, missions and goals for individuals, groups, organizations and a whole enterprise. It also deals with inspiring people about the benefits of making significant advances and achieving higher levels of sophistication. These are complex topics that do not always follow processes and prescribed methods. They are not easy to learn and apply. Leadership development focuses on transforming the incumbent leader from a competent manager into a dynamic, inspiring and sophisticated strategic leader who can be the master of the realm. In contrast, management development involves subjects that are easier to teach and learn. It is based on established theories and practices that are generally accepted by the mainstream of intellectual thought and management professionals. Management development typically involves acquiring knowledge and experience about the strategies, operations, processes and activities pertaining to the conduct, flow and administration of business. It involves learning about assets, resources and perspectives of the company, the organization, and possibly the enterprise. It involves just what the words imply; it is more about managing than leading. In simple terms, one manages things and leads people.

Too many leadership development programs and related approaches are really about management development; teaching people to be good and effective managers and how to apply the management constructs. Management development is important, but limited in affecting positive outcomes and the potential for long-term success, especially for the individual leader, because the focus is on theories, methods and practices. Leadership development focuses on the person and how he or she thinks, makes decisions, and behaves with respect to other people and the future.

Leadership development includes understanding one's self and enhancing every aspect of one's repertoire. It also includes enhancing one's abilities to interact positively with other people. Interpersonal dynamics involve engaging and inspiring people to become what they want to be and helping them reach beyond their existing capabilities to enjoy the realization of their aspirations and dreams. These two areas generally involve micro-perspectives (about one's self and dealing with other individuals) and the macro-perspective (about how to lead other individuals and organizations). One critical distinction that business leaders can make to dramatically enhance their prospects for success is that people in an organization are unique and should be treated accordingly. They are not property or resources that are acquired or disposed of. People represent intellectual capital that requires support, development and nurturing. They are the essence of the organization and success and the reason for achieving it.

The micro-perspective involves knowing one's own capabilities and being. It also involves dealing with people on a one-on-one basis, i.e., interpersonal skills. The macro-perspectives involve working with teams, groups of people and bigger organizations. This includes developing people and organizations and engaging in group dynamics; leading people to perform complex tasks and activities. The macro-perspectives involve more inclusive aspects like organizational and enterprise dynamics which include business units and entire companies with their extended enterprises. In each category the focus is on people and how the leader engages in improvements and developments. Figure 4.1 provides a representation of the categories.

Leadership development is a precursor to management development. The overall starting point for both includes foundations of leadership and the requisite personal and professional capabilities for being a leader and a manager, respectively. The former includes the background, beliefs, precepts, principles, philosophies, values, and qualities of the leader. The latter involves experience, knowledge, capabilities, skills, talents, behaviors and methods used in managing organizations. There are overlaps between the two.

Leadership development begins with self-examination and awareness of one's aptitudes and abilities. This includes determining how to enhance one's personal quali-

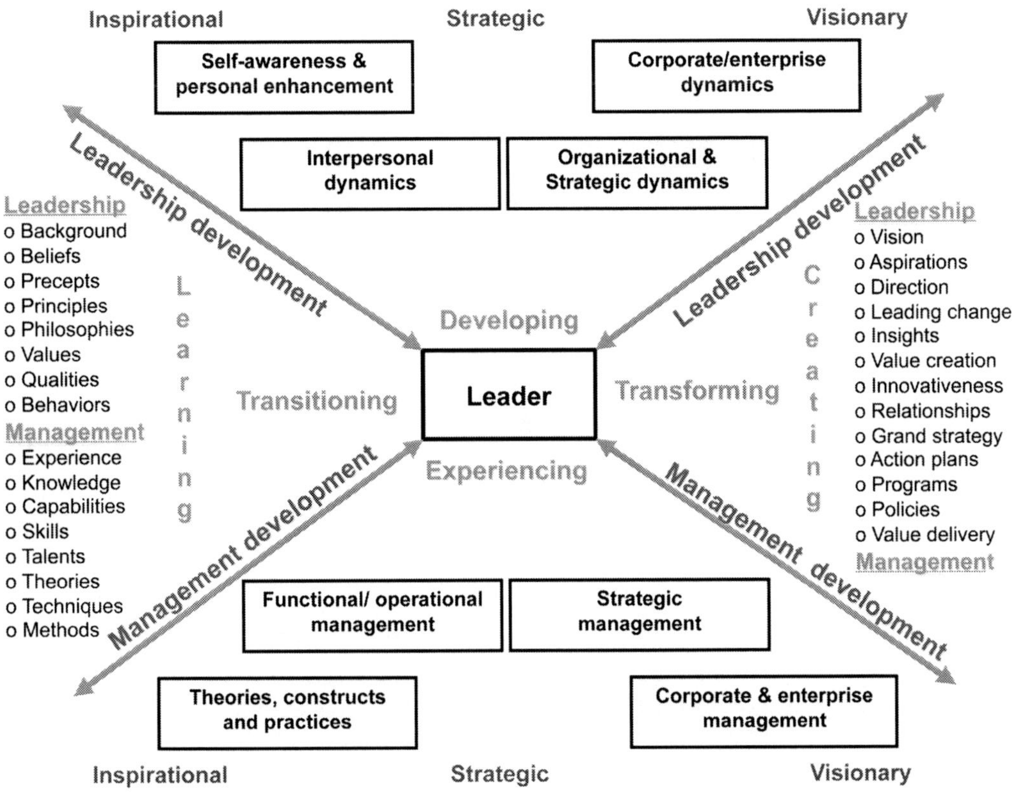

Figure 4.1 Linkages between leadership development and management development.

ties and strengths and to mitigate weaknesses and limitations. It should be followed by education, training and learning how to understand and relate to other people and how to lead them from an interpersonal perspective. This is the micro-perspective of leadership development involving the individual and his or her direct relationships with other people on a one-on-one basis.

Concurrently or independently, leaders should engage in management development learning fundamental theories, generally accepted practices, and prevailing management constructs involving the management and administration of groups and organizations. Management development often deals with learning the methods, techniques and processes for producing the desired outcomes and performance of the organization and ensuring that the company is managed and controlled properly. Management development from a micro-perspective involves the direct roles and responsibilities of supervisors, first line managers and how they engage in functional/operational management. Functional management typically involves managing one of the internal dimensions of the organization like finance, marketing or production. It usually has a limited scope and a specific agenda.

Leadership development and management development can be integrated from the very beginning and it may be one of the best approaches for enhancing personal growth and learning, especially when the individual realizes the differences between leadership and management. As stated previously, leadership generally focuses on people and management focuses on things. It is critical that both depend on leaders/managers to inspire the organization, to achieve the desired outcomes, and to go beyond the simple requirements of the particular situation or time. As the leader/manager matures and becomes more knowledgeable and sophisticated, leadership development and management development tend to merge into a fuller understanding of the micro- and macro-perspectives. At higher levels in organizations, companies and enterprises, it becomes difficult to separate leadership aspects from the management ones, especially as the strategic aspects become more critical for achieving success. Leaders have to learn how to create, develop and build the organizations and engage in the strategic management. They have to lead and manage.

Leadership development and management development have to co-exist on an ongoing basis as the individual reaches the higher levels. From a strategic leadership perspective the individual must be able to lead change across all of the internal systems and the extended enterprise. Likewise he or she must be capable of managing the strategic aspects of the entire corporation and all of the enterprises. The highest level strategic leaders/strategic managers engage in visionary strategic leadership to create new realities and a more exciting future for the whole organization, the extended enterprises and all of the people therein. Ultimately leadership development involves the full spectrum of all of the qualities and requirements necessary to achieve success, including all of the constructs associated with leadership and all those associated with management. Remember, leadership aspects are more open-ended and depend on perspectives, whereas management aspects are more specific and can be mapped out using processes and prevailing methods.

The main categories of leadership development

General framework of the main categories of leadership development

Leaders and potential leaders focus on improving the foundations of leadership and management underpinnings. Dedicated individuals can make rapid improvements through formal education and focused learning processes. Given their relative low starting point they typically make dramatic improvements during the initial phases of leadership development and management development. However, as progress is made it becomes more difficult to maintain the same rate of improvements. As overall competencies and capabilities are improved, the development approaches must shift toward enhancing strategic and enterprise leadership aspects and shifting from being a grass-roots leader to a strategic one. Eventually a rare few transform themselves into executive leaders with a high-level of leadership and strategic management know-how and aptitude.

Given that the focus of this book is on the pursuit of sustainable leadership (PSL), the remainder of the chapter is on leadership development and not management development. Management development includes many specific theories, constructs and practices pertaining to how to operate and manage businesses and other types of organizations and runs the gamut from functional and operational management, finance, marketing and product innovation to strategic and corporate management. These areas are the topics typically covered in typical master of business administration (MBA) programs and other management development approaches.

Leadership development can be divided into categories:

- Basic Level (Level "0")-Self assessment and the development of one's self.
- Functional Level (Level "1")—Interpersonal dynamics and the development of building and engaging in relationships with individuals and groups, especially functional areas and operations.
- Strategic Level (Level "2")—Organizational dynamics and the development of interrelationships with organizational structure, business units, value systems and the entities thereof.
- Corporate/Enterprise Level (Level "3")—Corporate/enterprise dynamics and the development of interrelationship with the organization and the extended enterprises.

While each of these categories involves extensive details about what can or should be developed over the course of time, the focus here is on the main elements that are critical for achieving and sustaining success. The basic level involves knowing and developing one's internal strengths, knowledge, capabilities, skills and talents, overcoming one's limitations, improving the learned qualities of leadership, especially competencies and capabilities and reducing one's weaknesses to the extent possible. The functional level involves becoming a more competent and qualified leader and knowing how to relate to other people, especially subordinates, peers and superiors. It also includes learning how to deal with direct external relationships, particularly those involving customers, suppliers and stakeholders. The strategic level involves mastering leadership principles, philosophies and approaches and becoming a strategist who creates solutions and systems for the whole organization and its internal and external connections. It also includes building relationships across space and time. The corporate/enterprise level involves the full integration of all relationships across space and time. It includes creating new solutions and even new paradigms that dramatically increase the positives of the whole and eliminate the negatives. It is an extension of the strategic level that includes leading the whole company and all of its extended enterprises.

The basic and functional levels involve the general leadership development approaches, which work well during the early development period, but may not adequately provide the specific development requirements that an individual needs as he or she matures and moves along the pathway toward higher levels of responsibilities, especially those involving strategic leadership of business units and companies. While there may be a fundamental flow from developing one's personal qualities and self to learning and acquiring the competencies and capabilities to engage in strategic and enterprise leadership, it is also clear that leadership development is a continuum in which each of the levels necessitates ongoing enhancements, improvements and dramatic leaps in one's leadership qualities and abilities over time. Moreover, leadership development becomes more complicated and necessitates more sophisticated constructs as leaders or potential leaders progress because each succeeding levels builds upon the previous and the requirements become more arduous and demanding as people advance to higher levels of responsibilities and positions.

Figure 4.2 depicts the four main levels in the hierarchy of leadership typical in many business and organizational situations and settings. The construct of levels does not suggest that there are only four levels nor does the notion of levels imply that each of the level takes approximately the same time and effort to prepare for, attain, and transition to the next level. There are incredible variations based on the actual realities that leaders and prospective leaders face. While the depiction shows more or less steady progress as a person transitions from level to level, leadership development aspects are typically not equal. Each level involves is own degree of difficulty and can be stated in terms of certain essential requirements, competencies and capabilities.

An individual can make significant progress during the early levels only to be stymied due to failures to overcome certain inadequacies and limitations or because the individual cannot attain or master certain critical requirements of leadership at a given level. Moreover, even in cases in which there is steady progress, higher levels of leadership usually take considerably more time to obtain than lower levels. While the basic

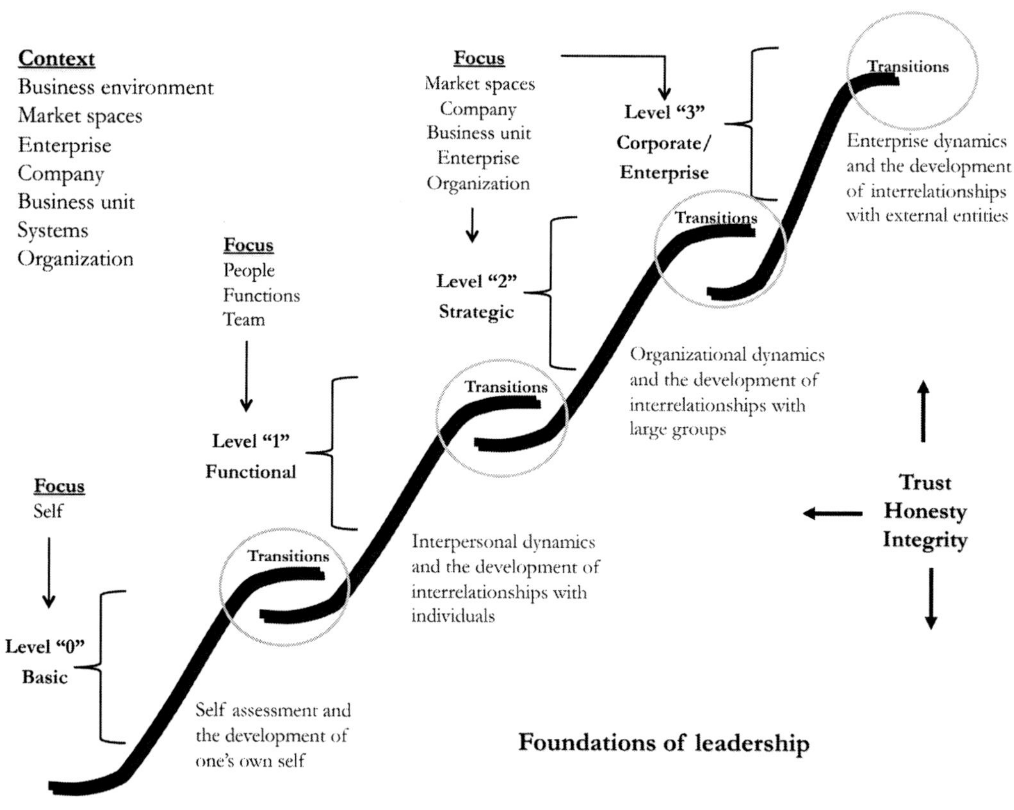

Figure 4.2 The main levels (categories) of hierarchy of leadership development.

and functional levels can be defined for the typical situations, individuals should map out their own steps toward obtaining higher levels of leadership. As stated above, it becomes increasingly more challenging to attain the subsequent levels of leadership. It is also important to realize that few leaders, if any, actually achieve all of the requisite leadership aspects at each of the levels.

It is more likely that the successful leaders are the ones that obtain most of the essential aspects before they concentrate and/or transition to the elements of the next level. Moreover, successful leaders continue to make progress in all of the qualities and roles and responsibilities as the progress from level to level. There is no precise formula or specific set or matrix of leadership aspects and there are many potential stumbling blocks. There are numerous examples of excellent leaders of functional organizations who are unable to become strategic leaders of more diverse groups, business units, or whole companies because they are uneasy with or cannot relate to people they do not know personally or deal with more intangible aspects of strategizing and leading change. Moreover, as one progresses from the lower (basic) levels of leadership to the higher (corporate/enterprise) levels of leadership, the opportunities to obtain more senior positions diminish dramatically. For example, a company like ConocoPhillips, which has approximately forty thousand employees, may have five thousand first line supervisors/managers, five hundred strategic leaders and one hundred in the highest level of the executive (corporate) ranks.

Note that the "S" curve analogy provides an excellent perspective on what it takes to progress from one level (category) to the next, but it is one that may mislead people into thinking there is a process and that anyone can progress systematically through the levels. It is not that easy. It adequately portrays the rising levels as one goes from the fundamental aspects of one's self (basic level) and the functional level to the strategic level and beyond. It also depicts the notion that each succeeding level is built upon the foundations of leadership and the developments of the previous levels. The main challenge is that required developments at each level cannot be exactly mapped out or measured. Each level is not just another step in a process, but a complex array of numerous elements that may take years to achieve with no guarantees that any given leader can successfully get to the next level or even stay at a given level. Moreover, as the world changes and becomes more complex, leaders in general have to devote significant time and effort keeping pace with changes. The incumbent has to find the ways, in which he or she is going to advance.

As leaders and potential ones progress from the lower levels to the corporate/enterprise level, the required knowledge, skills and talent multiply many times. Moreover, there may be higher levels than those suggested as globalization, complexity and turbulence continue to accelerate in importance during this century. In the future, executives, especially those in the giant global corporations, may have to engage in even broader social, economic, ethical, technological and environmental aspects with government officials, social leaders and others. For instance, corporate executives may have to spend a considerable amount of their time and energy solving global problems like climate change and terrorism. The notions of a global strategic leadership level or sustainable strategic leadership level may become critical perspectives for large global corporations.

Context drives what leadership means and what leaders have to do to become successful and maintain their positions. The overarching aspects also include the foundations of leadership, which underpin leadership from the basic levels to the highest levels possible. Regardless of how important the leader becomes or how high he or she rises in the organization, the fundamental principles, philosophies and values still apply and honesty and integrity are among the most crucial factors for achieving and sustaining success. Indeed, the basic and functional levels are the underpinnings that provide the basis for ongoing success.

Flaws and weaknesses in one's basic and functional aspects often lead to failures in the long term that are often viewed from the perspectives on the higher levels, but ones that may be caused by inadequacies at the basic and functional levels. Think about certain leaders at Enron who engaged in making inaccurate reports among numerous other inappropriate behaviors. It can be argued that the causes of their flawed behaviors were based on the lack of embedded principles pertaining to the fundamentals of leadership. As discussed in the previous chapter, trust is the crux that makes the business world work well and business leaders successful. Trust is what makes building relationships possible and the glue that makes them endure. The most critical aspects pertaining to each of the levels are discussed in the subsequent subsections.

Level 0-Basic: Self assessment and self development

Knowing oneself is not only an initial element, it is an ongoing requirement. It involves self-assessment and self-awareness. Leaders have to have a great understanding of who they are and what they stand for. Again, this involves the foundations of leadership (as discussed in Chapter 1) and developing the fundamentals of being a leader. Warren Bennis, a leadership expert, suggests that leaders have to know themselves before they can be effective in leading others. He stated that:[4]

> [The] only workable equation for anyone aspiring to selfhood is: <u>family + school + friends</u> = true you . . . In this way, rather than being designed by your experience, you become your own designer. You become cause and effect rather than mere effect.
>
> Self-awareness = self knowledge = self procession = self-control = self expression.
>
> You make your life your own by understanding it.

Self-assessment is a huge challenge. There are many techniques that can be used. However, regardless of the techniques used, it is crucial to be open, honest and forthright. The biggest fool is the person who tries to fool himself or herself. Self-assessment should involve examining the elements in the foundation of leadership and how the individual has progressed over time in terms of the underpinnings of leadership and what are the required qualities to be successful going forward. Some of the key questions are:

- What are your principles, philosophies, values and qualities?
- What has to be improved or dramatically modified based on the conditions and trends?
- How much time and effort is required to make progress?
- What are the necessary actions?

While it is difficult to map out all of the critical elements, one can develop a check sheet containing some of the most important aspects. It should include critical questions and explore many different perspectives that a developing leader should contemplate and be guided by. Remember you are the architect of your future. As Bennis indicates, the individual leader is the designer and responsible person for his or her own leadership development program. Moreover, one's leadership development is not a random walk from point A to Z, but a well-orchestrated action plan that involves understanding oneself and having a framework for knowing where you are going, for creating your own pathways to higher levels, and for achieving successful outcomes in the short term and in the long term.

Unfortunately, self-assessment is often only used when someone is seeking a new position, especially when the person is unemployed. The approach usually focuses on the tangible qualities of leadership like capabilities and competencies. These provide a sense of what a leader knows and how well he or she can perform rather than examining all of the aspects that make the individual who he or she really is. While focusing on the immediate situation (the new job) is a sensible approach, it is equally important to assess and understand one's deeper self. The latter is critical for determining required development plans and actions and what the priorities are. Moreover, the roots of limitations or problems may result in barriers to exciting new opportunities and/or may be the causes for poor results. The underlying causes of difficulties may be embedded within the intangible qualities like lack of confidence or lack of empathy for other people. Such limitations may retard growth and improvements in the more direct aspects of leadership. For instance, it may be impossible to inspire other people, if they perceive a leader to be disingenuous, deceptive or worse. One's limitations are often not readily apparent to an individual, since he or she may not believe them to be very important or they are masked by other aspects that seem more important. Moreover, the individual may view certain limitations or weaknesses as his or her strengths. For instance, a "take charge and get results at all costs" type individual (leader) places a high value on tangible outcomes and may not even perceive the damage that he or she is causing other people and the organization in the process, especially if the harm relates to employees and not to business objectives. Such individuals often obtain outstanding performance in the short term, but they may be consuming the vibrancy of the organization and eroding the viability of future outcomes. Their careless approaches make success less sustainable and they leave unhappiness in their wake. Unhappy people often spend a lot of time discussing and dealing with their unhappiness, which detracts from future successes and does not enrich anyone. Their contributions become less fruitful.

Self-assessment is a lifelong mechanism that should be used frequently to ensure that true achievements are being made and that progress is being obtained at rates sufficient to stay ahead of changes in the business environment. Moreover, as a leader advances through the levels of leadership, he or she must enhance his or her understanding of what is necessary, appropriate, required and expected to succeed at the present level and how to get to the next level well before it becomes fully apparent what needs to be done. Often it is too late to make up lost ground when a superior suggests that an individual needs to have more experience in a certain area or that he or she should improve his or her educational background and/or capabilities. Even if it is not too late to overcome some of the tangible aspects, there may not be any signs or indications that suggest what one must do to improve the tangible aspects.

The intangible aspects are even more difficult to orchestrate. Leaders usually find it difficult to obtain outside input or feedback about intangible qualities like passion and confidence when discussing areas requiring improvements. Other people may talk to you about your attire (appearance) or your lack of knowledge in a given area, but rarely do they openly discuss whether ethical perspectives are limiting your potential or whether you are too self-centered, lack concern or caring for other people. Moreover, certain problems are often tolerated at the basic and functional levels, but are totally unacceptable at the higher strategic levels. For instance, a leader that uses inappropriate language may get away with it when he or she is managing a small and relatively homogeneous group that does not seem to mind the negative aspects; however, as one advances to higher levels those attitudes and behaviors are often offensive to more and more people and they are tolerated less and less. Unless corrected during the early levels, such weaknesses may become real barriers to long-term success. It is incumbent on the individual to take stock of both the tangibles and intangibles and determine the ongoing improvements and changes that must be made to continue effective personal and professional development and to enhance one's prospects for sustainable success.

Self-assessment should lead to self-awareness. It is a means to a means to an end. Self-awareness of one's positive and negative qualities and aspects of leadership lead to understanding and direction for improvements, enhancements, developments, and even radical changes. The concept is that if one is aware of his or her underlying characteristics and qualities of leadership and the positive and negative aspects thereof, then he or she can organize, develop and implement the improvements, further developments and/or radical changes necessary to achieve success. Moreover, self-awareness provides the insights and evidence to make a determination about the type of changes required to exceed expectations.

Table 4.2 provides a sense of what leaders should concentrate on given their positions, situations, circumstances, and the conditions and trends in their external and internal contexts.

The graphic is not intended to be prescriptive or to provide a precise mapping of leadership development approaches, since each individual's opportunities and challenges are unique; however, it is intended to offer a general sense of the appropriate

TABLE 4.2 Types of leadership development approaches

<table>
<tr><th>Personal situation</th><th colspan="4">External opportunities and challenges</th></tr>
<tr><th></th><th>Attractive with high potential</th><th>Less attractive with modest potential</th><th>Unattractive or limited potential</th><th>Regardless</th></tr>
<tr><td>Mostly positive</td><td>Enhancements</td><td>Improvements</td><td rowspan="2">Dramatic changes</td><td rowspan="4">Learning</td></tr>
<tr><td>Mixed-more toward the positives</td><td colspan="2">Major improvements</td></tr>
<tr><td>Mixed-more toward the negatives</td><td colspan="2">Radical developments</td><td rowspan="2">Find a new situation?</td></tr>
<tr><td>Mostly negative</td><td colspan="2">Radical change</td></tr>
</table>

methods and recommended choices. Moreover, each category may be useful regardless of the opportunities and challenges and one's personal situation. For instance, enhancements and improvements are always useful except that they may not be good enough in more dynamic and less advantageous situations. If the context is mostly positive and one's personal situation and circumstances (aspects) are also positive, then enhancements and improvements are usually appropriate and may be adequate. If the context is generally positive, but one's personal situation and circumstances have many negative aspects, then more dramatic developments are necessary. If both context and one's personal aspects are mostly negative, then radical developments or changes are absolutely critical for getting on track and obtaining success. They are especially important for higher levels of development.

Regardless of the perspectives, learning is always relevant and a way to improve one's prospects and to make real gains. In the worst case, if very little is working properly or beneficially one should seek new situations with better prospects for success. For instance, if one is not well suited to be a singer, a nuclear scientist, or a mathematician, then all of the educational efforts, training programs and learning activities may not result in positive outcomes regardless of the investments. The individual may be better suited for other endeavors.

Leadership development programs during the early stages of development usually concentrate on enhancements and improvements because one's situation is usually focusing on context and one's position is relatively open-ended. While the requirements for success at the beginning of one's career are relatively easy to understand and achieve, the overall requirements for leadership development is significant. The leader has much to learn and experience.

Basic level learning and development focus on the fundamentals of leadership. They include enhancing one's qualities of leadership and developing additional skills and talents. The focus is typically on capabilities, knowledge and learning more about leadership and one's own self. It should include the basic aspects of leadership like learning how to plan and create new programs and approaches for leading change. It should also include the underpinnings of being an entrepreneur who has the abilities to operate without a lot of structure and support mechanisms. When these critical elements are missed during early development, it may limit one's creativity and ability to think outside of the norm. Young leaders, especially those working in large corporations, often become dependent on the systems and structures of the corporation and fail to develop the wherewithal to operate in a more open-ended environment.

The basic level is the training ground for learning how to be the future leaders of businesses and the organization. Effective leaders have to be good developers and educators of other people and the organization. These are among the most important skills and competencies that should be learned and honed early in one's career. They are parts of the fundamental approaches that focus on other people and shift one's perspectives from the self to the whole. Great leaders know how to take care of other people and subordinate their own well being to support the well being of whole.

Leaders are decision makers. Decision making is a fundamental that cuts across the full spectrum of leadership from the most insignificant operational aspects to the most significant strategic decisions involving the future direction of the whole enterprise. Again, these are competencies that must be acquired from the earliest stages of leadership development and reinforced over time through ongoing experience and learning. Young leaders need practice and experience in making good decisions. As they gain experience and knowledge, they can weigh the outcomes of their decisions and gain confidence in their abilities to make decision and/or to make adjustments as necessary as they analyze the results. One rarely becomes faultless in decision making, but one should become more adept and confident as knowledge and experiences are gained.

Level 1-Functional: Interpersonal dynamics and the development of relationships

The functional level is an extension of the basic level in which the leader focuses on developing interpersonal relationships with subordinates, superiors, peers, customers and external stakeholders. The functional level involves learning how to relate to people and how to lead them effectively in achieving superior outcomes, extraordinary performance and sustainable success. The functional level includes developing the knowledge, skills, capabilities, competencies, etc. used in engaging people to achieve objectives and accomplish tasks and activities. It also includes learning the skills and knowledge necessary to implement action plans and development programs and to execute day-to-day operations. It involves those they are in direct contact; it usually involves people they have involvements with on a one-on-one and small group basis. The leadership development approaches involve what is required to lead people, not just on the management of tasks and activities. Again, there are distinctions between management and leadership.

Functional leaders must have broad perspectives and be able to understand and deal with opportunities and challenges. They must be competent, innovative and technologically sophisticated leaders who have the mindset and insights to think broadly and to know how to develop new landscapes for meeting the needs and dreams of all customers, stakeholders, and society. One's depth of technological and business leadership is one of the most important factors for achieving sustainable success. The functional level involves developing the capabilities and knowledge to lead in complex business situations. However, in today's rapidly changing world, leaders must become the "masters of their domains" not just competent managers. They must go beyond the obvious leadership aspects pertaining to the prevailing situations, and acquire the qualities needed to lead change in complex and challenging business environments.

Functional leaders must become innovators and creators of new ways of leading. True leaders must maximize their leadership qualities to the extent possible and reinforce their abilities to lead change. They must be at the forefront of creating value and building relationships. They have to have the ability to integrate business operations and to make decisions that improve the prospects of their businesses faster than their peers, markets or competitors. While many functional leaders are concerned with the financial outcomes of their organizations, dynamic leaders focus on discovering opportunities and exploiting them to create sustainable solutions and advantages and enduring success. It demands exceptional leadership knowledge, skills and capabilities to realize the extraordinary outcomes in the short term without sacrificing the prospects for the future.

Level 2-Strategic: Organizational dynamics and the development of relationships with business units

The strategic level focuses on systems, organizational dynamics and interrelationships with large groups and business units. Leadership development at this level involves becoming a strategist and an architect of organizational development and global change. It also involves being the builder of the organization and the provider of the means and mechanisms to achieve success. A strategic leader builds relationships across the organization and integrates the organization and its enterprise into a whole. As one progresses through the levels of leadership, the transformation to a strategic leader is a significant change in perspectives and approaches.

As one rises toward the strategic and enterprise levels, it becomes more and more challenging to be fully in line with the expectations of the external business world and the roles and responsibilities of the various positions one holds. Therefore, more dramatic developments are often critical for advancing and succeeding at the higher levels. As more is expected, more becomes required of leadership development. Strategic leaders have to accelerate their leadership development to be in concert with reality. Leadership development is cumulative as one develops from the basic and functional levels to the higher strategic and enterprise levels. It is an integrative function in which strategic leaders have to incorporate all of the lower level aspects as they grow and mature through learning and experience. It is akin to becoming an expert in mathematics. As the individual learns more advanced subjects like calculus and differential equations, he or she must maintain competencies in geometry and trigonometry. And, as one advances in mastery of the subjects, it becomes more difficult to learn the higher levels of knowledge. Table 4.3 depicts a sense of the transition or transformation at higher levels based on three critical elements: learning, experience and knowledge. It provides a sense of what is most appropriate, but is not prescriptive.

TABLE 4.3 A general sense of the transition or transformation in leadership development

Learning	Experience and knowledge		
	Less intense	Intense	More intense
More intense	Basic level	Functional level	
Intense		Strategic level	
Less intense			Corporate level

Transitions and transformations are often subtle. Like most aspects involving leadership development, it is not an "either-or" situation. It is a continuum in which the leader continues to make significant advances in learning and becoming a master of leadership at the same time focuses more and more on gaining real world experience and knowledge. This is particularly critical when engaging larger groups in organizational settings and with specific entities like business units.

Strategic leaders combine their knowledge of leadership and management as they engage people within and outside the organization to achieve results in the short term and to realize the vision and aspirations in the long term. Strategic leadership generally involves the high-level transformational aspects like aspirations and strategic direction. Strategic management also involves strategic direction, but focuses more on strategies and actions.

Leadership development at the higher levels becomes more difficult to exactly specify. It includes all of the underpinnings previously discussed. It involves becoming a visionary and a strategist who can lead large organizations and build relationships with all of the external entities supporting the organization. Strategic leaders have broad capabilities and knowledge. They depend on their expertise and experience when engaged in decision making and dealing with other people. They are the masters of strategic thinking and setting direction. Specific details about the higher levels of strategic leadership are spelled out in the next chapter.

Level 3-Corporate/enterprise: Holistic views and the development of relationships with entities

Corporate/enterprise level leaders have to have the knowledge, experience and capabilities to orchestrate the design and development of new business models or even paradigms for proactively inventing the future of the organization. Leadership development at this level involves understand the prevailing context so well that the leaders can lead positive change. It focuses on strategic innovations, discovering new solutions, and developing new systems and structures. It includes radical changes to the enterprise, the technologies, products, and processes.

Enterprise level leadership focuses on the whole business environment, the networks of partners, allies, and participants, the corporate vision and strategic direction, governance, and other facets down to the operating systems and functional areas of the organization. It involves creating extraordinary value through the strategic alignment and integration of the entire enterprise and through strong strategic leadership of the corporation. It also involves creating sustainable enterprises that are holistic; ones that focus on sustainable solutions and success. It involves making dramatic improvements and positive changes to the full scope of relationships and linkages of the supply networks, customers and stakeholders, and support service providers. Strategic leaders at this level engage in sustainable development to envision, create and develop sustainable solutions and outcomes that balance the performance objectives of the present with the needs and expectations of the future, and the financial outcomes with the broader social, economic and environmental objectives. Enterprise level leadership also involves the total integration of the whole business enterprise and the deliberate linking of the internal organization(s) with all of the value networks, strategic partners, and constituencies. This connectedness works to further the overarching objectives of the enterprise: to create value and sustain the benefits of investments, contributions and achievements over the long term for customers, stakeholders, value networks, employees, and shareholders, and to create innovative solutions for all. Attaining this level of integration depends on a comprehensive understanding of all of the forces (internal and external) that drive change, and responding to them in ways that enhance the positive attributes of the enterprise and mitigate the negative impacts and consequences. Visionary leadership, technological and product innovation, and organizational integration are critical to this task.

Enterprise level leadership involves leading and managing change and integrating the full spectrum of the business environment. This includes the social, economic, technological, environmental, and market considerations and implications. It also includes the strategic leadership, governance, and the strategic direction of the corporation, its management systems and all of the business units and operations. This holistic view transforms 'supply and demand' management thinking of the last century into a more sophisticated framework that is based on value creation, social responsibility, sustainable development, ethics, inclusiveness and transparency among many other factors. The strategic focus shifts from short-term financial rewards to a more balanced perspective that also includes creativity, leading change, business strategies, innovation management, risk mitigation, and strategic leadership.

Reflections

The business world is ever changing; innovative leaders must continuously improve ahead of expectations. Successful leaders have to be at the forefront of change and lead in the development of new businesses, technologies, products, methods, and techniques. Leadership means actively engaging and energizing people in realizing extraordinary results on an ongoing basis. Extraordinary outcomes are obtained through people, the organization and the enterprise. Leadership necessitates an integrated and innovative approach. Integration of the whole means creating internal and external relationships that are inclusive and enduring. Leadership implies that participants are in sync and that approaches and actions across the enterprise are in line with each other and are of the same kind and quality. Innovation involves making dramatic changes and big improvements that have positive outcomes with respect to customers, stakeholders, and the organization. It is an essential leadership construct for leading change, making investments, managing risks, and creating value. While the actual management constructs depend on the type of innovation (business, technological, product or process), they start with the imagination and insights. Imagination is a high level of thinking and how to create solutions for making dramatic and even quantum improvements. It involves thinking based on what could be rather than what is happening. Insights involve understanding reality and discovering the true nature of a situation. They are about understanding the underlying factors that are causing change and discovering new solution.

Leadership development is the never-ending quest to become an outstanding person and leader with the qualities and mindset to create solutions and achieve success. It focuses on the future and what the individual must learn, experience and know to obtain the higher levels of leadership. It involves an intense drive to become an individual with the wherewithal to lead people and change.

Notes

1. Winston Churchill, *The Second World War, Volume 1, The Gathering Storm* (Boston, MA: Houghton Miffin Company, 1948, pp. 298–321).
2. Daniel Goleman, "What Makes a Leader," Harvard Business Review, January 2004, p. 88.
3. W.D. Ross, *ARISTOTLE: a compete exposition of his works & though* (Cleveland, OH: Meridian Books, 1959, pp. 188–193)
4. Warren Bennis, *On Becoming a Leader* (New York, NY: Basic Books, 1989, 2000, p. 64).

References

Bennis, Warren (2000) *On Becoming a Leader.* New York, NY: Basic Books.

Churchill, Winston (1948) *The Second World War, Volume 1, The Gathering Storm.* Boston, MA: Houghton Miffin Company.

Ross, W.D. (1959) *ARISTOTLE: a compete exposition of his works & though.* Cleveland, OH: Meridian Books.

5

Sustainable Strategic Leadership

Introduction

Sustainable Strategic leadership (SSL) provides the foundation, perspectives, and decision making for establishing strategic direction and governance, providing the guidance and inspiration for the organization, and taking advantage of strategic positions among numerous other essential requirements. It is a dynamic construct that varies from the fundamentals of dealings with people to the more profound and complex responsibilities and obligations for leading change. The fundamentals of SSL include the core beliefs and underpinnings, the leader's credentials and experiences and his or her perspectives and decision making approaches.

Over the centuries business leaders have focused on discovering, developing and exploiting opportunities, especially ones that promised extraordinary profits and exceptional growth. Such business leaders were typically looking for the "pot of gold" or the "magic formula" that would lead to great success and competitive advantages over their rivals. They used their acumen to uncover new opportunities through inventing and developing new technologies, opening new markets, designing and commercializing new-to-the-world products, starting new ventures, and developing innovative financial arrangements. Such business leaders also purchased other companies and businesses to expand their positions. The literature is replete with famous stories of strategic leaders of the past who created new means and mechanisms to realize exciting new opportunities and expand the business horizons. They used their imaginations, insights, creativity and enthusiasm to become more innovative, dynamic and successful than their peers and competitors. Some of most invigorating examples include:

The Pursuit of Sustainable Leadership, pages 115–138

- David Sarnoff, the CEO of Radio Corporation of America (RCA) during its formation and development years, led change by creating some of the most innovative technologies during the early twentieth century. His strategic leadership focused on the development, commercialization, and integration of a broad range of technologies and business endeavors dedicated to bring advanced radio and television (TV) technologies to the world. RCA's investments included the development of black and white and then color TV and the establishment of the NBC network. Sarnoff realized TV sets in people's homes were of little consequence unless there were supporting entities the provided content (programs), repair services and industry standards. He recognized that RCA had to provide solutions not just products.
- Alfred Sloan, Jr., one of the most innovative strategic leaders at General Motors (GM) between 1919 and 1946, was instrumental in establishing General Motors Acceptance Corporation (GMAC) in 1923. Sloan and GMAC turned constraints into opportunities. GMAC eliminated one the main barriers in purchasing a new car by providing credit. Most people could not afford to pay cash for the purchase, but they could afford to pay in increments over a number of years.
- Juan Tripp, one of the founders and executives of Pan American Airlines, realized that there were huge opportunities for flying passengers to distance locations in the Pacific Rim and South America, if the right solutions and systems were available. He understood that an airline was more than airplanes, pilots and attendants. He went beyond the prevailing view of the economic mission of an airline and built an infrastructure of hotels and restaurants to provide passengers with the full complement hospitality services they needed during long trips.
- Steve Jobs and Steven Wozniak, the founders of Apple Inc., designed, developed and produced some of the first personal computers (PCs). Their great genius went beyond their obvious technical skills and expertise. They had the foresight to perceive the underlying needs for PCs and that the market potential was huge if computers could be made small enough, affordable, and relatively easy to use. While their new-to-the-world inventions were not perfect solutions, they provided benefits that were unavailable during the late 1970s and eventually helped bring computers to the average person.

The business world is very turbulent and becoming more complicated as globalization takes hold. The business "meltdown of 2007/2008" is a culmination of the lack of strategic leadership, poor management, ineffective governance, and faulty decision making among other deficiencies. Too many contemporary business leaders and strategic decision makers rely on archaic philosophies, theories and methods for managing their business enterprises. Many such leaders are out of synch with reality. They tend to follow rather than lead. Many still manage using simple constructs like focusing on core competencies and outsourcing the non-core areas to global suppliers without understanding the business environment and the long-term implications of their decisions.

Today, many economists and strategic analysts point to the technical problems associated with the failed financial instruments such as hedge funds and sub-prime mortgages as the root causes of many of the collapses and debacles. However, the real root causes may be the failures of the business leaders across many industries and sectors who are still using fairly similar conventional strategic leadership theories and practices. In the past, scholars, practitioners, analysts and investors had an implicit assumption that most executives and business leaders generally knew what they were doing and had a fundamental understanding of their businesses and industries. Business research groups and independent ranking organizations conducted hundreds of surveys of company executives and other strategic leaders to determine their perspectives on the proper conduct of business. Such surveys and rankings were based on the assumption that the collective wisdom of the mainstream business leaders would shine the light on the proper perspectives and the best approaches for managing and leading business enterprises. However, based on the need to "bail out" many of the largest financial institutions, banks, the automobile companies, and others, one now has to challenge the assumptions that most business executives know exactly what they are doing. It can be argued that the business environment in all of its dynamism is moving faster than what traditional strategic leaders can keep pace with given their predilection to focus on the present and near term. Moreover, many of strategic leaders rely on managing based on their existing positions and situations rather than leading change for the future. In fact, it is apparent that many of today's strategic leaders have not realized the importance of having a broad understanding of the business environment, keeping ahead of the rapidity of changes and leading their enterprises instead of following mainstream thinking or their competitors. Given the current state of affairs in many industries and corporations and the rapidly changing global business environment, the elements of strategic leadership and how strategic leaders act and make decisions require profound changes. Strategic leaders have to be more inclusive, innovative, and sophisticated. They have to be the masters of the realm and the architects of the future.

The chapter includes the following main topics:

- Mapping out the elements of sustainable strategic leadership.
- Identifying a framework for sustainable strategic leaders.

The Critical Perspectives of Sustainable Strategic Leadership

Overview

True strategic leaders are fiduciaries who put their duties and responsibilities to their organization, enterprise, customers, stakeholders, employees and shareholders at the forefront. They are uncompromising about achieving sustained success and ensuring that all entities and individuals are successful in their own right to the extent possible. They are revolutionaries with an entrepreneurial spirit and a "trail blazer" attitude. They lead rather than just manage and they expect the best outcomes for everyone. Most importantly, they lead by example, they "walk the talk," and they respect and reward people. They avoid making tradeoffs in which some win and others lose or short-term gains are made at the expense of long-term vulnerabilities or increased liabilities.

SSL requires proactive actions. Strategic leaders have to exhibit SSL. True strategic leaders engage people, set direction, build relationships, inspire employees, guide subordinates and peers, develop future leaders, and ensure that requirements and expectations are exceeded among a litany of other roles and responsibilities. True strategic leaders have a duty to provide "due care" of people, assure their well being, and ensure that are accorded due respect and dignity. They lead from the front and are courageous in driving positive changes in the business environment and within their domains. Most importantly, they exhibit their fiduciary duties to protect, preserve, and succeed. They have to embrace the pursuit of sustainable leadership (PSL).

Leadership style

Leadership style involves the personal choices that the incumbent leader makes in determining how he or she leads and manages in an organizational setting and in dealing with external context and the extended enterprise. While there are several key theories about leadership style, it can be argued that there are as many alternatives as there are leaders. In his article on leadership style, Dail Fields, professor at Regent University, outlined several theories and the subsets within each. He called them alternative leadership models; they are as follows:[1]

- Personal characteristics—the leader adapts a style based on personal traits and characteristics. For instance, achievement-motivated individuals are driven by their goals and aspirations and assume personal responsibility for outcomes and performance. Charismatic leaders use their personal traits to motivate followers to obtain the desired ends.
- Behaviors—individual lead by example and by being guided actions and directions. There are several subsets to the model:
  - The path-goal theory—the concept is based on the assumption that followers will embrace the strategic direction and goals set by the strategic leaders and will achieve the appropriate performance and outcomes. Followers expect their leaders to provide guidance during execution and bestow commensurate rewards upon realizing success.
  - Telling, selling, participating, and delegating concept—this theory is based on the generic process associated with getting followers involved in the formulation and implementation of strategies and actions. The focus is mostly on implementation. It suggest that leaders play a strong role upfront in mapping out what has to be done and slowly entrust followers with the ultimate execution.
  - Transactional—the concept is based on the interactions between the leader and the followers. The focus is on the exchanges of information, activities and responses. The leader provides direction and guidance on the basis of the contributions of the followers and makes adjustments accordingly. Positive contributions are encouraged and rewarded, and negative ones are reduced through interactions and learning.
  - Transformational—the concept is based on obtaining the followers' acceptance and adherence to the leaders' or organizations' shared vision. It involves getting followers to embrace the strategic directions and to make significant contributions to radical changes and dramatic improvements. It involves inspiring followers and providing long-term benefits based on achieving strategic success.

- Leader–follower exchange—This theory focused on the relationship between the leaders and the followers. The focus is on establishing a solid rapport between the leaders and the contributors. It is the trust that is developed over time that facilitates achieving positive results and ongoing success.

Field's list is a microcosm of the numerous models pertaining to leadership style. While many of his elements are generic, one's style should be unique in the true sense of the meaning of leadership style. Each individual leader should create and hone his or her development of a particular style that is customized to one's capabilities, competencies, and qualities/characteristics. He or she should make it his or her own. Table 5.1 identifies and provides an overview of a number of selected characteristics pertaining to leadership styles.

TABLE 5.1 Selected characteristics of leadership style

SSL characteristics	Conventional characteristics
Broad—being able to handle many variables and a wide-ranging scope of one's business domain; being able to deal with many opportunities and challenges simultaneously.	**Narrow**—limiting the scope of one's endeavors to those that can be comfortably handled at a given time; having a limited capability to manage multiple elements.
Proactive—leading change and being on the cutting edge before forced to do so by business environment; making decisions and taking actions expeditiously.	**Reactive**—focusing on what the mainstream leaders are doing; delaying decisions as long as possible to reduce uncertainties and gain additional information and confidence.
Empowering—allowing followers as much latitude and freedom of actions as prudently possible; delegating the execution to a broad array of contributors.	**Authoritative**—creating hierarchical schemes in which all key decisions are made by the leader(s) or a small group of senior managers; governance is a top down approach.
Systematic—obtaining a myriad of inputs and employ analytical approaches to identify opportunities and challenges and to select deploy the best approaches.	**Emotional**—following one's feelings, emotions or intuition rather than using logical or rational approaches; taking actions based on the inclinations of the moment.
Creative—using innovative methods in managing and following logic and underpinnings that provide new mechanisms for discovering and executing solutions; thinking about what could be instead of what is.	**Conventional**—using conventional methods, techniques and processes that are based on experiential knowledge and know-how; having a historical basis for decision making.
Confident—being self-assured; having the capacity to make informed decisions and take the necessary actions; being able to take bold initiatives and actions; believing in one's self.	**Cautious**—requiring significant amount of time and efforts to assure that all decisions are appropriate and that actions will lead to the desired outcomes.
People-oriented—focusing the people of the organization and those of the external business world; recognizing that it is their intellectual capital that creates value and sustains success.	**Finance-oriented**—focusing on the business objectives and strategies as the prime directives in decision making and actions; assuming that bottom line is the underpinning to success.
Risk taking—having the capacity to act with some uncertainties; willing to accept a reasonable level of risks, but with mitigation.	**Risk adverse**—requiring a high level of certainty and assurance of success before taking actions; unwilling to accept the possibility of failure.

The left side provides some of the salient characteristics pertaining to the PSL; the right side provide a sense of the more conventional characteristics; however, context as discussed in Chapter 1 plays a role in what characteristics are most important in a given situation or circumstance. The table presents just two sides of the various characteristics. The two sides tend to be opposite ends of the characteristics, but they are not necessarily the extremes. Moreover, the identification of the two sides does not imply that there is a "happy middle ground." It does not suggest that strategic leaders should find the "golden mean' or the balance. The proper choices are dependent on one's situation, capabilities, and competencies. There are few, if any, universally appropriate or best characteristics that are guaranteed to work in every case. For example, being a risk taker may work well for the leader of a research and development (R&D) center that is engaged in developing new technologies in consumer electronics, given that speed to the market is critical for success. And, being risk adverse is generally the desirable approach, if one is responsible for operating a nuclear power plant or operating an airplane. Moreover, strategic leaders may need to be risk takers in certain situations and risk adverse in others. For example, the R&D leader at a major pharmaceutical company may be more than willing to risk one billion dollars in developing a new product that has to potential to return ten billion dollars in cash flow over its product life, even though the R&D program has less than a twenty percent probability of succeeding. Yet, the same leader should not risk the well being of a single person in developing and commercializing the new product.

Most strategic leaders understand their background and settings and create a leadership style that fits their situation the best. While strategic leaders should develop their own unique leadership style, their choices should be internally consistent and based on context. For instance, military leaders usually have to be proactive and confident among other characteristics in a combat situation. But, the same leaders may have to adapt their leadership style when the context and circumstances change. Military leaders who are responsibility for administrative matters may have to be more deliberate and performance-oriented then those engaged in commanding combat troops.

The foregoing discussion implies that strategic leaders have to be flexible and adaptable. This is especially true in a fast-paced business world in which change is the expected case. It is crucial for effective strategic leader to avoid getting caught in a time warp; a situation in which strategic leaders are in perfect synch with the present, but they are unprepared to handle change, i.e., they have a high probability of being unable to adapt to future requirements. If one tries to maximize the present, it often results in suboptimal outcomes in the future. Moreover, it is folly to become too rigid in one's leadership style given that the business world is turbulent and there are rapid changes going on. However, there are extremes in the various categories or characteristics that are generally unacceptable regardless of the situations or circumstances. They include being arrogant, dictatorial, egotistical, impulsive, careless, and timid among numerous other negative traits. For instance, many senior business leaders go beyond being confident, proactive and other positive characteristics and assume that they know everything and can make all of the decisions without input and reflection by others. They become self-centered and autocratic and try to dominate their organizations and enterprises. While in the short term they may achieve certain levels of success, in the long term they often have difficulty maintaining success because in such situations people simply become disengaged and let the "dictator" types make most of the decisions and dominate the actions. One of the major concerns with such approaches is that there is usually no one modifying inputs, suggesting alternative courses of action, or even taking corrective actions until well after the organization is mired in intractable problems or stagnation.

In most contexts, sustainable success is derived from the participation and contributions of the whole organization and enterprise not just the results of what high-level strategic leaders formulate and implement. It is based on the intellectual capital, the strategic thinking, hard work and the results of the compounding of the positive actions of all contributors and recipients. Professor Amy Edmondson of Harvard Business School indicated that effective leaders need to be truthful, adaptive, empowering, and innovative. The following are some of her insights:[2]

> Fostering an atmosphere in which trust and respect thrive, and flexibility and innovation flourish, pay off in most settings, even the most deadline-driven. When managers empower, rather than control; when they ask the right questions, rather than provide the right answers; and when they focus on flexibility, rather than insist on adherence, they move to a higher form of execution. And when people know their ideas are welcome, they will offer innovative ways to lower costs and improve quality-thus laying a more solid foundation for their organization's success.

PSL demands strategic leaders with leadership characteristics that are multifaceted. They must be proactive and aggressive and take preemptive actions to lead in the quest of excellence. They must take a broad view of their business domains and be fast acting in their decision making and in executing strategies and initiatives. They must enjoy being on the cutting edge of change and in developing new solutions that have more positives and fewer negatives. They have to be people-oriented and respect and recognize the great contributions of their employees and the other contributors in the enterprise. They have to be confident in their leadership and competent and capable in all endeavors and if they have any shortcoming they must work tirelessly of overcome them through learning and new experiences. They must be practical and achieve the desired outcomes and the associated performance.

Good intentions are not good enough. Improvements, new developments, enhanced solutions, innovative technologies and myriad of other positive outcomes that lead to sustainable success are the true measures of the leaders' abilities to create great outcomes. PSL also demands strategic leaders who are thoughtful in their decision making and actions. They must ensure that they safeguard the well being of people and the natural environment. They must not risk causing damage and degradation to people and the natural environment, or destruction and depletion of natural resources and the ability of the biosphere to sustain life and the diversity of species.

A Framework for the Sustainable Strategic Leadership

The fundamental elements and flow

SSL is an open-ended construct that involves leading people in the present, setting the stage for future success and engaging the organization and the enterprise in the strategies and actions to realize the desired outcomes and requisite performance. SSL is not a prescribed process, but a way of thinking, behaving, acting, engaging, making decisions and ultimately leading. It is esoteric and it is difficult to spell out in great detail what it takes to be a sustainable strategic leader. However, it is crucial to understand that leadership in general and SSL, in particular, involve more than just occupying positions, they involve leading and being a true leader. SSL is always relevant and is the precursor for strategic thinking, management and action. It involves underlying considerations that define what kind of leader one is and how the leader views his or her roles and responsibilities in the company and its enterprises. Moreover, SSL establishes the values, principles and philosophies that set the standards for perspectives, strategies and actions. It includes the experiences and qualifications of the person and his or her capabilities and competencies to lead and management.

Figure 5.1 outlines the main elements of SSL. The fundamentals also include one's leadership style and strategic logic used to lead and make decisions. Strategic

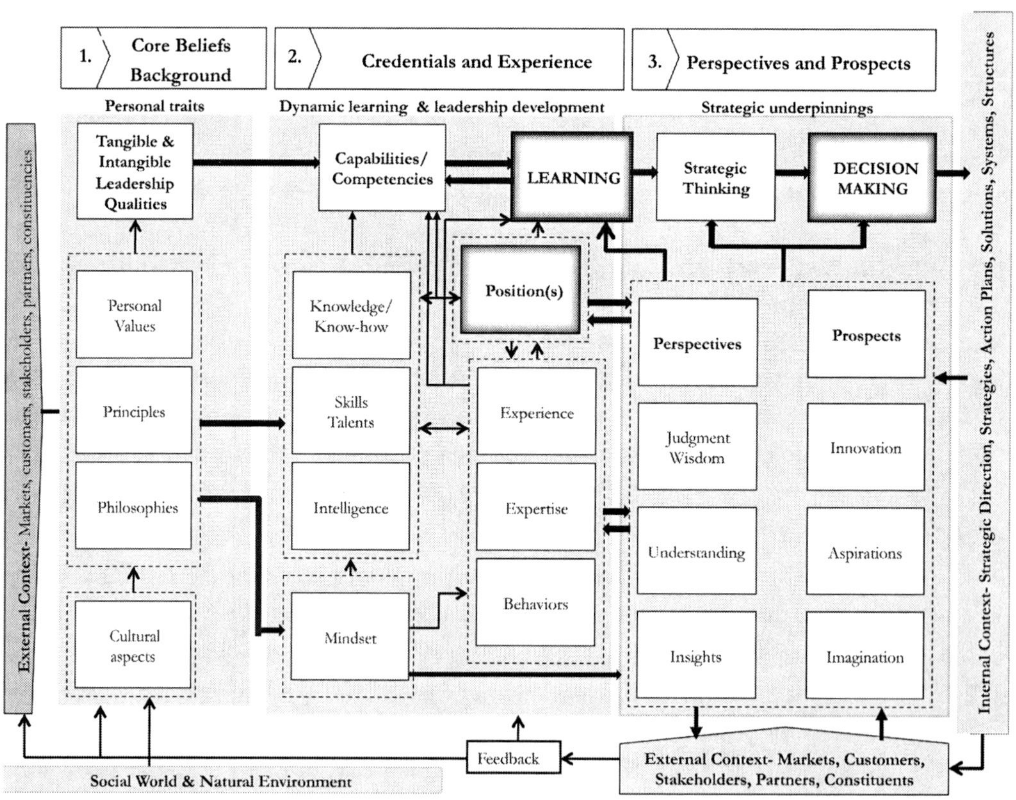

Figure 5.1 Main elements of SSL decision making.

logic focuses on one's temperament, perspectives and prospects. The fundamental considerations (elements) concentrate on the philosophical, psychological, practical and physical makeup of the strategic leader and how he or she fits into the business environment, business enterprise, value delivery system and the organizational aspects, i.e., external and internal context, respectively.

Core beliefs and personal background

Core beliefs include the individual's personal makeup, views, standards and unchanging ideals (for the most part). They include personal values, principles, philosophies, and cultural aspects as discussed in Chapter 2. While some of the discussions in this section are similar to those in Chapter 2, it is important to reiterate some of the main points. They provide the foundation and are part of one's leadership qualities. Personal values are the preeminent elements that are easy to formulate, but are among the greatest challenges for many leaders because one has to adhere to them over the course of time during which there may be many diversions Personal values include one's ethics, truthfulness, honesty, integrity and openness to scrutiny. They also include how one responds to other people and the respect given to them. Personal values are easy because all one has to do is to articulate one's beliefs and adhere to them. Truthfulness and honesty are among the most effective leadership qualities, since they are simple and respected across the globe. People expect to be told the truth and want to deal with leaders who are known to be truthful. But, telling the whole truth is not always straightforward. Many leaders believe that they have the right personal values; yet, when it comes time to communicate the negative side of the strategic aspects and operations or when challenged by unpleasant situations, they hedge and fail to tell the whole truth. Truthfulness, honesty and openness necessitate more than not telling lies. They also involve avoiding deceptions and misleading communications that are factually correct, but are not quite precise. For instance, strategic leaders may promote a new product (say a hybrid car) that is "clean and green" because it is more fuel efficient and generates less pollution. However, the messages may mislead consumers into thinking that they are buying better products when in reality the new product is only slightly more beneficial if it has an air conditioner and it is typically driven on the superhighways. This leads to the probably of creating significant problems by telling only the positive side of a story. Such problems are particular concerns for marketing and sales leaders who are tasked with promoting the company's products and service. The typical marketing messages usually articulate the benefits that customers receive, but they often fail to discuss the negative aspects; they do not tell the whole truth because they do not warn customers about the potential harmful effects, defects, burdens and/or problems. Honesty and truthfulness are powerful because they facilitate building lasting relationships. People, regardless of context, want to work and collaborate with leaders who can depend on and the veracity of their statements can be relied on.

Principles are the underlying beliefs that are strongly held and are presumed to be true. The beliefs that all people have human rights and deserve to be treated with dignity and fairness are among the most important basic principles. Other principles include one's duty of care of the well being of other people and the environment and the obligation of leaders to insure that their decisions are proper and have validated before being executed. This includes the precautionary principle that suggests one should err on the side of caution when in doubt or there are serious concerns about the negative effects of the decisions. Having well thought-out principles facilitates decision making since they provide a solid logic of underpinnings and reasons for selecting the desirable approaches. Strategic leaders who follow well-established principles and use them when making decisions are less likely to engage in "trial and error" approaches or not know why they failed in a given situation.

Principles shed light on what is fundamentally true and critical for making good decisions. Principles guide decision makers when there is uncertainty in what is important or what has to be done. Some of the most important business-related principles include focusing on people not just money and assets and ensuring that solutions are sustainable. They include being inclusive in one's view and having a holistic scope of the business enterprise. Having broad perspectives allows strategic leaders to have comprehensive understanding of reality; thus, reducing the possibilities of missing key inputs and requirements. Principles are generally timeless.

Philosophies are more malleable. They are generally one's personal view of what is critical and necessary for success. They are the fundamental ways of thinking that a given leaders holds to be appropriate in guiding decision making and taking actions. Each leader may develop one's own philosophies, but many leaders often adopt generally accepted philosophies like the notion that maximizing profits is one of the most important aspirations of a business. Great care has to be exhibited when assuming that such philosophies are correct or if the leader simply accepts the mainstream views and goes along with what is perceived to be valid. Leaders need to determine their own philosophical views. They need to think through what they know to be proper and appropriate ways of acting and behaving. Good leaders adopt philosophies that are based on ethical and moral perspectives. The more comprehensive, encompassing and well articulated one's philosophies are, the more likely they provide the leader with wisdom and judgment in making good decisions.

Making everyone successful, especially customers and stakeholders, is a critical philosophical perspective. Rather than trying to convince people that your products and services are the best choices using fancy marketing campaigns and the like, strategic leaders can simply concentrate on what do customers or stakeholders need and expect and what do they require for achieving success via the company's solutions. A corollary to this perspective suggests that if the company's offering, i.e., solutions, cannot make customers and stakeholders successful, then strategic leaders must seek alternate approaches or they should not engage in the actions and activities. Focusing on the success of others is a key to differentiating one's positions versus others, especially competitors. In many ways, such thinking reverses the typical management approaches of concentrating on the company's positions and achievements rather than the success of customers, stakeholders, communities, employees, and other contributors.

Being a good corporate citizen is a simple concept, yet it is an effective way to reinforce one's success as a strategic leader. It is difficult to precisely define what a good corporate citizen is, but thinking in terms of the obligations and responsibilities of being a good citizen can facilitate making good (effective) decisions about the whole enterprise.

Understanding one's cultural background is an important consideration when determining who you are and your fundamental beliefs. While it is impossible to generalize about cultural aspects, one's background, religion, upbringing, social status, and education among numerous others play key roles in developing one's personal views and leadership qualities. There are few absolutes and many pathways can lead to success.

Personal values, principles, one's philosophies, and cultural background all help form an individual's leadership qualities, especially the more intangible ones like intuition and compassion. Leadership qualities include the confidence that the leader has in making decisions, the courage to make difficult choices and stick with them, the empathy for people, and the wisdom he and she has in making good decisions. Leadership qualities are varied and it is difficult to say exactly what is necessary to set the stage for long-term success. They are especially powerful means to assure consistency, accountability and adherence to proper governance.

Credentials and experience

A leader's credentials and experience include his or her skills, talents, knowledge, know-how, intelligence, positions, expertise, professional experiences, and behaviors. They include the lessons learned, views, and mindset gained over time, especially due to actually holding leadership positions or being a leader based on situations or circumstances. They translate into capabilities and competencies that the individual possesses and how they change through ***learning.*** This section involves dynamic SSL aspects since effective and competent leaders are always learning, gaining new knowledge, and encountering new experiences.

Unlike the core beliefs and background that focus on the underpinnings and one's background, credentials and experience involve having leadership positions and producing positive outcomes. Strategic leaders must be competent and have the appropriate competencies and capabilities to lead their organizations and enterprises. These are imperatives. It is vital that strategic leaders are prepared and qualified for the positions that they hold. It is unacceptable to take on a leadership role in an organization without the necessary credentials, capabilities, and competencies. Too many strategic leaders accept positions that they are not qualified to handle. They may have several competencies like understanding financial management and strategic management, but they often did not have the full complement of competencies and capabilities and they are often unable to execute all of the responsibilities. Even when the incumbent is competent and capable, he or she must seek learning to gain the knowledge and know-how to fulfill the roles and responsibilities.

SSL involves having knowledge and knowing how to use it. The requisite knowledge that a strategic leader must have depends on one's position and level of leadership. Higher levels demand more knowledge and know-how. Knowledge includes specific information about the external context-the business environment, markets, the industries, competitors and the extended enterprise. It also includes all aspects of the internal context-the solutions, systems, structures and relationships. Know-how implies that one has the capacity to obtain superior performance and favorable outcomes. It includes the ability to formulate and implement plans and actions. There are numerous strategic leaders who know a lot of detail information and can plan well. They know what needs to be done, but they are unable to execute properly.

Skills and talents are important elements in a strategic leader's portfolio of credentials and qualifications. Some of the most important skills and talents pertain to dealing with people and leading organizations. Effective strategic leaders hone their skills to be in concert with the main driving forces and key factors of their industries and enterprises. For instance, executives in banking and stock trading must be particularly astute in financial affairs and risk management. On the other hand, strategic leaders in the automobile industry need to understand design considerations and manufacturing methods along with market requirements and marketing techniques. In each case, there are a myriad of such items that strategic leaders have to have special skills and expertise in.

Having the right mindset and being willing to take on challenges for the organization and the enterprise are among the most critical elements of true strategic leadership. But, it is challenging to articulate exactly what are the proper mindset should be. For instance, it is difficult for strategic leaders in companies that are company-centric to think about the broader perspectives of being market-centric or enterprise-centric so they can visualize the proper strategic direction for the greater good and to think about sustainable success. Mindset is not intended to be fixed or rigid. It is imperative that strategic leaders who believe in sustainability go beyond the present situations and focus on the long term and how to create and implement solutions for all of the contributors and recipients. It is intended to covey the thought processes and the underlying beliefs that one holds and deploys when thinking about the future and making decisions today. For example, strategic leaders at Johnson and Johnson (J&J) seemingly have a good perspective on how to make good decisions because they generally follow the company's fundamental beliefs as stated in "the Credo." What is noteworthy about the Credo is that it starts with the external basis for thinking about what is important (patients, doctors and nurses) first, focuses on the importance of communities, and then proceeds to key contributors like employees and suppliers at the end. It is clear from the Credo what J&J believes to be important. The Credo facilitates governance since the key aspirations are mapped out. The Credo helps strategic leaders to determine how they should make key decisions.

Gaining new knowledge and know-how through education and training is important. But, there are real limits to how well one can achieve the practical side of strategic leadership without actually engaging in the demands, trials, tribulations, and joys of the real world. Having the right positions and gaining the requisite experiences are essential for long-term development and growth. Most people acquire a majority of their knowledge, know-how and skills through learning on the job. This is the practical side of acquiring the credentials and qualifications for being a strategic leader, both with respect to one's current roles and responsibilities and one's desired future positions. While practical experience is vitally important for developing the qualifications of strategic leadership, one's ongoing experiences have to include further advancements and not just more of the same old experiences. One of the biggest traps is the belief that one is always obtaining additional experience as he or she accumulates more time in a given position. In many situations, having repetitive years of the same experiences produces marginal benefits after a given period of time. Indeed, it can be argued that staying too long in a given position may actually limit one's long-term potential, since the incumbent is not gaining new or different experiences. But, such situations depend on the person's objectives and realities, i.e., to be a subject matter expert or a well-balanced strategic leader, narrow or broad, or something in between.

The main benefits of having a given position and the acquired experiences are often dependent on the rate of change in the business environment and industry. If the rate of change is slow and most of the innovations are incremental, then the experiences are usually relevant and beneficial. However, if the rate of change is fast, then one's expertise and real world experiences have to outpace the rate of change. Old experiences, even knowledge and know-how, may become irrelevant as radical changes necessitate new ways of doing things, new knowledge, and new capabilities. For instance, digital photography made most of the old chemical processes obsolete and one's knowledge and know-how in managing such processes and operations are less valuable.

Expertise is proficiency in specific areas. Strategic leaders are typically generalists who have broad knowledge and capabilities. But, they often have to have specific areas of expertise like finance, marketing, law and numerous others. Many strategic leaders are selected on the basis of their specific expertise given the critical needs of the company. For instance, if the company engages in executing many mergers and acquisitions, a strategic leader with a financial background or one that is lawyer may be the preferred candidate. While this seems to be sensible both from the perspectives of the company and the strategic leader, there may be tendency to focus too much on the most critical area(s) instead of a person having credentials in many areas. Moreover, such a candidate may be narrow in his or her thinking; thus, leading to skewed perspectives and decision making. Since expertise is particularly vulnerable to changes in the business environment, it is imperative that strategic leaders acquire many areas of expertise and continue to develop them.

Strategic leaders have to exhibit proper behaviors at all times, if they wish to be viewed as creditable. People follow leaders who they believe to be authentic and worthy of being the leaders. The behaviors of strategic leaders have to mirror the core beliefs and values that they articulate.

Learning is the pivotal element in developing highly capable and sophisticated strategic leaders who have the capacity to create sustainable outcomes and success. While the requisite learning is difficult to fully articulate, it is clear that strategic leaders have to be on the cutting edge of knowledge, know-how, skills, and expertise, especially in a fast-paced business world. As the rate of change accelerates, strategic leaders must learn at a rate that is faster than the rate of obsolescence. The relevancy of one's knowledge, know-how, expertise and skills is dedicated by context and context continues to expand via globalization, technological change, economic and social upheavals, and new regulatory mandates.

Many leaders believe that they can rely mainly on their strengths to reach their goals. However, such beliefs are deceiving, since they seem to work well in the near term, but may leave the individual vulnerable in the long term. Moreover, there are certain weaknesses and difficulties that are a relatively easy to correct in the early stages of a career, but they often become almost impossible to positively affect as one matures in an organization. For instance, if a person has trouble making formal presentations to a large audience, it is fairly easy to overcome such problems by learning how to address groups of people in non-threatening situations like in an MBA class at the local university. The general expectations for a twenty-year old person are usually low and if mistakes are made they are quickly forgotten. People in general do not expect a young leader to be highly polished in all areas of leadership and the skills and capabilities that go with it. However, the same is usually not the case for a forty-year old, middle-level manager who has been able to avoid such situations during his or her early career. At some point in the hierarchy of leadership, such skills and capabilities usually become important and necessary. Having failed to mitigate such difficulties when they are easier to deal with may result in the death knell of one's rise in the ranks.

Learning is a lifelong necessity. There is never a point where one can say he or she knows everything necessary to be an effective strategic leader. Leadership development and the associated learning paradigms are typically provided to promising young leaders in their twenties and thirties. While this seems to make sense since such individuals usually have demonstrated their potential to lead and have significant time ahead of them in their careers, say thirty-five years, it is imperative that all leaders, especially the more mature strategic leaders who developed their credentials during earlier periods, continue to obtain new knowledge, know-how, skills and expertise through learning and leadership development. While it would take significant amount of market research to determine the true capabilities and competencies of today's strategic leaders, it is not unreasonable to deduce that they are not all in synch with the realities of the twenty-first century and/or have the requisite competencies, capabilities and sophistication to lead complex organizations in turbulent times.

Professor Edmondson suggests that learning is a source of competitive advantage in the information age. She argues that many old line industrial organizations like GM were slow to understand that great execution depends on effective learning not just the efficiency of getting things done.[3] Edmondson advocates ongoing experimentation, reflection and innovation as one engages in execution. She suggests that:[4]

> A focus on getting things done, and done right, crowds out the experimentation and reflection vital to sustainable success.
>
> My research identifies a different approach to execution-what I call *execution-as-learning*-that promotes success over the long haul.
>
> ... From a distance, execution-as-learning looks a lot like execution-as-efficiency. There's the same discipline, respect for systems, and attention to detail. Look closer, however, and you find a radically different organizational mind-set, one that focuses not so much on making sure a process is carried out as on helping it evolve, building four unique approaches into day-to-day work.
>
> First, organizations that focus on execution-as-learning use the best knowledge obtainable (which is understood to be a moving target) to inform the design of specific process guidelines. Second, they enable their employees to collaborate by making information available when and where it's needed. Third, they routinely capture process data in an effort to discover how work is really done. Finally, they study these data in an effort to find ways to improve.

Learning is the bridge between the prevailing business world and the approaches and methods used to obtain results and the new ways necessary for achieving success in the future. The emphasis of learning is on being able to manage in the present and to adapt to change into the future. Strategic leaders cannot assume their full responsibilities and execute them or make proper determinations about strategic direction and what has to be done unless they are competent in all of the areas they engage in. There are no excuses for not having the competencies and capabilities necessary for making strategic decisions and taking the actions. While most strategic leaders depend on specialists and senior professionals to facilitate strategic formulation and implementation, to assist in the governance of the company, and to ensure proper performance and execution, it is imperative that the high-level strategic leaders personally have sufficient capacities to assure that the decisions are valid and are implemented properly.

Being competent and having the appropriate capabilities are always hard to precisely determine and like the previous discussions about what one knows, they are dependent on context and circumstances. Many strategic leaders may be competent in steering the company in the right direction and achieving success during stable social and economic times. They may be good strategic managers and have the skills and capabilities to keep the organization and enterprise afloat during smooth sailing. However, many such business leaders may only competent if the underlying business conditions and circumstances are favorable. They may really be less than fully competent or even incompetent if the business climate changes and becomes more turbulent and less predictable. Many executives and strategic leaders are unable to deal with high levels of uncertainty and changing business environments. This is especially the case for individuals who depend on set approaches for decision making or a standard repertoire of strategies, actions, and tactics.

An individual's capabilities and competencies should always open to scrutiny to determine if they are in concert with the prevailing and expected conditions and trends. It is incumbent upon all leaders, especially high-level ones, to ensure that they are competent in fulfilling all of their responsibilities. While lower level leaders are generally reviewed periodically and given guidance and development opportunities, the same is not always the case for high-level strategic leaders. Indeed, high-level strategic leaders are often assumed to be competent without any checks and balanced until there is a meltdown; then it is too late and many people suffer, especially employees and shareholders. Therefore, it is absolutely imperative that board of directors and the appropriate committees thereof make formal reviews of all senior leaders. Moreover, they should require that senior leaders make improvements, adaptations, and radical modifications as part of their ongoing leadership development.

Perspectives and Prospects

Strategic leaders are the theoretical strategists and architects of the future for their organizations and enterprises. They envision what has to be done to exceed expectations and create an environment that leads to sustainable success. Strategic leaders set the perspectives about reality and how all of the entities, organizations, and individuals are interconnected and what relationships and interactions are necessary to make the endeavors successful. The perspectives also include how changes may play out over time and what the expected consequences of the changes may be. Many strategic leaders have a good sense of what needs to be done and are more than capable of formulating and implementing the right strategies and actions plans, but many strategic leaders are unable to think through all of the implications and the long-term consequences. For example, the strategic leaders at Circuit City had an aggressive growth strategy of opening hundreds of new stores, but they failed to fully appreciate the vulnerabilities associated with their strategies during an economic downturn.

Perspectives are multifaceted and dynamic. They have to be based on all of the key contributors and recipients of the company's solutions, systems and structures. Most of the strategic thinking of the past focused on a narrow set of essential players like customers and competitors without regard to the complexities of the real world. Decisions that are just based on the realities of today may be faulty tomorrow. Strategic leaders in the past often felt compelled to act on the needs of the present and discount the importance of long-term consequences. While it seemingly makes sense to focus on the present if one is in a crisis situation, even in such cases it is crucial to think through all of the ramifications so that the best options are identified, deliberated and validated and the best choices are made that fit the needs and expectations, both the short term and the long term. Perspectives have to include the broad views and future considerations based on the potential consequences of one's decisions. For instance, coal is a plentiful fossil fuel, especially in the US, and it is an inexpensive fuel source for electric power generation. Coal resources provide cost-effective solutions, if one just thinking about the economic factors. But, there are many forces that limit its applications. Certain stakeholders like environmental groups oppose the use of non-renewable resources and ones that exasperate concerns about climate change. Such organizations make it difficult and time consuming to obtain permits to build new plants.

Prospects are future outlooks and the probabilities of given situations occurring. Strategic leaders often concentrate of the positive prospects that present opportunities for success. Being optimistic and taking positive actions are desirable traits, especially ones associated with being proactive and fast-acting, but it is also necessary to think about the negative aspects that are always present in the business environment. While it is impossible to prove that one of the causes of the global business "meltdown in 2007/08" was due to the failure of strategic leaders to contemplate the down side, there is a lot of evidence that suggests that many strategic leaders, investors and decision makers believed that markets and economic factors would continue to be positive. People often make seemingly good assumptions like the markets will continue to rise based on the fact that they have been increasing for more than five years. Such evidence is often insidious, since past results do not predict future possibilities. Indeed, it is often just the opposite; the further one goes out into an economic expansion that more likely it is that the expansion will slow down if not stop.

Strategic leaders have to understand and develop the underlying logic of what they are trying to accomplish. While seeking growth and maximizing profits have dominated strategic thinking over the last century, the strategic logic has to be more multifaceted than just expanding one's businesses, making money, or increasing share price and market capitalization. It has to be based on creating value and making everyone success to the extent possible. Strategic leaders have to have positive attitudes toward change and recognize that good is never good enough and that there are always more challenges to manage and more improvements and developments to be made. Strategic thinking involves both intangible and tangible aspects. The former involves how the leader views the real world and perceives the opportunities and challenges he or she faces. The latter involves one's being, capabilities, competencies and abilities to learn and engage in the realities of the business world and the prospects for the future. They are typically coupled together when strategic leaders are involved in making decisions and taking actions.

Strategic thinking involves putting the pieces together using a systems perspective, framing the dimensions of the enterprise, contemplating how everything works or should work, developing new ways of doing things, and creating innovative solutions. Strategic thinking involves a high-level perspective of the total picture of any situation in terms opportunities, challenges, risks and prospects and determining what can be done and how to do. It entails understanding the essence of reality and delving into the depths of the conditions and trends. It also involves going beyond the prevailing situations and determining what is advantageous and what are the desirable expectations. In this regard, strategic thinking implies considering what could be not just what is.

Strategic thinking and decision making are based on insights, imagination, inspirations, aspirations, innovation, judgment and wisdom which are critical attributes that strategic leaders need to develop and exploit. Insights provide the perspectives and lessons gleamed from assessing the business environment or a portion thereof that lead to a broader understanding of reality and how to manage the situations and make appropriate decisions. They are also based on a comprehensive understanding the organization and enterprise in terms of what is desirable and possible beyond what is being done. It involves out-of-the-box thinking for finding opportunities to make dramatic changes and improvements.

Imagination is the next step in the sequence. It involves thinking in abstract terms about creating value and new ways of doing things. It also pertains to the ability to solve or dissolve complex difficulties and challenges. Imagination is used to view the business world through different lens and to contemplate new solutions; ones that eliminate the underlying causes, not just ones that resolve the issues and concerns or make the effects and impacts tolerable. It involves going beyond problem-solving techniques of the past that simply masked the symptoms but ones did not eliminate the problem(s). For instance, establishing rigid controls over the activities of employees such as using time clocks may assure time is spent on the job, but such controls may not address productivity issues and the effectiveness of the outcomes. If the underlying difficulty pertaining to poor performance is due to a lack of strategic leadership such as little empathy for the workers and their well being, then more stringent controls exasperate the situation and make finding the real solutions even more challenging. Probably, the most common mistake is the leader's view that deficient performance and/or poor attitudes are due to a lack of motivation rather than a failure on the part of leadership to inspire people and to give them the respect and recognition they deserve. Often strategic leaders spend considerable amounts of money on having consultants motivating workers, when in reality the strategic leaders need to spend time energizing the workforce.

Inspiration involves a compelling awareness that a strategic leader has an obligation to create, develop, produce and deliver extraordinary and sustainable outcomes that benefit recipients and contributors across space, time and generations. Inspiration is multifaceted. Firstly, inspiration involves inspiring employees, contributors and others to accept the challenges facing people and to achieve as much as possible. It involves spreading the excitement and the drive to go beyond the norm and to produce positive outcomes for one's purposes and the broader purposes and needs of the people involved. Secondly, the strategic leader has to be inspired to lead change and work toward the pursuit of sustainable success. In this sense, it is an inner-personal conviction that the pursuit of excellence and sustainability are inherently proper, highly desirable and necessary for one's success and the success of the organization and enterprise. Thirdly, inspiration involves what is driving the individual leader to make dramatic improvements and developments and to never accept the status quo or just marginal gains. Such inspiration is hard to define. It is based on the realization that success is an intangible that transcends money and goods and involves making the business world and one's part in it better places for everyone to live.

Aspirations are the underlying dreams and ambitions of the leaders and his or her organization and enterprise. While aspirations may be articulated in the form of goals and objectives that make them understandable and reachable, aspirations are high-level aims, targets, desires and quests that may not be obtainable in the near term, but are highly beneficial and advantageous when they are realized. Sustainable success itself can be characterized as an aspiration. It is almost impossible to attain true sustainable success in the present given the huge challenges involved, but it may be accomplished in future generations. The pursuit of sustainable success is akin to building the Interstate Highway System in the US or the dramatic recovery of Europe and Japan after World War II. The compounding effects of multiplicity of efforts across space (geography) and time (decades) resulted in achievements that few could have contemplated at the start.

Judgment and wisdom are wide-ranging elements that are the most esoteric of the fundamentals of SSL. They involve determining the proper perspectives about reality and long-term possibilities and having the ability to discern what the situation(s) truly is, what the most critical aspects are, and what the essence of the decision making process has to be. Judgment and wisdom involve forming objective views of the situations, circumstances and the future consequences and possessing the capabilities to map out options and select appropriate criteria for determining what the best possible solutions are. They also involve weighting all of the factors, understanding what is necessary and appropriate in terms of the means to obtain the solution and the required ends, and having the wherewithal to make the proper determination(s), i.e., decisions and solutions. Many strategic leaders have the "right stuff" to be good leaders, but the lack good judgment and wisdom. The underlying difficult often has to do with their core beliefs, their leadership style, mindset, and integrity. If they are not open and honesty and they are self-centered, they often skew their perspectives toward to wrong ends. Such leaders often think about themselves and their "friends and associates" first and attempt to ensure that most of the benefits and gains are distributed to a small clique of people including themselves. Indeed, it can be argued that such leaders do not exercise good judgment at all, since they are biased and are not acting for the greater good, whether it is for shareholders, customers, stakeholders, employees and others.

Sustainable success necessitates innovation, especially in fast-paced business world. As the business environment changes and new requirements become necessary and old ways become obsolete, strategic leaders have to become more adept at innovation. This does not mean they have to be inventors or designers. But, they should be the architects of the systems and structures, the individuals who map out what is necessary and appropriate. They exhibit leadership by laying the foundation and establishing the protocols for subsequent actions and outcomes.

Strategic thinking involves putting the pieces together using a systems perspective, framing the dimensions of the enterprise, contemplating how everything works or should work, and developing new ways of doing things and creating innovative solutions. Strategic thinking involves a high-level perspective of the total picture of any situation in terms opportunities, challenges, vulnerabilities, and prospects and determining what can be done and how to do. It entails understanding the essence of reality and delving into the depths of the conditions and trends. It also involves going beyond the prevailing situations and determining what might change and what the expectations might be going forward. In this regard, strategic thinking implies considering what could be not just what is. Strategic thinking links one's learning, competencies and capabilities with the perspectives and prospects of the present and future. Perspectives are how the leader views the business environment. Prospects are the opportunities for success.

Ultimately, the quintessential essence of strategic leadership is decision making. Decisions are the choices that leaders make to set direction and determine what is crucial for success. Decision making is art and a science. The art lies in the minds and hearts of the leaders. The art depends heavily on the fundamentals of leadership and the qualities of the leaders. It includes all of the elements from the core beliefs and background to the experiences and perspectives of the leader. Moreover, simply having a strong intellect and being well educated are not enough for making good decisions. It also takes having integrity and exhibiting proper behaviors. The focus in these areas is related to the heart. The heart involves having empathy for other people and ensuring that everyone is considered when making decisions. The science rests with the theories, concepts, processes and practices involving decision making. The science of decision making involves a plethora of inputs, methods, thought processes, and techniques. A strategic leader's decision making is usually based on his or her knowledge, capabilities, experiences, learning, strategic thinking and perspectives.

Effective decision makers are holistic in their perspectives and embrace the whole enterprise when making their choices. Effective strategic leaders/decision makers are true to their fiduciary responsibilities to assure the sustainable success of their organizations and enterprises. Moreover, they recognize that decision making is not an event, but a continuum. They know that sustainable success is not just an objective but a never ending aspiration.

Historically, much of the focus of strategic leadership was on the leader's experience and know-how. Today, learning is also a key factor, especially in enhancing one's capabilities and competencies and being in synch with the rapidity of change. It reinforces one's intellectual capital and the currency of one's strategic thinking, wisdom and judgment, which are essential for making relevant and good decisions.

The Notion of Full-Spectrum Strategic Leadership

True strategic leadership implies fulfilling one's obligations to the whole enterprise and everyone included therein and assuming the appropriate responsibilities for all facets of one's domain. True strategic leadership does not imply a top down hierarchy of superiors and subordinates, but more of a horizontal perspective of the full spectrum of responsibilities from horizon to horizon. This includes resolving the related problems and challenges and participating in the development and deployment of sustainable solutions based on the full spectrum of needs and expectations of the society, market spaces, business environment, the social/human world, and the natural environment.[5] As discussed in my book, *Full-Spectrum Strategic Leadership: Being on the Cutting Edge through Innovative Solutions, Integrated Systems and Enduring Relationships,* the notion of full-spectrum strategic leadership (FSL) is a holistic leadership approach that includes all of the critical responsibilities; top down, bottom up; across the business environment and time; and, the served and latent customers and stakeholders.

FSL takes an inclusive view that runs the gamut from the micro-environment of the internal organization to the macro-environment of the external world. The full spectrum perspective radiates from horizon to horizon with each element in the array being significant and necessary for the well functioning of the organization and enterprise and the attainment of success. It implies that true leaders are not empowered to rule nor have command and control over people, but they are really fiduciaries who have the duty to serve and support the whole enterprise and to assure that sustained success is achieved. True leaders are people-centric and market-centric. They put others first and themselves last. Full spectrum strategic leaders are responsible for setting strategic direction and for assuring the execution of the mission. They focus on sustainable success and achieve it through value creation and extraordinary performance. The crucial perspectives involve people and markets.

Figure 5.2 depicts some of the salient aspects of FSL.

FSL involves connections and relationships in a non-traditional and non-hierarchical way. While higher level strategic leaders typically have superior positions, the key perspective pertaining to FSL is to realize that everyone is important and each person deserves respect and recognition. Any high-level leaders who thinks that he or she knows what to do in every situation or can make all of the decisions is deceiving himself or herself in a false sense of importance. True strategic leaders depend on the capabilities and resources of the whole organization and enterprise when making decisions; therefore, it is critical that all inputs and people are given due regard and respect.

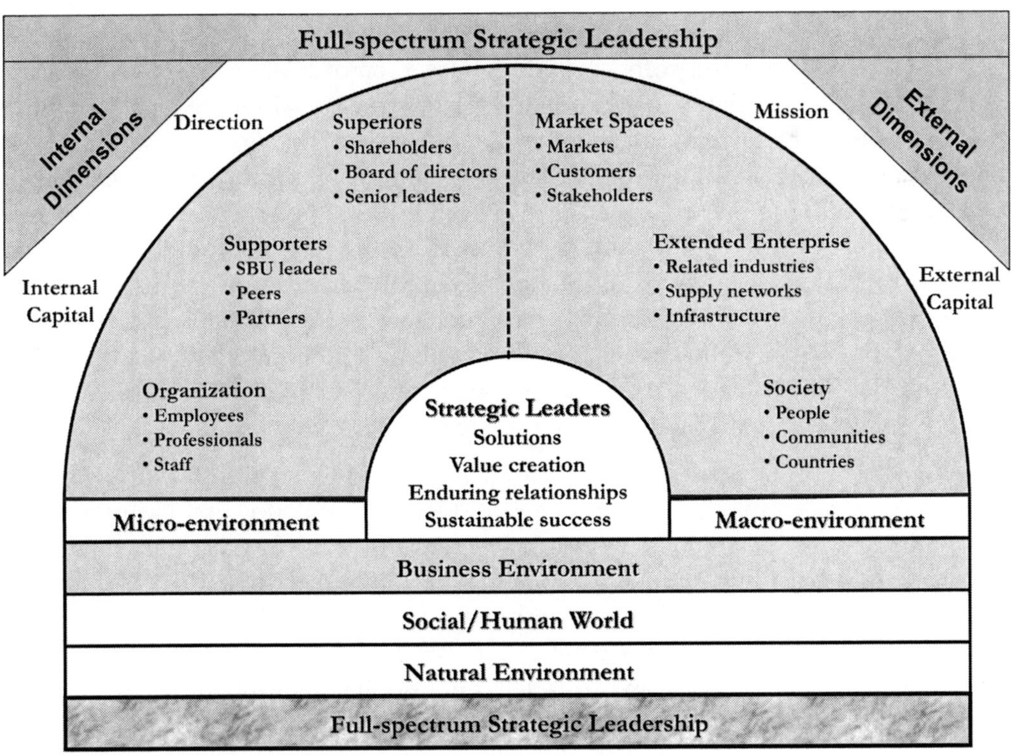

Figure 5.2 Full-spectrum strategic leadership[6]

True strategic leaders know that the micro-elements of the organization and all of the key contributors and supporters are the essential in creating, developing, producing and delivering value. Subordinates are not underlings who are servants for the high-level managers to use or are simply suppose to respond to the bosses' whims; rather they are the intellectual capital, the core competencies, and capabilities of the organization. Subordinates are not at the bottom of the organizational pyramid, but they are the key contributors that make businesses successful. While higher level leaders may be the strategic decision makers, they are not superior to everyone else; they are generally the people who are entrusted with the well being of the organization. In reality, high-level leaders are actually subordinate to their nominal subordinates, since they have an absolute duty to assure everyone's proper development, progress and well being.

True strategic leaders based on the principles of FSL realize that they depend on peers, partners, and other business leaders for advancing their organizations and enterprises, achieving their goals, sustaining success and building long-term relationships. In a complex and turbulent business world, strategic leader often engage such people in the discovery of new opportunities, in setting strategic direction, and in executing strategies and action plans. They know that it takes a diverse team of highly capable and dedicated people across a broad spectrum of realities. This provides effective strategic leaders with broad-based insights for strategy formulation and additional means and mechanisms for strategic implementation.

Furthermore, every strategic leader has superiors that he or she is accountable to and has to follow. Superiors may include the shareholders and the board of directors for executives and company officers and high-level senior leaders for lower level strategic leaders and general managers. Similar to the traditional hierarchical structures of the last century strategic leader report to superior and carry out the legitimate requests and orders of the superior(s). However, unlike the old top-down approaches, FSL involves more interactive and holistic relationships among leaders that are built on mutual respect, recognition and trust. Superiors obviously have duties and obligations that set them at higher levels in the organization, but they are not at the top with others at the bottom. Rather, they have higher level responsibilities like ensuring proper governance and the appropriate accountability to shareholders, board of directors, external entities that have regulatory control or oversight, and other stakeholders that share in the proper functioning of the organization.

From an external perspective, true strategic leaders focus on the business environment, market spaces and the extended enterprise. They assure that customers and stakeholders are satisfied and successful. They reach out to the extended enterprise and work with the entities and people to also make them successful. They use collaboration and cooperation instead of exploiting their positions and/or influence to exert power over weaker people. They realize that most situations are temporary and that one's power ebbs and flows. They are equally comfortable in dealing with external and internal situations and with people regardless of context.

In an even broader perspective, FSL includes all of society and the communities of people; locally, nationally, regionally, and globally. While most strategic leaders define their domains and what they can reasonably take on and accomplish for the greater good of humankind, it is imperative strategic leaders embrace holistic view and reach out beyond the narrow confines of markets, customers, supply networks and operations. With such perspectives they have the opportunity to contribute to society beyond just selling products and providing services by assisting in developing solutions for the broader issues and problems. Such leadership enriches one's capacity to understand the underlying needs and expectations of customers, stakeholders, people and society.

True strategic leaders lead by example and take the initiative. They are willing to stand in front of the organization and take responsibility for their decisions and actions. While they empower people across the enterprise to participate in decision making, they know that they are ultimately accountable for the decisions and actions of the organizations and enterprise.

Reflections

SSL is an evolving construct. While certain core elements and requirements never change, the expectations of business leaders are most likely to become even more demanding. As markets become more diverse and social, political, economic, environmental, and technical changes accelerate, strategic leadership, not just strategic management, is essential for staying ahead of the expectations and challenges.

SSL is complex and ever-changing. It is challenging to articulate all of the elements that are necessary for mapping out what strategic leaders are and what they have to do. Given the prevailing turbulence and crisis in the business world today, it is valid to say that there are fundamental problems associated with conventional strategic leadership. While industry analysts discuss the financial problems as the underlying difficulties, the lack of true strategic leadership at the helms of many of the global corporations around the world may be the real difficulty. There are too few leaders and too many followers. While such statements are always difficult to prove, the problems with inaccurate financial reporting in the aftermath of the Enron and WorldCom and the more recent financial crisis in the "sub-prime mortgages" and other problems are indications that too many corporate leaders simply follow the prevailing thinking of the mainstream or are narrowly focused on the marketing and financial aspects. Many of the business leaders are really not leaders at all. They may be the executives of their organizations, but many of them lack the courage and conviction to lead. Many of them are stuck in a "time warp" based on the strategic thinking of the last century. Strategic leadership is the decisive factor that can make or break the realization of desirable outcomes and the achievement of sustainable success. Strategic leaders engage in the relentless quest toward perfection, i.e., SSL, FSL and true strategic leadership.

Notes

1. Charles Wankel, *21st Century Management: A Reference Handbook, Volume 2* (Los Angeles, CA: Sage Publications, 2008, pp. 272–290). Dial Fields article is titled "Developing a Leadership Style to Fit 21st-Century Challenges.

2. Amy Edmondson, "The Competitive Imperative of Learning," *Harvard Business Review,* July–August 2008, p. 67
3. Amy C. Edmondson, pp. 60–67.
4. Ibid, p. 62
5. David L. Rainey, *Full-Spectrum Strategic Leadership: Being on the Cutting Edge through Innovative Solutions, Integrated Systems and Enduring Relationships* (Unpublished, 2012, p. 100).
6. Ibid.

References

Collins, Jim (2001) *Good to Great: Why Some Companies Make the Leap . . . and Others Don't.* New York, NY: Harper Business.

David L. Rainey (2012) *Full-Spectrum Strategic Leadership: Being on the Cutting Edge through Innovative Solutions, Integrated Systems and Enduring Relationships.* Unpublished.

Wankel, Charles (2008) *21st Century Management: A Reference Handbook, Volume 2.* Los Angeles, CA: Sage Publications.

6

Concluding Comments

Introduction

The pursuit of sustainable leadership (PSL) runs the gamut from the foundations of leadership and the selection of principles and philosophies to leadership development and being a high-level strategic leader. PSL pertains to the personal and professional makeup of the individual leader and his or her leadership principles, philosophies, capabilities, and approaches. It involves qualities, attitudes, behaviors and actions of the strategic leader and his or her abilities to lead people based on innovative ways of thinking, leading and making decisions. It involves having the confidence, courage, conviction and commitment to truly lead in unique ways. It is being open, honest and accountable. Most importantly, PSL involves achieving success and making people successful. It is the never-ending quest for excellence and achieving outstanding performance based on the recognition that perfection is a distance dream.

PSL is an exciting life long journey. Even the most senior strategic leaders of large corporations have to engage in new learning and experiences, if they want to stay abreast or ahead of the rapidly changing global economy and the compelling demands of the business environment and market spaces. The social, economic, ethical, technological, and environmental forces are moving at incredible speeds and in many directions. Sustainable leaders cannot make assumptions about reality; they have to have the wherewithal to assess the prevailing state of affairs and the future expectations, make determinations and quickly decide what the strategies, solutions, actions and activities have to be. They need to be constantly on top of the opportunities, challenges and risks in an ever more complicated and turbulent business world in which change is the norm.

The Pursuit of Sustainable Leadership, pages 139–145

Perspectives on Leadership Constructs

Leadership constructs in the context of this book may be divided into three main categories: ones that are timeless; those that are most appropriate for short-term situations; and, ones that are dynamic involving change. The discussions focus mainly on the first and third categories, especially those pertaining to sustainable strategic leadership (SSL).

The first category includes those that are inherent and do not change over time. Generally, such constructs involve the absolutes of leadership like honesty, openness, integrity, moral turpitude, and ethical behaviors. It also includes all of the "must do" mandates like protecting human well being, compliance with laws and regulations, and the proper governance of the organization.

The second category includes leadership constructs that are most useful for short-term strategies, tactics and action plans. For instance, discounted cash flow thinking and the associated techniques involve effective financial management mechanisms for achieving short- and intermediate-term results, but often fall short or lead to misleading conclusions when analyzing investments that have long development time-frames and long-term implications. The difficulty is that long-term outcomes depend on many additional variables that may not be significant considerations in the short term, but they may morph into critical factors in the future. For instance, the development and deployment of new-to-the-world technologies usually take many years, even decades to bring to fruition. In the long term, they may have significant positive effects and dramatic improvements on the nature of customer demand and the competitive scene. In the short term, however, technological innovations (also referred to as radical innovations) and the associated technology developments are usually not significant factors in the market spaces and competitive landscape, since it takes considerable time to fully develop any new technology and new-to-the-world product. For example, nanotechnologies are expected to provide innovative products like producing clean water from the ocean; water that is pure, affordable, and plentiful. But, it may take more than ten years and numerous development projects to realize the possibilities. Conventional marketing and financial management techniques may indicate that the rewards are questionable; yet water is a scarce resource that is becoming more critical over time. Conventional short-term oriented techniques are not wrong per se, they are often misapplied. These statements have to be modified by the recognition that there are cases in which innovative technologies and products are introduced within just a few years.

The third category involves more dynamic leadership aspects and techniques; ones intended for the fast rate of change and long-term implications. The rate of technological and market changes have profound effects on the selection and adaptation of leadership constructs as well. If change unfolds over many years or decades, i.e., the rate of change is slow, business leaders typically adapt incremental improvements to their business and product portfolios and they try to keep them current and maintain stability. Conversely, if change is rapid, as in consumer electronics and telecommunications, radical innovations become critical for managing success. New technologies and products have to be developed quickly and flawlessly to stay on the cutting edge. Failure to maintain such innovativeness and achieve commercial success may doom even the most well endowed and successful corporations. For example, Kodak was one of the most successful corporations for decades and even one of the prestigious Dow Industrial for most of the twentieth century, yet it fortunes have slip dramatically as digital technologies impacted the dominance of its previous position as the market share leader in chemical-based photography. While strategic leaders at Kodak may have understood the strategic implications of digital technologies, they were slow to craft new solutions and strategies and implement changes.

The systems and structures of companies and business units have tremendous influences on the selection and application of suitable leadership and management constructs. In the days of vertical integration when the corporation produced most of the materials, parts and components for its products, the lack of true integration with suppliers and even customers was not deemed to be a critical factor. Suppliers provided raw materials that were generally commodities that could easily be obtained from a myriad of sources. The relationships between producers and suppliers were often adversarial and the lack of solid relationships was not always a significant problem, since the exchanges were based on short-term transactions that were often one-time or periodic events. Producers generally sought low cost structures and leveraged their purchasing power to extract the best terms and conditions. If such actions caused the suppliers to be less effective or unsustainable, the buyer was not concerned because it had numerous other options to fulfill its needs. Most exchanges were based decoupled approaches that were done at "arms length" with little interaction and concern for the other party. The relationships with customers were also taken for granted in many industries. It was often assumed that customers were "locked-in" and did not have any real choices. This was reinforced by the fact that most of the competitors followed essential the same strategies and practices. Moreover, for most twentieth century mainstream leadership and management constructs focused on the company and its relationships with customers; they were narrowly defined by the immediate or short-term business situations, and included only the direct linkages and exchanges (the product-market perspective). For instance, marketing concepts and approaches typified this situation with extremely narrow perspectives about conveying only the positive aspects of the messages and information pertaining to the products and services being promoted. Most companies highlighted the positive attributes without much consideration about the negative implications. The general theme was to produce products, and then try to convince customers to buy them at a given price. The main objectives were to increase revenues, margins and market shares. While customer satisfaction was recognized as an important metric, it was deemed important as it related to achieving the primary goals—profits, cash flow and growth. The focus was on company-centric outcomes. External goals were viewed as secondary, and social and environmental responsibilities were tangential if they existed or they were managed as an aside, if they were mandated by governments.

In the 1980s, the static constructs of the hierarchical structure and vertical integration gave way to horizontal integration. As companies became more horizontally structured, a more balanced perspective pertaining to both the internal and external dimensions evolved. Business leaders expanded their strategic thinking to be more inclusive of the external contributors and recipients and the relationships with them (holistic perspective). Additionally, as the scope of the supply networks expanded and customer expectations became more complicated, management constructs that just focused on internal operations became less relevant. The connections and interactions between entities, i.e., between suppliers and producers and between producers and customers, became much more important for ensuring the proper execution of processes and achieving success. Indeed, information exchanges between the various entities became very important as well. The management constructs had to become broader to keep pace with the changing realities.

Over the last two decades, the earlier versions of horizontal integration were replaced with the concepts of value delivery systems and extended enterprise and the broader perspectives of inclusiveness and innovativeness (the sustainable enterprise perspective). Such leadership and management constructs are based on the external context and what it means to the company or business unit in the long term. Sustainable enterprise perspectives shifts strategic management constructs from developing strategic direction based on internal capabilities, resources and the organizational structures to designing, developing and implementing business frameworks, strategies, and management systems that are dynamic, inclusive and innovative. This shift is one of the most important changes to occur in business management over the last quarter century. While product development and technologic innovation are important constructs for achieving success, strategic leaders have to ensure that the new technologies and products provide solutions.

Today, the situation is even more challenging. While some of the conventional leadership and management constructs are still useful, many of the older theories and practices are not relevant due to the extensive scope and global nature of business transactions and operations. Many of the older leadership and management constructs were developed during slower, less complicated times when corporations managed most of their affairs using internal resources and capabilities. They were based on narrow and mostly internal perspectives.

Leadership constructs can be characterized according to the perspective and fit with context from narrow to broad and according to the rate of change from slow to fast. Figure 6.1 provides a relative sense of how some of the leadership constructs mentioned in the book fit into context and the rate of change. It is not intended to be comprehensive, but to provide a sense of how some of the leadership constructs may be portrayed. The dashed lines indicate that the positioning of the constructs is relative and depends on context. The constructs in the bold lines are the main themes in this book.

The narrow perspectives of the past usually did not invoke much of a stretch for either the strategic leaders or the people of the organization and the enterprise. However, holistic perspectives with strategic innovations and sustainable solution require

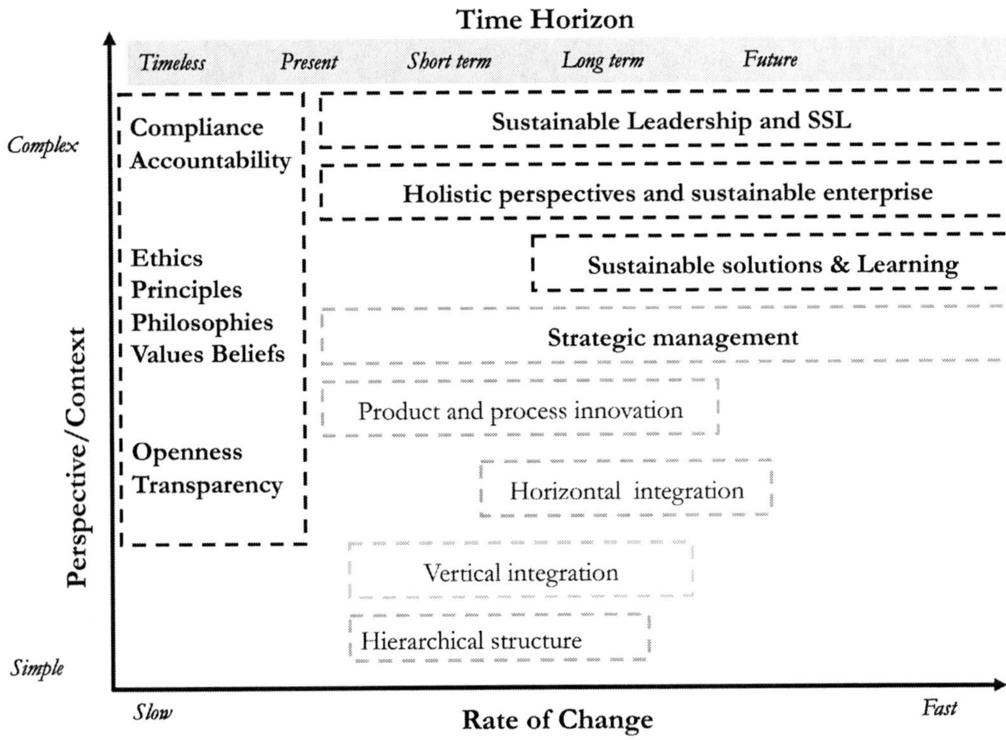

Figure 6.1 Comparative view of selected leadership constructs.

dynamic strategic leadership that instills courage, confidence, conviction, and commitment in the organization and across the enterprise. It takes PSL to transform an organization into a new reality. The more proactive the strategic direction, the more critical it is for strategic leaders to lead the way.

The stabilizing constructs include values, beliefs, principles, philosophies, ethics, and compliance with the overarching aspects of good governance. These are the timeless underpinnings that are generally accepted and rarely changed, management constructs that guide the strategic leaders and the organization in decision making and achieving results.

Concluding Comments

Leadership as discussed throughout the book is a complex subject matter that defies simple definitions and narrow perspectives. True strategic leadership, especially considering SSL, is even more complicated. It is a multifaceted construct that includes influencing, directing and inspiring people, obtaining solutions, delivering value, creating systems and structures, building relationships, and developing and rewarding people of the enterprise. It also includes setting the vision, direction, and agendas of the organization, initiating and orchestrating actions, achieving success, and leading change among many other facets.

The foundations of leadership discussed in Chapter 1 include an overview on the underpinnings of leadership and precepts. Perspectives on philosophies, principles and personal values of leaderships, the concepts of transparency, openness and accountability, and the critical qualities of leadership were discussed in Chapters 2 through 4. Leadership development was also discussed in Chapter 4.

Figure 6.2 provides a general sense of the opportunities and challenges of PSL and leadership development. The graphic is a broad generalization that is intended to provide insights and considerations about the opportunities and challenges of leadership development. As depicted most leaders find it difficult to maintain their growth potential as they progress through the levels.

Leadership development is open-ended in the sense that it is impossible to specify all of the developments required to achieve one's long-term objectives. While there may be many intermediate goals, there are no exact targets in which an individual can identify as ones that produce nirvana. Leadership development is the ongoing pursuit to obtain knowledge and learning with the realization that the world is ever changing and that one has to outpace change and be the architect of one's future, if the person wants to be a successful leader and maintain success over time.

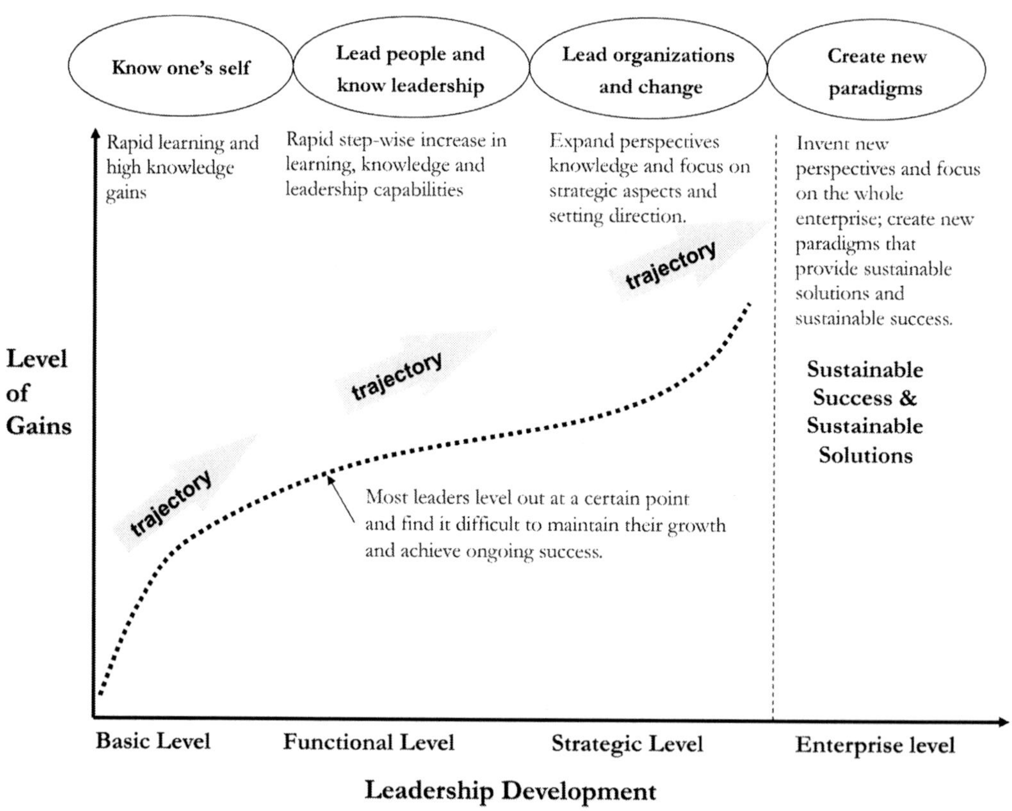

Figure 6.2 The dynamics of leadership.

Many prospective leaders make significant progress during their early development. They learn quickly and rapidly acquire new knowledge, skills and capabilities using self-reflections and learning. They learn how to understand people and lead them in an organizational setting. While many critical aspects of leadership pertaining to the basic and functional levels are not necessarily simple or easy to learn, most potential leaders are relatively successful in making gains and realizing an acceptable level of competencies and capabilities, especially ones associated with leading and/or managing small groups or teams. However, many promising leaders fail to continue to make sufficient progress as they mature and their potential to grow and develop flattens out. While there is no specific point at which a given individual's momentum slows down in his or her personal and professional development, many leaders lose energy somewhere along the mid-way of their development pathway and they have difficulties realizing their ultimate goals going forward.

The key for PSL is continuous development that takes a holistic perspective. The aim is to become an innovative strategist and inventor of the future. At the strategic level and beyond, the leader has to think out-of-the box about future needs and expectations as well the present ones. The leader has to discover new ways for achieving success though unique solutions and management constructs. By establishing the agenda and creating new paradigms leaders can aspire the highest levels of leadership which include leading change across the enterprise.

A commitment to lifelong learning and progress is one of the most important perspectives of PSL. The trajectory is onward and upward. The imperative is unceasing determination to become the leader who possesses the best qualities, imagination, insights and innovativeness as possible. Strategic leaders have to master the art of leadership and become multi-talented individuals who are on the cutting edge of theory and practice. They have to exhibit all of the positive qualities and eliminate most of the negative ones. While most leaders have some deficiencies, great leaders are the ones that work hard to overcome them to ensure that certain limitations do not stymie their potential.

About the Author

Dr. David L. Rainey is an internationally known author, educator, academic leader and business consultant. He is a leading authority on sustainable development, strategic leadership, strategic management, technological innovation, product development and energy management. He is a strategist and pragmatist working at the intersection of leadership, strategy, innovation, systems and solutions pertaining to the opportunities and challenges in today's turbulent business environment.

Professor Rainey has over thirty-five years of experience and leadership in industry and academia. He is a professor of management and the former chair of the Hartford Department of the Lally School of Management and Technology at Rensselaer Polytechnic Institute (RPI). He also served as Acting Vice President of Rensselaer at Hartford. Dr. Rainey is a visiting professor at the Technical University of Munich and an associate of "the Center for the Study of Corporate Sustainability", Instituto De Estudios Para La Excelencia Competitiva in Buenos Aires, Argentina.

Professor Rainey has advised companies on developing business strategies and radical technologies in the fields of biotechnology, energy systems, fuel cells, aircraft and submarine design, hydrogen peroxide applications, cryogenic processing, bioremediation, recycling, high temperature plasma-arc furnaces and many other technologies and products. He has consulted with more than fifty global corporations, including United Technologies Corporation, Sikorsky Aircraft, Toyota, BMW, Siemens AG, AT&T, Electric Boat Division of General Dynamics, Holnam, International Fuel Cells, Lego Systems, Pennsylvania Power & Light, Pfizer, Inc., and others. He has participated in the start-up of more than thirty entrepreneurial companies. He was a principal, owner and executive of GNA Industrial Furnaces, Inc., a systems engineering company, in Montreal, Canada that specialized in designing and producing equipment for the aluminum industry.

Dr. Rainey is the author of *Product Innovation: Leading Change through Integrated Product Development* (2005, ISBN 0-521-84275-1), *Sustainable Business Development: Inventing*

The Pursuit of Sustainable Leadership, pages 147–148

the Future through Strategy, Innovation and Leadership (2006, ISBN: 0-521-86278-7) and *Enterprise-wide Strategic Management: Achieving Sustainable Success through Leadership, Strategies and Value Creation* (2010, ISBN: 978-0-521-76980-8). The books are published by Cambridge University Press. His next books include: *Visionary Strategic Leadership: Sustaining Success through Strategic Direction, Corporate Management and High-Level Programs, Full-Spectrum Strategic Leadership: Being on the Cutting Edge through Innovative Solutions, Integrated Systems and Enduring Relationships,* and *The Pursuit of Sustainability: Creating Business Value through Strategic Leadership, Holistic Perspectives and Exceptional Performance.*

Dr. Rainey was President and CEO of a US subsidiary of Alfa Laval AB, a Swedish multinational. He was Vice President and General Manager of the U.K.-based Wellman Engineering Corporation, a manufacturer of process equipment for the automobile, steel, aluminum, and pulp and paper industries. He began his business career at Combustion Engineering, Inc. holding successive positions as research and development engineer, project manager and manager of strategic business planning.

Dr. Rainey earned a BS in Mechanical Engineering, a MBA, and Master of Science degrees in Engineering Science and Business Management. He earned a Ph.D. from RPI.

CPSIA information can be obtained at www.ICGtesting.com
Printed in the USA
BVOW061514100313

315083BV00004B/4/P

9 781623 961275